PROFESSIONAL PROGRAMMING CONCEPTS

"BRIDGES THE GAP TO PROFESSIONAL PROGRAMMING"

BUD PEMBROKE

MANAGEMENT INFORMATION SOURCE, INC.

COPYRIGHT

1107 N.W. 14th Avenue
Portland, Oregon 97209
(503) 222-2399

First Printing

ISBN 0-943518-87-3

Library of Congress Catalog Card Number: 88-12941

DEDICATION

This book is dedicated to the person whose wholehearted encouragement and professional assistance made this book a reality—my wife, Ellen Fenwick.

TABLE OF CONTENTS

DISK ORDER FORM
ON LAST PAGE
OF BOOK

FOREWORD

In this age of specialization, people often find that their view of the world is limited. When, out of interest or need, they venture into other disciplines such as programming, they find it necessary to supplement and widen their knowledge base. The intent of this book is to do just that for the student, amateur, or novice professional programmer.

Individuals who make their living by programming have a background of knowledge to draw from when approaching a task. This book gives you that underlying foundation of information by explaining common professional development techniques so you can program more effectively. Some of the techniques will apply to any programming task; others will relate more to large software development environments. In either case, you are provided with a logical and historical understanding of how professional programming is accomplished.

Although this book shows you the BASIC and C programming languages, it is not intended to replace programming language manuals; it is intended to supplement them. You are taken, step by step, through the creation of a program—from conception of the idea through debugging the finished code. Many concepts discussed in this book are fundamental to most programming languages.

This book begins with BASIC—the language most people begin with—and moves into the "professional" language—C. You might think of BASIC as a starting point and C as a destination, but the concepts covered in this book can give you the background to program in any language you might choose.

Although this book can be used for reference, you should read it while sitting in front of your PC. It includes samples of code in both BASIC and C that you should try on your computer as you read the text. These programs should act as springboards. Observe what they do and how they do it. Then, modify and experiment with them.

You can save considerable typing time and effort by taking advantage of the companion program disk. The program disk contains all the source code for the sample C and BASIC programs in this book. See the disk order form on the last page of the book.

The concepts discussed in this book apply to the IBM family of personal computers (or compatibles) with the MS-DOS operating system. Two specific languages are used: IBM-BASICA and Turbo C. Special emphasis is placed on Turbo C and Turbo C graphics. The languages were chosen because they are both readily available on PCs, and they have both been used as professional programming languages.

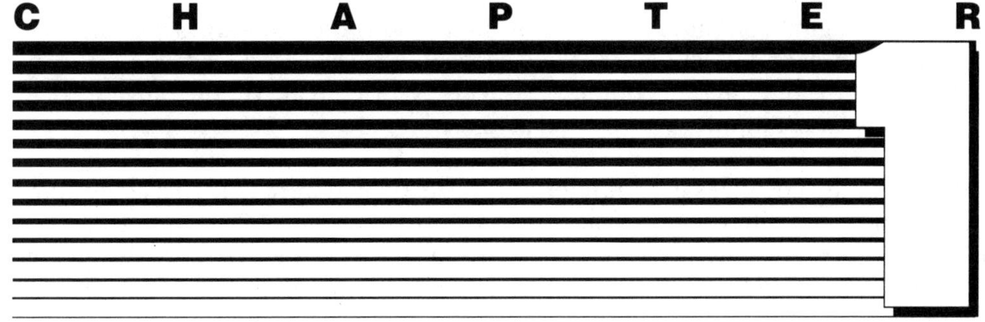

AN OVERVIEW OF PROGRAMMING AND LANGUAGES

Electronic digital computers as we know them today did not always exist in their current form. Computers have evolved as technology has advanced. Since the introduction of the digital computer during World War II, the advances in electronics and computers have been astonishing.

Because of the advances in computer hardware, people were able to use the computer in new and different applications. As more people used the computer, more ideas were generated on how to make further use of this slave to modern man. Today, because these new applications require additional and often greater programming effort than their predecessors, the programming industry must produce code faster and more cheaply than it has ever done in the past.

A LOOK AT PROFESSIONAL PROGRAMMING

What is professional programming? A profession requires specialized knowledge and, often, much schooling; programming is the process of preparing coded instructions to complete a task or solve a problem. To determine what professional programming is, take a closer look.

If it were 1958, you might see a man pick up what looks like a metal picture frame, about two feet square with holes around the edge. He attaches one end of a short wire to one side of the frame and the other end across to the other side. You watch him study the frame and then place another wire. After a little while, the frame has a maze of wires running back and forth in what appears to be a random fashion. You ask him what he is doing. He answers, "I'm programming." He walks over to a large "business machine" and pulls a similar metal frame from its side. "These wiring boards hold my programs." Across the room, you see a large rack full of more metal wiring boards. "Those are all my programs."

If it were 1968, you might see a woman sitting in front of a computer. On the computer is a long row of switches. She flips up the first switch in the row. A small light goes on. She moves down the line of switches, flipping some up and some down. She, too, is programming.

If it were 1978, you might see a man get up from a keypunch machine. He holds a rectangular card with little rectangular holes punched in it. He walks across the room to a table on which you see a small cardboard box meant to hold a stack of these cards. These cards contain his programs.

Today you are typing at a keyboard while watching the output on a screen. You, too, are programming.

All the previous examples involved preparing coded instructions for a mechanism. They all were programming examples, and it is quite conceivable that all of them produced the same result in the end. The differences were primarily in the method of input. Each person used a different method of getting the program into the machine or computer, and he or she probably used a different programming language to instruct the machine.

Programming is changing rapidly. In the past, children grew up learning a trade or profession, quite often from a parent. The knowledge learned lasted them a lifetime. In fact, it lasted for generations. Their grandparents had most likely passed it down to the children's parents. Changes or improvements came very slowly. This is no longer true. Changes are now occurring rapidly, and with each new change there comes a need for retraining.

The previous programming examples occurred within the working life of one individual. If at any point that individual had stopped retraining, within just a few years, he or she would have become obsolete and unemployable as a programmer. You might say that's okay because learning new things is good—it's stimulating. You're right, but there is a subtle distinction here between learning new things and retraining. When learning new things, you broaden your knowledge base. Yesterday, you knew one fact. Today, you know two facts. Retraining, because of obsolescence, does not broaden your knowledge base. You are simply replacing obsolete information with up-to-date information. Yesterday, you knew one job. Today, you still only know one job—you just do it in a different way.

There is a desire in human nature for stability and security. Human beings, at times, want what is known, comfortable, and stable. Professional programming cannot, at least for any length of time, satisfy this need. Professional programming is a dynamic, stimulating, and exciting career. It requires a lifetime of training, but, in the end, you still know only one job, and that job will be obsolete tomorrow.

PROGRAMMING CLASSIFICATIONS

Programming could be classified into a myriad of groups. For example, there is programming for the banking industry, the airline industry, and the medical profession. Just name an industry and there will be a group of programmers that specializes in applications for that industry. This book, however, discusses two general classifications: applications programming and system software programming.

Applications programming uses the computer as a secondary tool to satisfy primary needs. For example, the primary need of the banking industry is to account for and keep track of all the monies under its control. Thus, all programs produced to directly aid the banking industry in satisfying this primary need are applications programs. Applications programming tends to be performed in **high-level languages**—languages such as FORTRAN and COBOL that are designed for humans. The high-level language used may be especially designed for the industry involved, such as the programming language MUMPS, which was designed for the medical profession.

System software programming produces either the tools used by applications programmers or the programs that control the computer itself. In other words, the programmer who produces a language such as COBOL is a system software programmer, and the programmer who uses COBOL as a tool is an applications programmer. System software programmers, today commonly called **software engineers**, tend to work with low-level languages. **Low-level languages** are those designed for a specific computer. They are the assemblers and macro languages. There are exceptions to this rule—the most notable being the C language. It is not designed for only one computer, and for reasons that will be discussed later, much of today's system software is currently written in the C language.

THE FUTURE OF PROGRAMMING

New developments in hardware can and most likely will drastically change the future of this profession. It would be presumptuous of anyone to try to predict exactly what will happen in this dynamic field; however, it is possible to look at the trends and get a feeling for the direction programming might take in the future.

First, there is human nature. For example, have you noticed the resistance to switching to the metric system of measurement? In general, people like what they are familiar with and tend to resist change. Programmers tend to stay with the language they know, the operating system they are using, and the computer manufacturer they are familiar with. When programmers or managers need to make a decision about a company's future computer acquisitions, they will be influenced by what they are familiar with. Also, switching to a different computer or different language might require the conversion of years of previous programming efforts. As a result, there is a tendency among programmers to resist change.

Second, as mentioned previously, programming has changed tremendously in the last 30 years. These changes were brought about by technological advances. Technological changes are coming now at a faster rate than ever before and will continue to change the profession. It can be assumed that in spite of the human tendency to resist change the programmer will change, perhaps reluctantly, right along with the job.

The third trend concerns the effort to reduce the cost associated with programming. Today, the cost of programming is increasing while the cost of the hardware is decreasing. To counter this trend, the computer industry is attempting to find a way to keep programming costs in line. The effort seems to center around two questions: how can programs be produced faster, and how can the skill level necessary to produce the programs be lowered?

Based on these three trends, applications programming as it is known today will most likely disappear. New types of languages will be developed to lower the skill level required to program. Spreadsheet programs are examples of the beginning of this trend. These new languages will allow professionals in any field to do their own programming. Perhaps such programming isn't even programming by today's standards. Put another way, professionals will be able to perform the tasks necessary to get the desired results from the computer, or they will be able to hire semiskilled individuals at lower rates of pay to perform the tasks for them.

For some time into the future, there will exist isolated pockets of resistance—areas in which applications programmers will function in much the same way as they do today. These pockets will gradually die out as key individuals retire or their equipment becomes obsolete. These pockets will tend to be in companies or professions that are static in nature and do not experience a high growth rate, thus allowing existing computer equipment to continue to satisfy their needs.

There will still be system software programmers around—at least those who are willing to continue to retrain regularly. They will be more efficient and produce their programs at a faster rate as a result of new languages and a more systematic approach to programming. Some of the software they currently write will no longer be necessary because more and more of the functions currently accomplished with software will be incorporated directly into the hardware design.

Does all this mean that professional programming is a poor choice of profession? No. In many ways, it's an excellent choice. Computers are still a growing industry. The want ads will tell you that. There's a current need for professionals in the field of programming because there are more computer-related tasks to perform than there are time, money, and staff to perform those tasks. (It's for this very reason that the profession will be forced to change.) Also, the predicted trends will not happen overnight; conventional programming positions will exist years into the future. If you want to be a professional and if you're good, one of those positions will be yours. The point is that to stay in the industry you will need to constantly learn the new technology.

A GENERAL LOOK AT PROGRAMMING LANGUAGES

Begin by examining the tools of a professional programmer: the programming languages. A programming language is an established method by which the programmer directs the computer to perform a desired task. There are currently at least four generations of programming languages.

First-Generation Programming

The first-generation language is the language of the computer. Today's digital computers have been built to understand what is called **machine language**. Each computer or microprocessor has its own machine language. Machine languages use the binary number system and are therefore comprised of just two symbols: one and zero (see Appendix A for an explanation of binary and number base). Every instruction in a machine language is made up of only these ones and zeros. For the number one, the current flows. For the number zero, the current does not flow. Everything is either on (one) or off (zero). There is no in-between. These ones and zeros are referred to as **bits**. All communication between man and machine must take place with different combinations of bits.

Think of a computer as being like a row of mailboxes in the post office. Each mailbox can hold one binary number. That binary number is a machine language instruction. The computer will look in each box to see what it is supposed to do. For example, if the first four bits in a mailbox are 0011, the computer is wired to add the contents of two other boxes. If the first four bits are 0101, then the computer is wired to subtract some box from another. This is all that the computer understands. The computer is wired to interpret the contents of these mailboxes or memory locations and then perform a task, depending on what it finds there. Remember the woman flipping switches earlier in the chapter? She was programming in machine language by setting the bits one at a time in memory.

Binary numbers (machine language) may be well suited for the computer, but for humans they pose problems. First, it takes many digits to represent a relatively small number. For example, the number 549 takes ten digits to represent in machine language: 1000100101. Second, machine language is difficult for a human to read and understand at a glance. One of the first things early programmers did was write a program to convert binary to octal (base eight) or hexadecimal (base sixteen). They chose these number bases because they are easily translated to and from binary. Now programmers can write 1000100101 as 1045 octal or as 225 hexadecimal (hex). If you ever need to analyze a memory dump, you will be looking at the machine language of the computer that has been converted to octal or hex. This is much easier for humans to read, but it is still machine language. It is still not very meaningful to humans; it is just a little easier to handle.

Second-Generation Programming

The next step was to develop a program that would let humans type in something that was meaningful to them and then have the computer translate that entry into the ones and zeros it could understand. This is the second generation of computer languages. These translating programs are called **assemblers**. For each binary or machine instruction that the computer is wired to understand, the assembler has a corresponding word that is meaningful to the human. Consider the following example:

Machine Language	**Assembler Language**
0011 0001 0010	ADD A,B
0101 0001 0010	SUB A,B
...	...

The assembler simply reads the human words and substitutes the corresponding machine language binary code in its place. The assembler then stores the results in the computer's memory. The human version of the program is called the **source code**, and the machine version is called the **object code**.

In some cases, the same group of instructions is needed over and over again. Input and output routines (I/O) and multiplication are good examples. Many of the early computers could not multiply; they could only add. Whenever programmers wanted to multiply A and B, they had to write a program to add A to itself B times. As a shortcut, programmers decided to include **multiply** as a word the assembler could recognize and translate, but, instead of being translated into just one machine language instruction, the word was translated into a small group of machine instructions that would add over and over until multiplication was completed. Languages that translate into these groups of instructions are called **macro languages**. They are still considered second-generation languages and, for the most part, are identical to assembler language.

Third-Generation Programming

The next logical step was to move away from machine language altogether. After all, why does a programming language need to resemble the language of the computer at all? A language was needed that would speed up programming and be a real human language—one that would allow the programmer to use mathematical equations with real words and maybe even English sentences. So the third generation of programming languages was developed. These languages took many forms and have many different names—FORTRAN, COBOL, BASIC, etc.—but they all do the same thing: they take some form of strictly formatted human language and translate or compile it into the machine language of the computer.

If the programmer follows the strict format of these third-generation (or **high-level**) languages correctly, the source program will compile. Then, if the logic is correct, the object (or machine language) program will run on the computer. The important thing is that one line of code that humans understand might generate 5, 10, or even 50 machine language instructions. This allows programmers to increase their productivity. These third-generation languages are called **compilers**.

If a programmer had a large program to run, it might take the computer anywhere from a few minutes to a few hours just to compile the program. Then, after all that time, the programmer might find that the program could not run because a word had been misspelled. The whole process would need to be repeated after the correction was made. To speed up this process, an alternative approach was conceived that, instead of producing the machine language, just interprets the human language program and jumps to an already existing routine in the computer to do what the human language wanted. This process works fine. These so-called **interpreters** start executing a program immediately—no more waiting for the compile.

There was one problem, however. Even though the program started running immediately, it would run much slower than the compiled version. Interpreters have been known to run 10 to 50 times slower than the compiled version of the same program. This is because each instruction is interpreted just before its execution. If the program contains a loop, the same instructions are interpreted over and over again. Both compilers and interpreters are used today. You should use the one that best suits your needs at the moment. You might use a BASIC interpreter to write your program and debug it and then use a BASIC compiler when the program is done and ready to run on a regular basis.

Many third-generation languages were developed. The "computer wonks" or "hackers" of the day developed languages to work the way they thought languages should work. Most of these third-generation languages are now forgotten, but a few caught on and are still being used. Each was conceived and developed with some purpose in mind, but because their original purposes were not the same, these languages vary greatly in their ability to handle any given project.

Those that can be used to accomplish one type of task easily are often difficult and cumbersome to use on another. FORTRAN (FORmula TRANslator) was designed for scientists and is great with equations and mathematical calculations; however, it is not as good at handling large amounts of data. On the other hand, languages such as COBOL (COmmon Business-Oriented Language) and MUMPS (Massachusetts general hospital Utility Multi-Programming System) were designed to easily handle the large data files for businesses or hospitals but were found wanting when it came to algebraic calculations. To date, there is no universal programming language. No language is all things to all people. This book concerns itself with just two programming languages: BASIC and C.

BASIC was designed at Dartmouth College in 1963 for instructional purposes and as a language was quite limited. In fact, the name BASIC is an acronym derived from Beginners All-purpose Symbolic Instruction Code. It did, however, contain some features that caused the rapidly growing computer industry to quickly embrace it. BASIC was relatively easy to use, and it was interactive. Because of this popularity, additional features were soon added. The original limitations and the appropriateness of the acronym no longer exist. It still has strengths and weaknesses, but BASIC long ago established its place in the world of programming languages.

The second language discussed in this book is C. C has been described as a "hacker's" or programmer's language, which is probably true. Only a "real" programmer would bother with it. It was not designed to make programming easy so that anyone could do it; it was designed to get a job done. Designed by a programmer at Bell Telephone Laboratories in the early 1970s for use in the lab, it has a minimum of frills or "user-friendly" features. In some ways, C seemed to reverse the trend of trying to make programming easier, but it does have some desirable features.

Like most high-level languages of its period, it lends itself to structured programming (which will be discussed in the next chapter). There are two important points about C: just about anything that can be done in the machine language can be done with C (this is not true of most high-level languages) and C is transportable. A program written in C can be moved from one computer to another with little effort. Remember, each brand of computer has a different set of machine instructions. (With microprocessors, machine instructions change with the brand of chip used.) Therefore, the assembler language of each computer is also different. If you designed and wrote some software in assembler language for one computer and wanted to be able to market it to users of other brands of computers, you would need to rewrite that software for each different brand of computer you wanted to run it on. C, on the other hand, allows you the full power of machine language and at the same time is transportable from one computer to another. You simply recompile on the new computer, and you have a machine language copy of the program for that computer. For these reasons, much of today's software is developed with the C language.

Fourth-Generation and Beyond

In the mid-to-late 1970s, in a further effort to speed up programming and reduce the skill level required to program, the programming industry began developing fourth-generation languages. Although the goal was the same, different approaches were used in trying to achieve it.

Some of these new languages attempt to reduce the skill level from that of a programmer to that of the person using the end result. Suppose that instead of having to tell the computer *how* to do something, you could simply tell it *what* you want done. Other new languages attempted to shift the skill level to that of the analyst. These languages allow the analyst to generate screens and reports from well-defined databases, using data dictionaries. In fact, some of these fourth-generation languages have been referred to as **high-level database languages.** (A **database** is a collection of data files in which all related data is linked together without redundancy while easily allowing for the addition of new types of data. A **data dictionary** is the physical description of each data type stored in the database.) So far, there has been a small problem. Imagine the amount of "thinking" the computer must do to convert the *what* to *how*. These new languages tend to be slow.

It is possible that a fifth-generation will arise before a fourth-generation language really catches on. For example, in the area of human language processors, there are systems that will understand your commands regardless of words, syntax, or sentence structure used. As long as the statement is in acceptable English, the computer will understand and follow the instructions. Expert and artificial intelligence systems are examples of other pioneering areas of development.

Expert systems are systems that restrict themselves to one field of endeavor. They have access to all the currently accepted information in that field. They take these facts and with a heuristic approach (see Chapter 2) draw conclusions that in the past required significant human expertise. An example of an expert system is one that diagnoses a medical problem from the patient's symptoms. Another important development is **artificial intelligence** (AI), in which computer science is pursuing systems that would be capable of performing tasks previously thought to require human knowledge, understanding, learning, and reasoning.

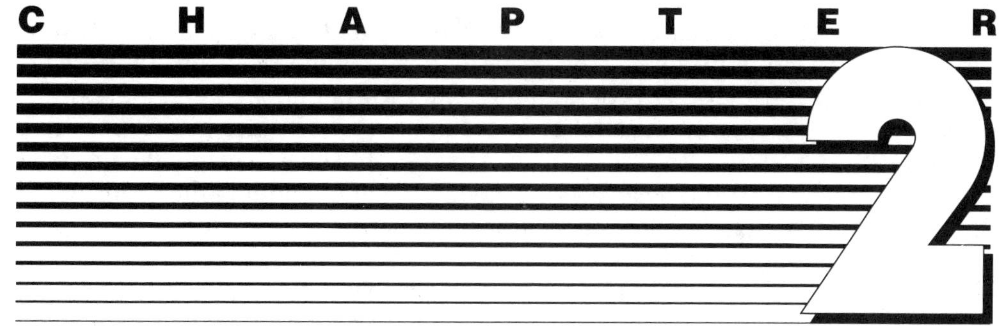

DEVELOPMENT TECHNIQUES

You have a program to write. Perhaps you've done a little programming on your own, but you're not quite sure of the best way to attack this problem. Or perhaps you have done considerable programming, but always under direction, and this time you're on your own. A number of techniques or aids are available. Soon you will look at a few of these techniques in detail. However, you might gain some insight on how they would best suit your needs by understanding the events leading to the development of these techniques.

Twenty-five years ago, computers were considerably more expensive, slower in execution time, and smaller in memory capacity than they are today. When you compared the cost of the computer or the cost of buying computer time against the cost of programming, there was no contest: the computer was by far the more expensive of the two. This meant that the smaller the program, the better. Each instruction that was removed from a program increased the speed of execution and saved precious memory. The average production for a professional programmer was seven lines of code per day. If you could jump back and reuse six lines of code at one spot and then jump to another spot and reuse a few more, you would. You would do anything that made the end result smaller or faster.

This meant that it was often difficult, even for the programmer who wrote the code, to go back and follow the program's logic. In today's vernacular, this type of coding is referred to as "spaghetti code." To make it easier to understand such programs, a **flowcharting** system was developed to graphically illustrate program flow and logic. It was thought that the best way to start a program was to flowchart the logic. Although conditions have changed and the incentive to produce spaghetti code no longer exists, flowcharting still has value and will be discussed later in this chapter.

A trend existed from the beginning of computer development for newer computers to be faster, smaller, and less expensive than their predecessors. At the same time, salaries were increasing because of inflation. The cost of labor (programming) eventually surpassed the cost of the computer.

Now it became important to reduce the cost of programming. The expense of modifying and debugging programs written with the convoluted logic of spaghetti code was high. Keeping the logic simple became vital. So what if the program took more memory? Memory was now cheap, and if the program took a little longer to run, no one cared because computers were so much faster than they had been. It was only important to produce programs that were easy to understand and to produce them quickly. The computer industry began looking for standarized code with simple, easy-to-understand logic that anyone could modify and maintain. It was from this environment that the concept of **structured programming** evolved—a set of rules and techniques designed to standardize and speed up programming.

Unfortunately, the disparity between the cost of the computer and the cost of programming continued to increase. When the microcomputer was introduced in the 1970s, this trend accelerated. The industry started to develop new programming languages—the fourth-generation languages discussed in Chapter 1. The programming industry now looked for a language that would make programming easier and thus speed up production. At the same time, still another phenomenon was causing the cost of delivering completed programs to climb.

The programs (or systems) being developed were becoming larger and more complicated. They were taking longer to develop. Some systems would take years to complete. Unfortunately, after such a long period of time had passed, the original needs had changed. The programs were obsolete on the day they were installed, which meant that additional programming was required to make them acceptable; thus, there were additional increases to the cost of programming.

One way to ensure that new programs are not obsolete before they are complete is to keep the end-user involved throughout the development process. An effective way to do this is to have the end-users review a prototype of the program early in the development process. Corrections can be suggested and incorporated in a new prototype, and the cycle then repeated. This approach to programming is called **prototyping**; however, for prototyping to work, you need a simple way to rapidly modify your programs. That is just what these new fourth-generation languages allow you to do. There are times, however, when prototyping can be effectively used with other languages as well, and the need to keep the end-user involved in development continues, regardless of what language is involved.

The techniques to help develop programs mentioned so far are only some of those used in the programming industry. There are others, such as data flow diagrams, HIPO diagrams, structured English, pseudocode, decision tables, and Chapin charts. Each is involved with one or more parts of the total task. To formally organize a group of these aids into one approach is to create a methodology.

A **methodology** is a set of aids, controls, and procedures that are followed to develop a program. Managers and their programming teams use methodologies to control the development of a large system of programs. Large programming departments use them to control all of their program development work. A few of the better known methodologies are Yourdon's structured design, the Jackson design methodology, and the Warnier-Orr design methodology.

The term "methodology" has recently taken on a slightly different meaning. There is a tendency to use it to refer to a group of products currently for sale to the computer industry. These products have been developed by different consulting and accounting firms in an attempt to ensure that their staffs and their customers' staffs will be successful in their development efforts. Any methodology of this type will consist of numerous volumes containing the design strategies, evaluation aids, procedures to follow, and sample forms that are to be completed as part of the control procedures. These forms document and ensure that each step of the procedure is carried out. Because of this additional work, the training involved in learning the methodology, and the methodology's purchase price, there is a potential increase in the cost necessary to complete a project, but, if followed religiously, the methodology tends to increase the probability of successfully completing a development task.

The concepts of flowcharting, structured programming, and prototyping mentioned earlier can effectively be used by the amateur and professional alike in program development efforts.

FLOWCHARTING

The process of using a **program flowchart** has a twofold purpose: first, as an aid to programming design and second, as a communication tool. There are times when the process you are trying to translate into a program is not clear in your mind. Perhaps the process is complicated enough so that without writing it down you have trouble keeping all the processes in mind. It is in this case that the flowchart has value as a programming design aid. If you have trouble following the logic of your own program, you can be sure others will have difficulty maintaining the program at a later date. Fortunately, program flowcharting can be a useful communication tool as well as a design aid.

Conventional Flowcharting

In addition to a program flowchart, which shows the program's logic, there is a second type of flowchart called a **system** or **operations flowchart**, and it documents the operation steps; that is, it graphically shows the computer operator how to run the system. Both types of flowcharts use the same group of symbols. (Templates with these symbols may be purchased in stationery or art supply stores.) The following is a list of these symbols:

(See Figure 2.1 on next page)

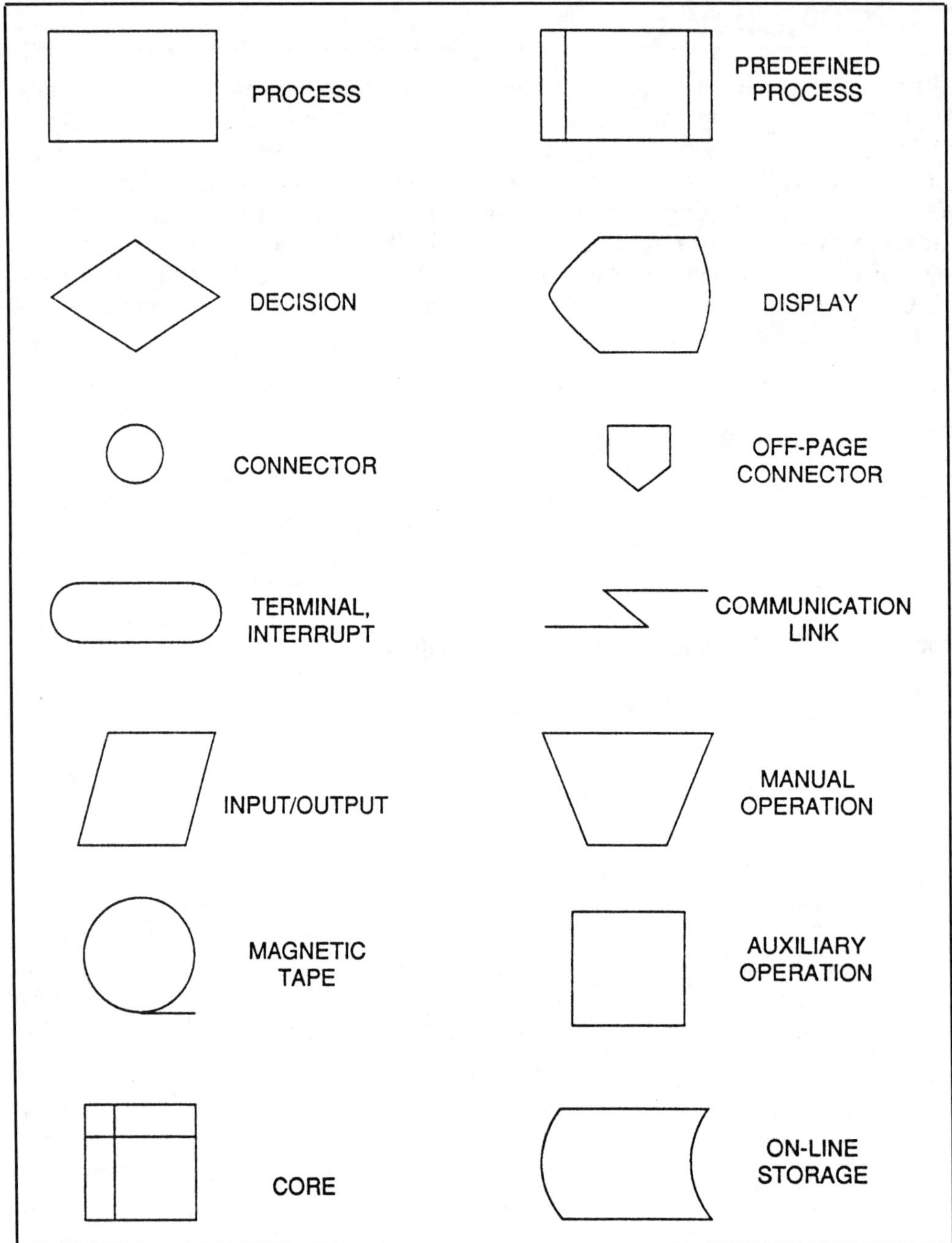

Figure 2.1 *Conventional flowchart symbols (as defined by American National Standards Institute X3.5 – 1970)*

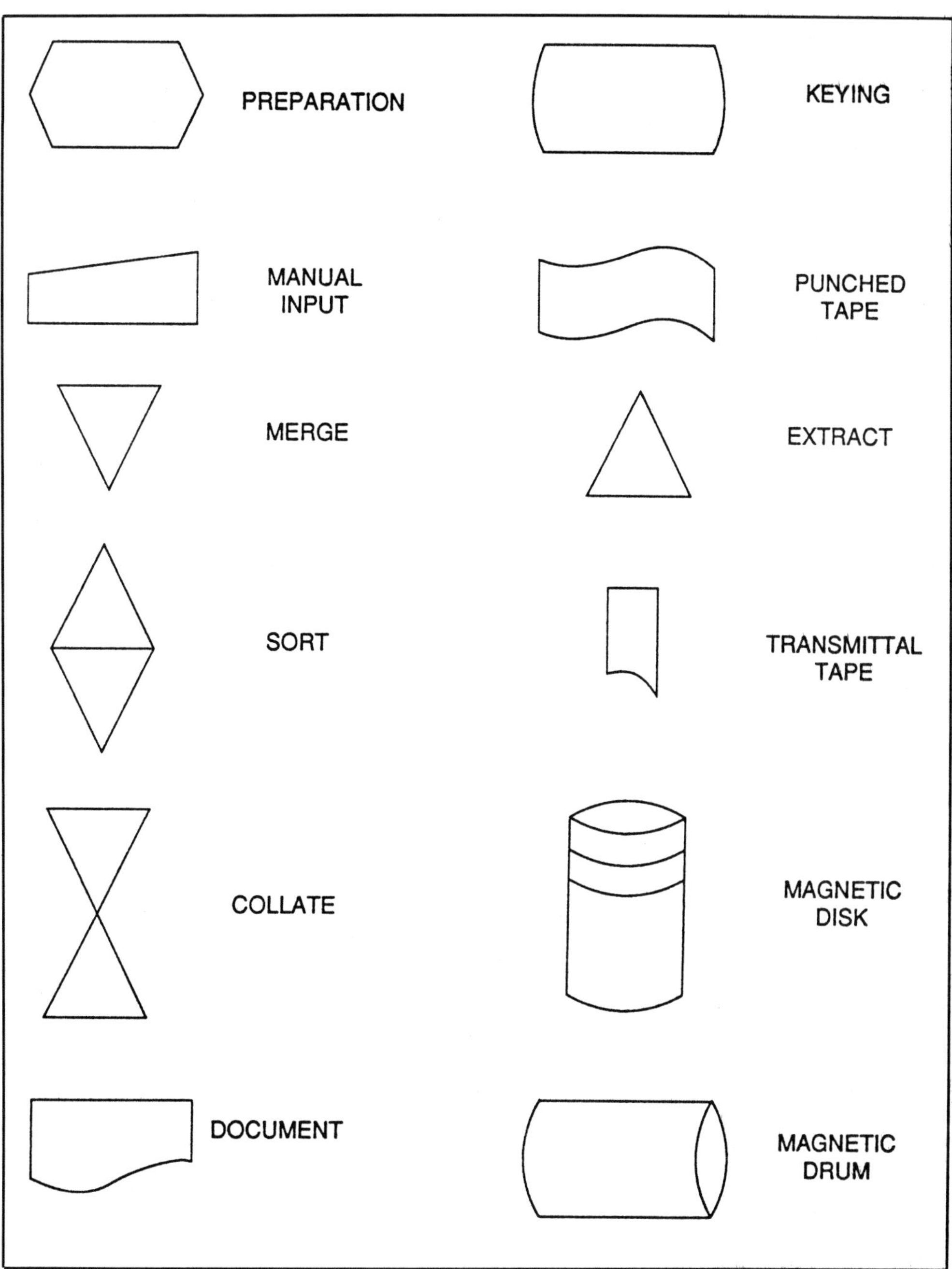

Figure 2.1 *(continued)*

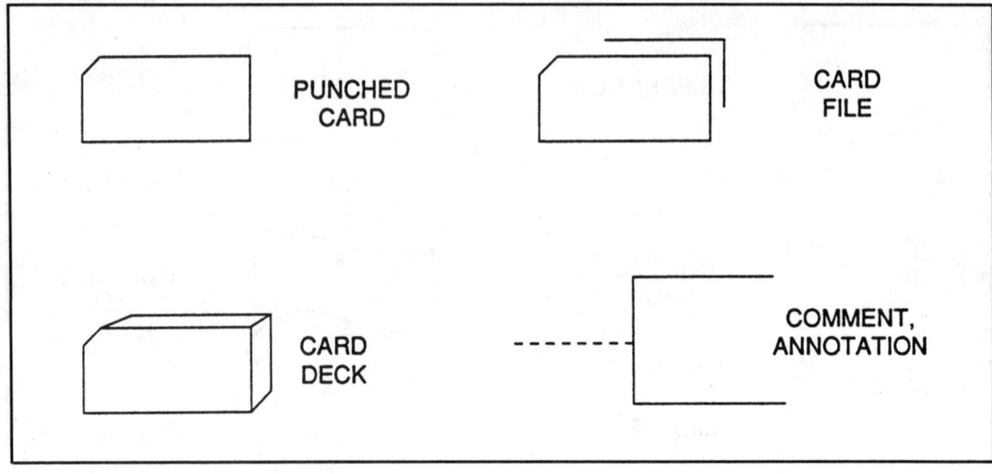

Figure 2.1 *(continued)*

As the old traditional batch processing has been replaced with on-line systems, the duties of the computer operator have changed, and the need for the system flowchart has reduced. Where still appropriate, however, the system flowchart takes the form shown in Figure 2.2:

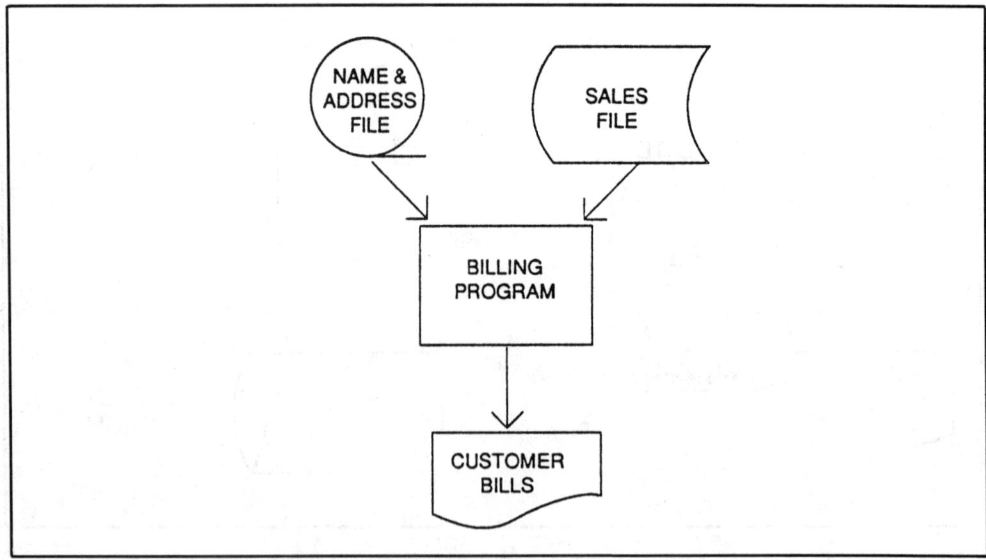

Figure 2.2 *Example of system flowchart*

Since the early days of programming, the conventional program logic flowchart has also become unpopular for many reasons. Simpler diagramming systems evolved that were designed around the concepts of structured programming or around the elements that the logic flowchart does not address (such as the flow of data). As programming systems grew in size, another limitation of flowcharting became apparent: with size, the flowchart becomes so complicated that it has little or no value. Substitutes for flowcharting were developed as a result of its unpopularity and limitations. They have taken various forms, including pseudocode and structured English. With these techniques, the program logic is written as if it were a program, but uses easy-to-understand English statements. Regardless of the unpopularity of logic flowcharting, it is still used, but its form has changed somewhat.

Structured Flowcharting

In the same way that early "creative" programming evolved into structured programming, the concepts of flowcharting have also evolved. Flowcharting has been simplified and structured. Although it still has limitations and is becoming less popular, structured flowcharting is used today. This book will confine itself to a discussion of structured flowcharting. Flowcharting need not be rigorously used in all programming as was once the convention, but it can still be effectively used as an aid to programming. If an elusive bit of logic is giving you trouble, you might find a visual diagram in the form of a flowchart useful.

The number of flowchart symbols traditionally used in structured flowcharting has been reduced. One new symbol has been added for "case" situations. These structured flowchart symbols appear in Figure 2.3:

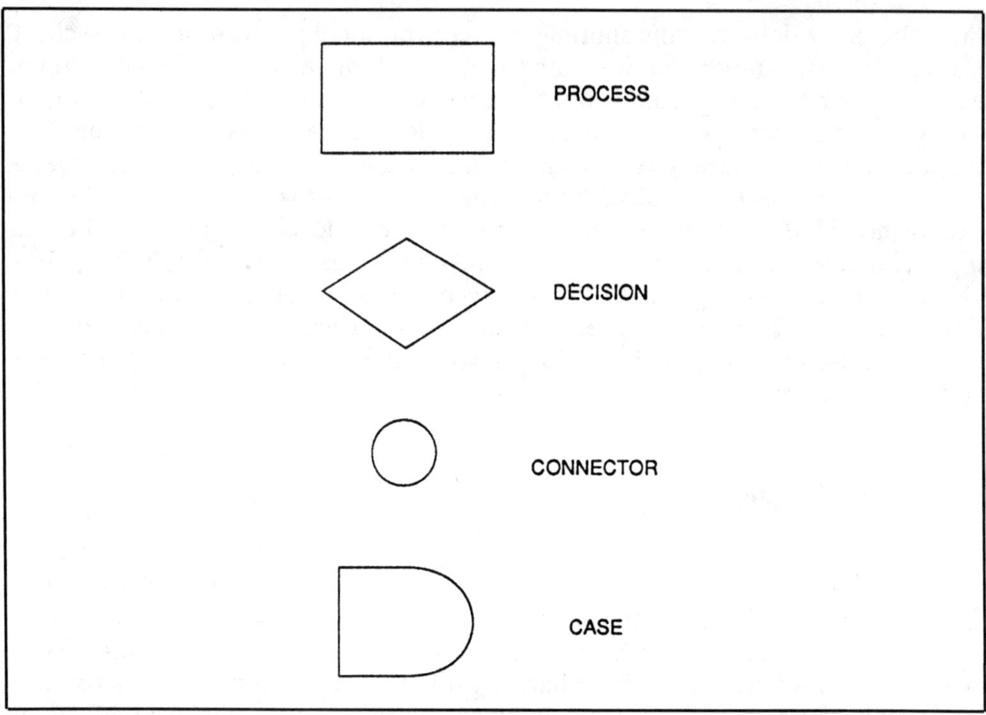

Figure 2.3 *Structured flowchart symbols*

For this example, assume that you have a screen that asks the user to select one of four options. The flowchart for this situation might appear as follows:

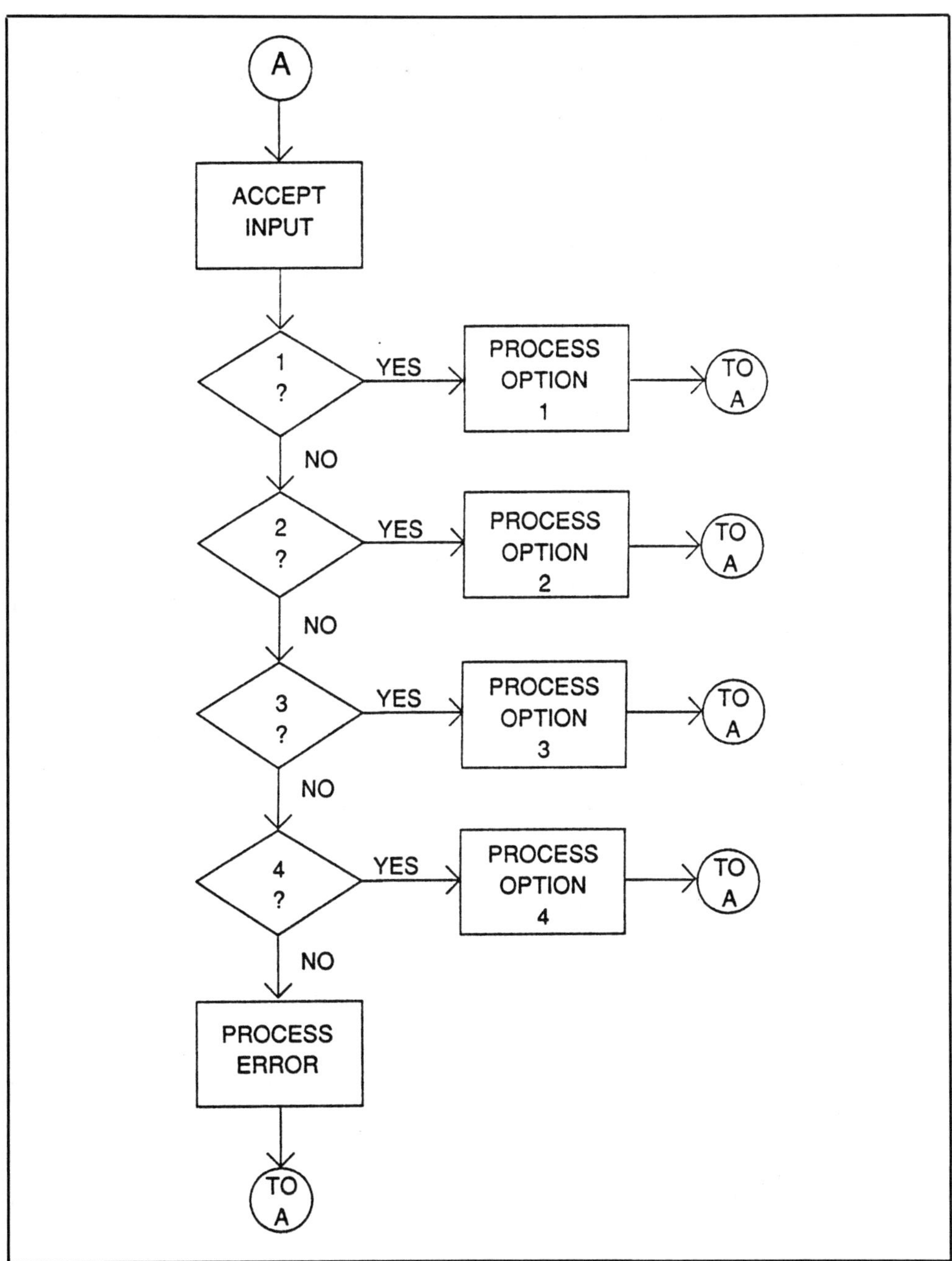

Figure 2.4 *Sample flowchart: select one of four options*

The example in Figure 2.4 could use four BASIC IF statements; however, note that the ON - GOSUB instruction was designed to be used in a situation in which selections are presented. This also happens to be the situation for which the case flowchart symbol was intended. Figure 2.5 is a sample flowchart for the same situation described for Figure 2.4, except that it uses the case symbol:

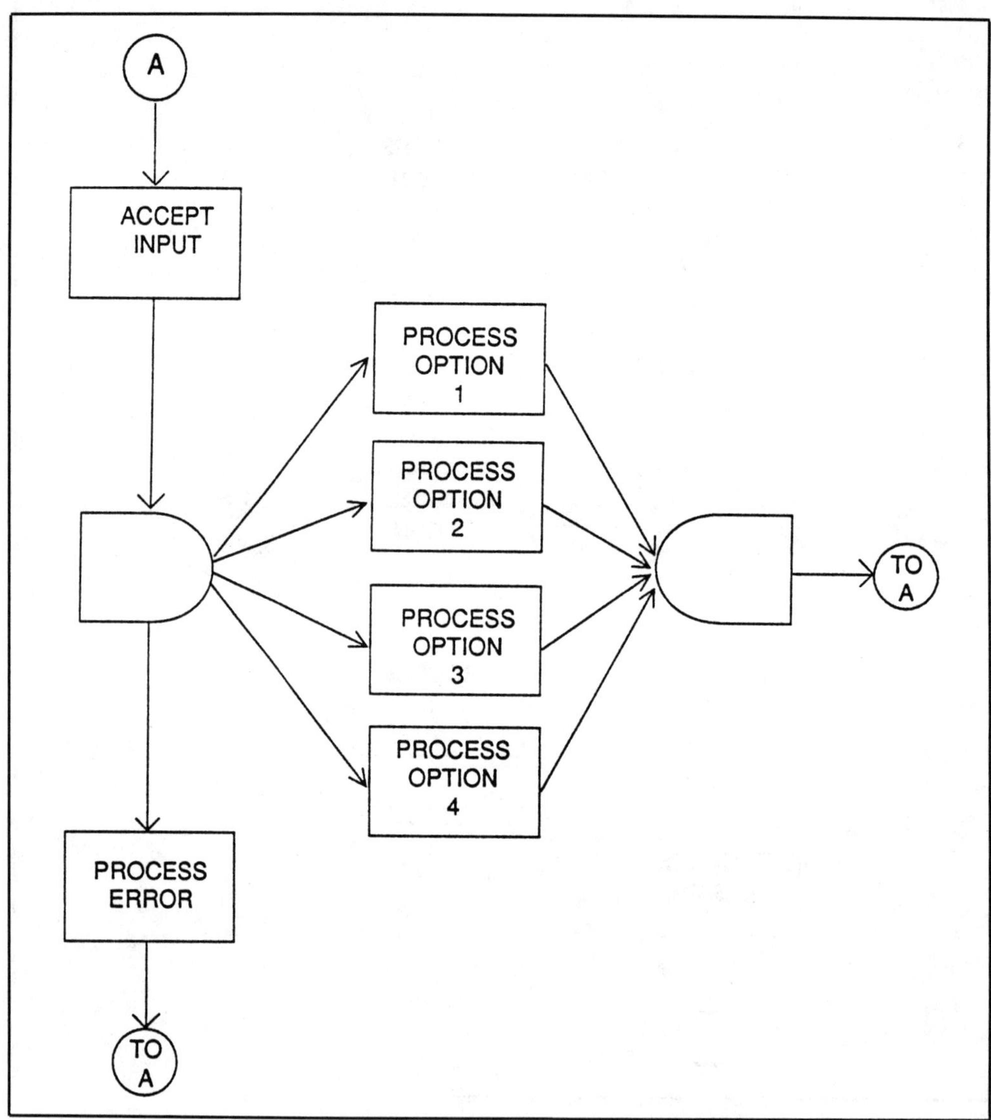

Figure 2.5 *Sample case flowchart*

The examples shown so far are more concerned with program flow than with logic. Consider an example that is concerned with program logic. Recall the earlier discussion of programmers needing to show early computers how to multiply. How did they go about it? You know that 7*3 is the same as 7+7+7 or 3+3+3+3+3+3+3. You also know that the computer knows how to add. With this knowledge, you can flowchart a routine that multiplies by repeated addition. It might resemble Figure 2.6:

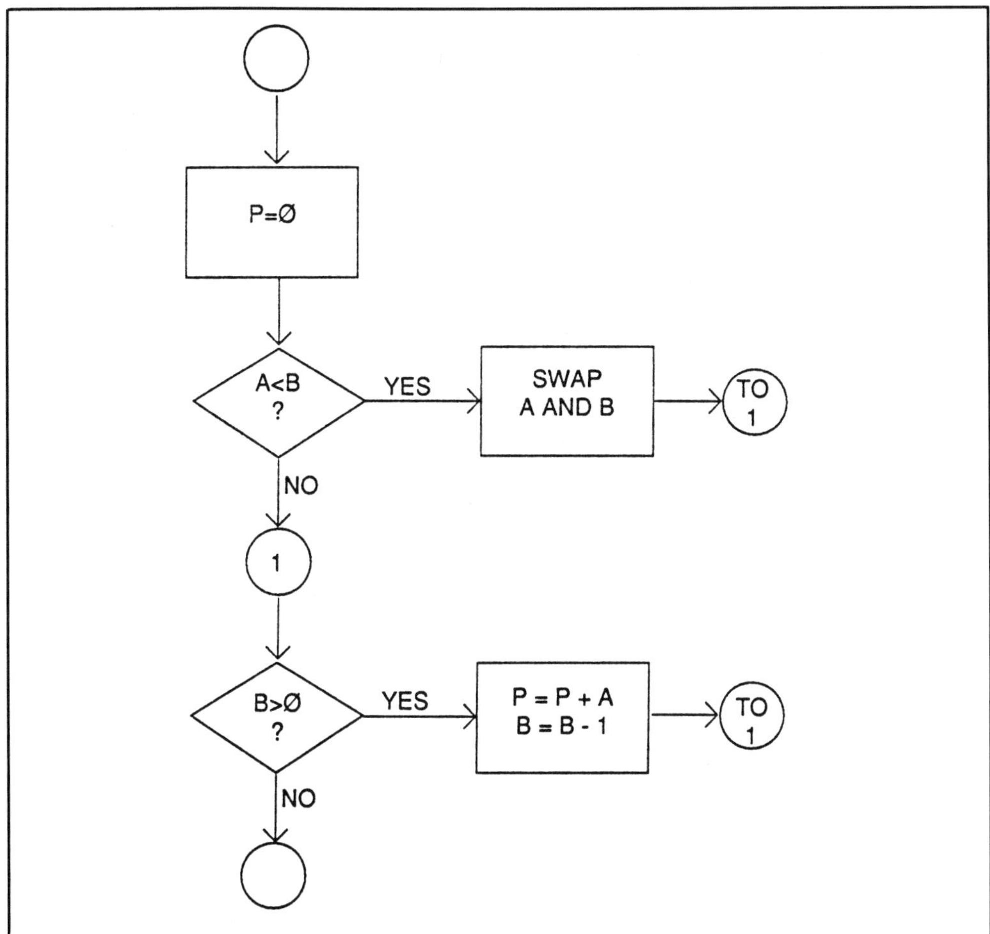

Figure 2.6 Flowchart to multiply A and B, using addition

If the first decision in the figure were removed, the logic would still work; however, it was included to make the routine more efficient. Suppose you wanted to multiply 3 by 4096. This first decision avoids a situation in which the computer would add 3 to itself over 4000 times and always chooses the simple alternative of adding 4096 to itself three times.

STRUCTURED PROGRAMMING

The concept of structured programming, as mentioned in Chapter 1, was the outgrowth of the spaghetti code era of programming. This was a time when programming was considered an art. As the limitations of the computer (speed and memory size) were overcome, the need to reduce programming costs took precedence, and the direction of the programming profession changed. With structured design, programming became a science—a set of procedures to help programmers think through their problems and at the same time make their code more readable and reliable. Readability improved the speed and ease with which a program could be modified or maintained. Reliability (bug-free code) speeded up development of a system. In the past, it was not uncommon for 50% of a programmer's development time to be spent in debugging new code. If a programmer could produce bug-free code the first time, production time could be cut in half. The question remains: just what are these structured procedures?

The concept of structured programming may vary somewhat from book to book and from company to company because the structured technique is evolving in exactly the same way that programming itself is evolving. However, the following concepts are generally classified as elements of structured programming:

- top-down design
- top-to-bottom logic flow
- modular design
- limited statement types
- self-documenting code
- top-down programming

Top-Down Design

A structured program system is designed in layers. First, you prepare the general overview of the total system, describing its main operations. This is sometimes called the **functional design**. Next, you prepare the **system design**, an intermediate level that breaks the system into functions or modules. What each of these modules will do is briefly described, but how it is to be done is not. Finally, the **detail design** is prepared, which describes exactly how each module is to be programmed.

Once the intermediate level of design is complete and all functions are known, the detail design and programming of each module can be accomplished simultaneously. You need not wait for module one to be complete before starting on module two. You already know the purpose of each module. This is a controlled approach to design that permits developers to involve as large a programming staff as desired. It is common for the programming staff to take an active role in the detail design in addition to the ultimate programming.

Top-to-Bottom Logic Flow

The logic flow of each module as well as the program system itself should start at the top and proceed in a straight line to the bottom. There should be no jumping around. It is important to keep the logic as simple as possible. What is simpler than a straight-line sequence of operations? Obviously, there must be some exceptions to this, but the exceptions are limited, well defined, and modularized.

Modular Design

The smallest or lowest unit of the top-down design is the **module**. All program systems will be made up of these building blocks. In BASIC, the element that best corresponds to the module is the **subroutine**. In C, the element is called a **function**. A module is to be used for one simple operation. Modules should be small in size (generally, less than a page of code in length), making it reasonable to use the structured logic flowchart, which works best for small pieces of code. All modules will have only one entry point and one exit point.

Only the data directly related to the operation is passed to the module; all other data is hidden from it. Limiting the size of the module and allowing only one entry and one exit point makes the module a stand-alone unit. It can be designed, programmed, and tested on its own. Once completed and tested, it becomes a known and trusted quantity that can be relied upon when incorporated into the total system. Keeping the module small and following the other principles of structured programming means there is a better chance that this module will be free of bugs when written.

Once a module is complete, the purpose of the module and the interfaces to the module must be well defined so other programmers working on the system can make use of it in their own programming. You can combine modules with other modules to create new functions, without needing to understand their internal workings.

Limited Statement Types

Not all programming instructions lend themselves to structured concepts. The ones that do lend themselves to structured concepts have been singled out for use while those that do not have been repudiated. One instruction in particular has been severely criticized: the GOTO command. The GOTO, and to some extent the IF instruction, has fallen from grace because indiscriminate use of the unconditional and conditional branch instructions caused the problems in spaghetti code. If the GOTO did not exist and the IF had been controlled, spaghetti code would not have existed. Some will say that the GOTO should never be used. Others are content to say it should be used sparingly. Languages such as BASIC that were developed before the evolution of structured concepts could not function as originally designed without the GOTO. New structured languages were developed and languages such as BASIC were upgraded to function in a structured environment. Although the GOTO can still be found in legitimate use today (especially in BASIC), it has received a considerable amount of adverse publicity.

In today's structured programming, there are only four basic statement types:

- sequence
- IF THEN ELSE
- do WHILE
- do UNTIL

The sequence is a fundamental operation of structured programming. Program flow is linear, from top to bottom. The flowchart of a sequence is as follows:

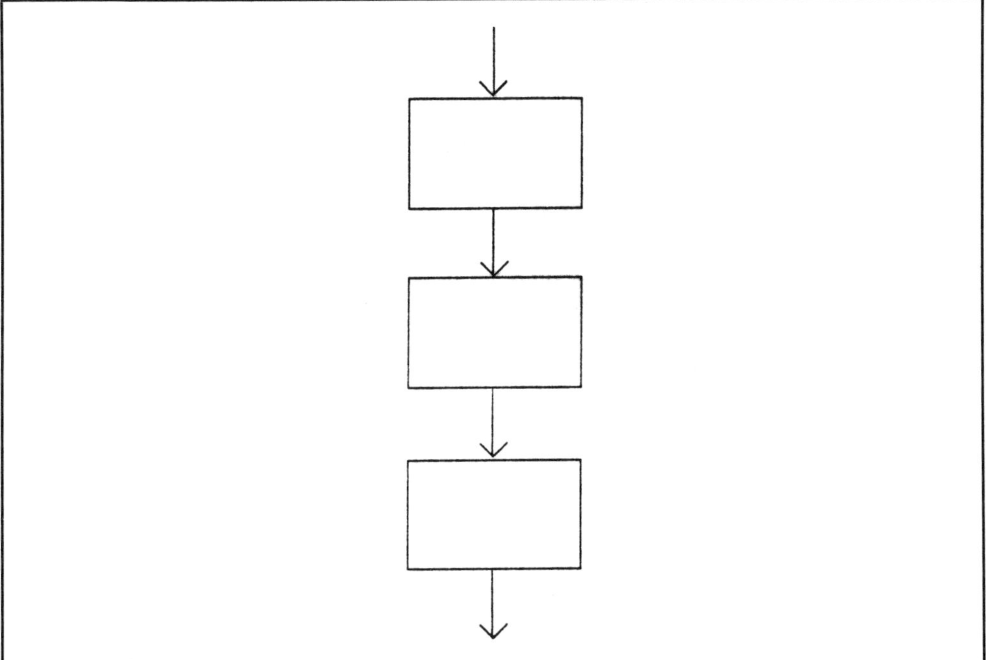

Figure 2.7 Flowchart of a sequence statement type

The remainder of the statement types seem to deviate from the linear top-to-bottom concept discussed here, but if you look closely at each remaining statement type, you will find they are all intended to function as self-contained units that, once completed, will continue the linear program flow to the bottom of the program. Actually, each of the remaining program types could be thought of as being contained within the operation blocks of the linear sequence in Figure 2.7. Without allowing these deviations from the linear concept, the main strength of the computer would be lost. Using them in a controlled fashion preserves this strength but creates a structured result.

The IF THEN ELSE statement is flowcharted in Figures 2.8 and 2.9:

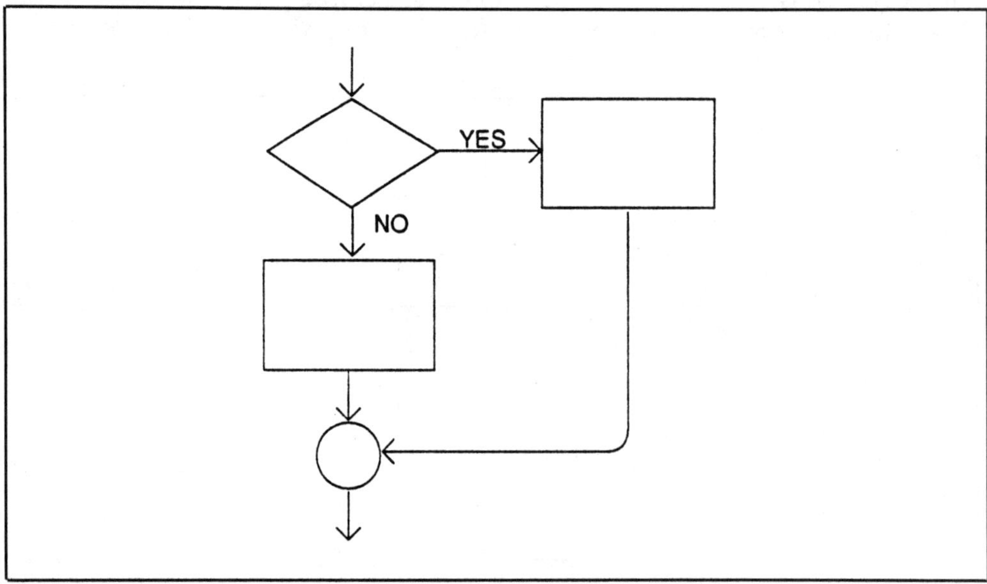

Figure 2.8 Flowchart of an IF THEN ELSE statement type

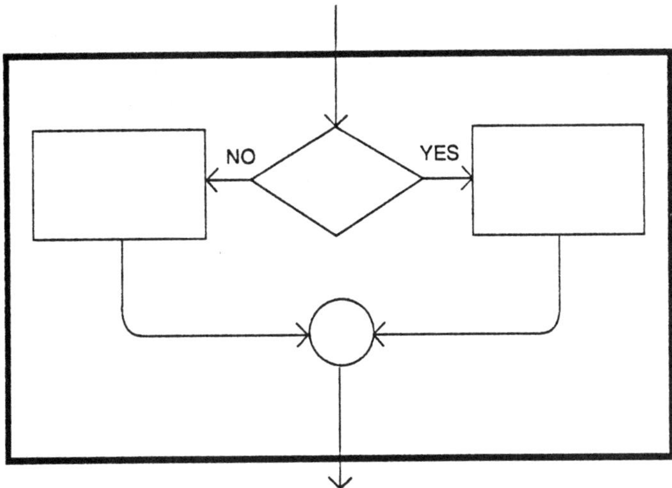

Figure 2.9 Alternate IF THEN ELSE flowchart

Figure 2.8 is the form you are familiar with if you use BASIC. Figure 2.9 is perhaps a better diagram of the concept. Actually, the two figures demonstrate exactly the same concept. The point is that the condition is tested. If true, the THEN branch is taken; if false, the ELSE branch is taken. But in all cases the program flow is returned to the main linear sequence, which means that the IF THEN ELSE statement used in this way is still considered linear. If used properly, it could be contained completely within one sequence operation shown in Figure 2.9 without affecting the top-to-bottom flow of the program.

When writing structured code in BASIC, you can sometimes use horizontal coding to keep from having to jump around in the program. As an example, examine the following BASIC IF instruction:

```
100 IF A=B THEN A=0 ELSE A=4*C
```

By using the ELSE option and keeping all the code horizontal, you eliminate the need to jump around between commands. The next example is the way you would have written the same code, using the original BASIC instructions. The ELSE option was not part of the original BASIC.

```
100 IF A=B THEN 130
110 A=4*C                    ; This is the ELSE option
120 GOTO 140
130 A=0                      ; This is the THEN option
140 ...
```

The do WHILE statement flowchart is shown in Figure 2.10:

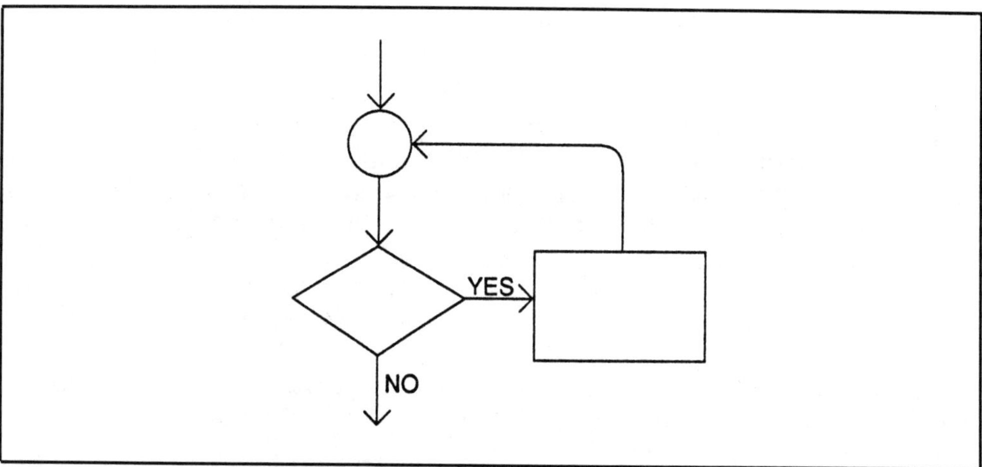

Figure 2.10 *Flowchart of the do WHILE statement type*

In this case, the termination condition is tested first. If it is true, the loop is executed, returning program flow back to the linear flow above the condition test. The loop is repeated until the condition proves false, and then the flow continues on the linear path down the program.

The last type of statement, do UNTIL, is similar to do WHILE but with two important differences. First, the statements in the loop are executed, and then they are followed by the condition test. If the condition fails, the program control is returned above the loop, and the loop is executed again. When the condition is true, the loop is ignored and program flow is allowed to continue downward. See Figure 2.11:

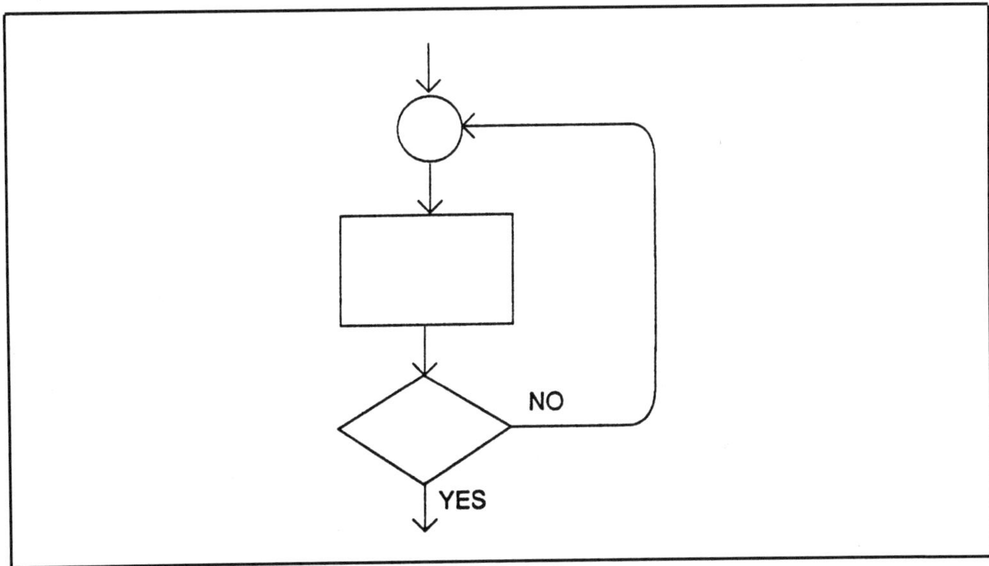

Figure 2.11 Flowchart of the do UNTIL statement type

The two types of loop statements, WHILE and UNTIL, can be constructed in both BASIC and C, using the instructions of the two languages.

Self-Documenting Code

The concept of creating self-documenting code is a logical outgrowth of the need for easy-to-understand programs. The elements that help accomplish this goal are rather simple.

Because flow is linear from top to bottom, indentations can be used to show momentary deviations from this flow. An example would be indenting the loop in a FOR statement in BASIC code as follows:

```
100 FOR X = 1 TO 10
110     Y = X*X
120     PRINT Y
130 NEXT X
140 PRINT "That's all."
```

You can use descriptive, meaningful words for variables and program names to help a program become self-documenting. Using comments to explain the logic of the program also improves readability.

Top-Down Programming

Top-down programming is the same concept as top-down design. You program in layers, writing the top level first. This is your main program, and it simply calls the appropriate modules. Examine the following BASIC code:

```
100 GOSUB 600                  ; Build screen
110 GOSUB 700                  ; Accept user input
120 GOSUB 800                  ; Compute result
130 GOSUB 900                  ; Display result
140 END
```

This is the complete top level of the program. Now, create stubs for each of the modules or subroutines called. A **stub** is simply an empty shell of the module. It contains only an entry point and an exit point. See the following examples:

```
599 ;**** Subroutine to build screen ****
600                                ; Temporary entry for stub
690 RETURN                         ; Exit to main program
...
899 ;**** Subroutine to display result ****
900                                ; Temporary entry for stub
990 RETURN                         ; Exit to main program
```

You have now programmed the top level of your program, including stubs for each of the modules. You have a complete running program. Run it and test it. Of course nothing will happen, but any syntax errors can be caught and corrected. Now that you know your main program works, drop down one level and start programming a module. When you have completed and tested the module, you can use it to replace the stub with a running subroutine. Again, not much will happen, but this time an input screen will be displayed. Program the next module and then the next, until you are done. If each of the modules is small enough, there is a good chance you could complete the whole program without an error.

PROTOTYPING

Many analysts and programmers prefer to work behind closed doors, isolated from everything but their computer. In their protected environment, they can design and program the most elegant of systems. As inviting as such an environment might sound to you, it can lead to disaster. The importance of end-users cannot be overemphasized. Keep in mind that you are developing the system for them. It is they who must eventually use the system to do their work and who will eventually make "your" system a success or failure.

The key to success is to give up proprietorship. Create an environment that allows users to take an active role in the development process. They are a valuable resource. Use them. Let users feel that it is their system – one that not only does their job, it does the job the way they want it done, and they helped design it.

User Involvement in Development

Today, there is more and more emphasis on the user in the development process. You use this vital resource effectively throughout development. Users without data processing experience can actually take an active and valuable role in the following areas:

- analysis
- design
- data administration
- testing
- installation and training

However, to take advantage of user input, the development staff must create an environment that makes that input possible. The analyst must rely on users for much of the information concerning the needs and requirements of the new system. Involvement with data administration allows the user to define data requirements, build data dictionaries, and capture and/or verify data. Involvement in testing relates to defining and building the test procedures and test scripts as well as the actual testing for verifying the validity of the system. For installation and training, users should also take an active role involving and instructing other potential users of the new system; however, it is user involvement in designing the new system that will be emphasized at the moment.

Users can certainly offer their ideas on a system's design, but without training in data processing, they can't be expected to know what options are really available. Often, a user will suggest an idea only to find it unsatisfactory once implemented. Or, once the idea is implemented, it can lead the user to an even better idea, which is where the concept of prototyping can be effectively used. Take the user's idea and build a sample or prototype of the idea so the user can actually try out the concept. Let the user evaluate the prototype and then make suggestions on improvement if it is unsatisfactory.

This approach obviously creates some problems, not the least of which is the potential damage to your ego. Someone has just criticized your program, your creation. You must realize that this isn't a rejection of you personally; it is a criticism of an idea that was probably the user's in the first place. Remember that the prototype was built for the purpose of evaluation and not intended to be a final result.

Prototyping Techniques

A major problem with prototyping is figuring out how to build a prototype of a proposed system and then perhaps scrap it and start over numerous times without allowing the time spent in programming to be prohibitive. If you use the conventional development approach, there is little chance of prototyping without wasting an excessive amount of time, but there is a solution.

Programming in a fourth-generation language makes prototyping easier. These languages were developed to speed up the programming process. Tools for rapidly building screens are often incorporated in them. They also tend to free programming from the limitations and restrictions of the file data. You can add data to files and not be concerned about having to change all modules that access the file. But prototyping can still be accomplished even if you don't have these luxuries.

You might try tools that would allow you to rapidly simulate the actual system. Tools such as report generators, query languages, and spreadsheets can be used for simulation; however, once you find what you want, you still must program the actual system in the appropriate language.

The best approach, regardless of the language you have to work with, is to design your development around prototyping. Structured design gives you a system of small, well-designed modules. It is possible to use the same modules in more than one system of programs; therefore, it is advantageous to create a module library. After you have programmed for a while, you should have a fair-sized collection of well-defined modules that are small and limited to a single function. Frequently, with a little additional programming, new prototypes could be written by simply putting together these modules from the library. These prototypes could be changed with equal ease.

One of the most difficult modifications to a system has always been changing the storage files. Adding new fields to a file record could have a disastrous effect on a computer system. All programs or modules that accessed that record would require modification. It might require changes throughout the total system. To reduce the effect of such a change, hide file and record data from all modules except a file-handling program. You can build the concept of a data dictionary within your file handling program so that file descriptions are created only once. To all other programs or modules, the data is simply a variable. Where or how it is stored is of no concern to any module that is not part of the file handler. This technique would allow you to produce a prototype of a system and simply have a stub for the file handler. Put some dummy variables in the stub that will be passed back to the modules when the file handler is accessed. In this way, the user could evaluate the prototype before much of the system was actually programmed.

In prototyping, it is important to get user feedback as early and as often as possible during development. Prototyping is an iterative process. You build a prototype, evaluate it, modify it, and then evaluate it again. With each iteration, the prototype is a little closer to the finished product.

Finally, a word of caution: prototyping is an effective technique to help produce user-friendly programs, but it has a built-in hazard. It is difficult to ever complete a system. Users and programmers can both get into a mind-set in which there is always some new idea or feature that could be tried or added to the system to make it better. They lose perspective on the real objective, which is not to keep changing the system to something a little better, but to produce a usable system and get it in operation. For prototyping to work, all participants must understand this objective, and they must personally accept the responsibility for ensuring that it is accomplished.

ANALYSIS

In the professional programming arena, the term "programmer" means many different things. At one extreme, it means a **coder**: someone who receives very specific instructions from an analyst in the form of flowcharts, pseudocode, or structured English. When a programmer is a coder, the detail design, algorithms, and program logic are already worked out. The coder simply translates the instructions into the programming language being used. At the other extreme, you find what is called the **programmer analyst**: someone who might do the work of both the analyst and the programmer. Between these two extremes, the work of programmers and the work of system analysts overlap to some degree. This in-between work tends to be in the realm of program design. Following is a flowchart of the development process to aid you in understanding the place of analysis:

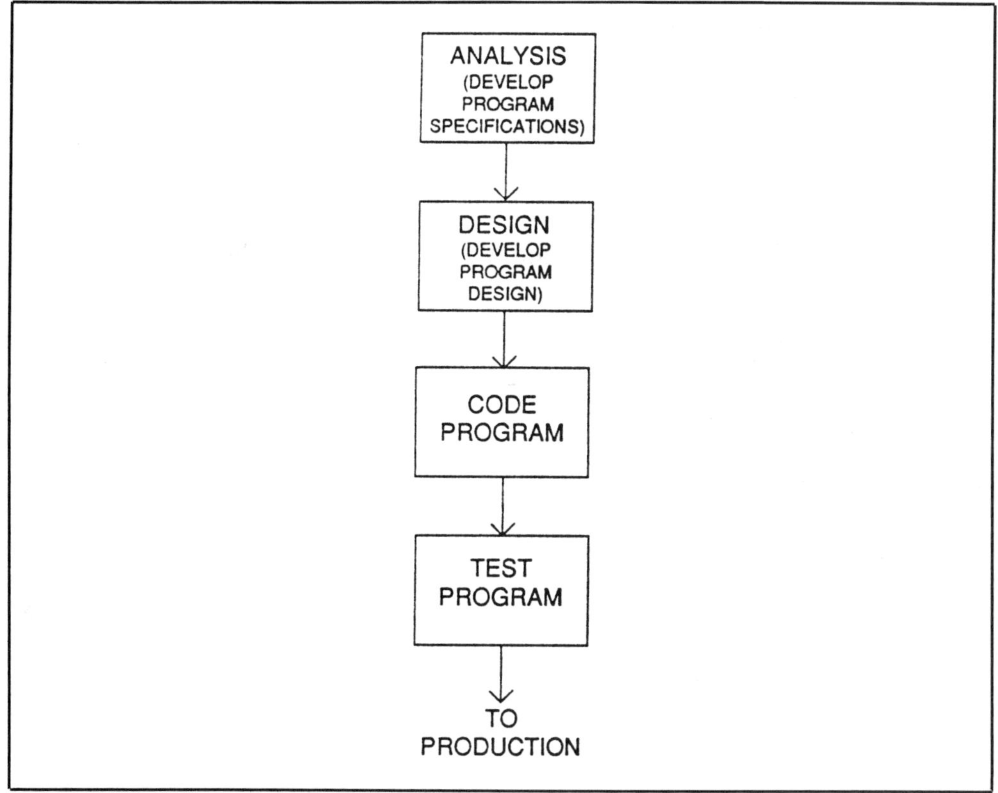

Figure 2.12 The development process

Figure 2.12 displays the four basic steps in program development. The design phase is one that is sometimes classified as part of the duties of the analyst and sometimes within the domain of the programmer. If you are tackling a programming task on your own, you are a programmer analyst by default and should have some idea about what is involved in analysis.

Definition of Analysis

Analysis is the study of a task or problem; it precedes and defines the action to be taken for resolution. A system analyst is generally responsible for analyzing user requirements and environment to produce the following:

- functional specifications
- system specifications
- program specifications
- test specifications

These specifications may be expanded to incorporate the following:

- labor requirements
- physical requirements
- performance requirements
- schedule
- budget
- hardware configuration

In addition to preparing all of the above, the analyst may also be responsible for ordering hardware, directing the programming staff, and even coordinating the total project. Books have been written on the subject of system analysis. The topic of this book is programming, but any good programmer must have some of the skills commonly associated with system analysis, and this chapter should give you sufficient insight to perform the analysis necessary for your own needs. If you have additional interest in tools of the system analyst, you might want to research the following topics:

- decision tables
- decision trees
- data flow diagrams
- data dictionaries
- HIPO diagrams
- structured English
- pseudocode
- Chapin charts
- Nassi-Shneiderman charts
- PERT charts
- Gantt charts

Interviewing Skills

The analyst is the interface between the users and the development staff. Because of this role, interpersonal communication, or the ability to relate to others, is high on the list of skills generally associated with the task of system analysis. There are other skills and knowledge required in analysis as well: knowledge of the user's field of expertise, a knowledge of data processing, and an analytical ability.

Remember that in a professional setting the people from whom you are attempting to gather information may well be hostile toward you and the project involved. They may feel threatened by a new system. Perhaps they fear their job will be eliminated, or through lack of experience or interest they don't want to learn or work with a new computerized system. Perhaps they want to keep the existing system because they were instrumental in setting it up. They could be the resident experts on the current system and feel they will lose prestige if a new system is installed. For these or any number of other reasons, you could find yourself working with a hostile group. A word of warning: no matter how good of a system you design, it will fail if you can't get the people who are going to be using the system behind it. This is one of the main reasons that your ability to relate to and communicate with people is so important. Following are some suggestions to follow when gathering information:

- Know how the company is organized.
- Work through the managers (don't start directly with users).
- Make an appointment for each interview.
- Explain the purpose of the meeting and the time required for it.
- Meet at their convenience and at their desk.
- Be prompt.
- Smile. Be positive and polite.
- Ask for their assistance (don't take it for granted).
- Don't act superior or criticize.
- Be an attentive and understanding listener.
- Try not to let the interview become a gripe session.
- Try to be objective and impartial (don't take sides).
- Have a prepared list of questions.
- Get their ideas.

- Ask if they know of points you failed to bring out.
- Summarize the interview, noting unresolved points.
- Where appropriate, give deserved credit to individuals.

Fact Gathering

The first task required of the analyst is to collect all the pertinent information from the intended users:

- What are the objectives of the project?
- What are the intended benefits?
- What are the limitations you must work within?

  Money
  Staff
  Equipment
  Space
  Time constraints
  Regulations or laws
  Current organization

- How is the task currently being accomplished?

  Procedures
  Sample input documents
  Controls used
  Volumes handled
  Time tables
  Staff required
  Sample output documents

- What are the user's ideas on a new system?

- What data will be input into the new system?

  Accuracy required of data
  Current volume
  Anticipated growth
  Record and field sizes

- What data must be saved on-line?

  Current volume
  Anticipated growth
  Record and field sizes
  Purge on what conditions?

- What is the intended form of new output?

- What is an acceptable response time?

For the application you are working on, some of the points just mentioned may not be appropriate, and other concerns may apply. These you must recognize from your knowledge of the particular application. If you do not already have such knowledge, you should acquire it to a degree that allows you to adequately analyze the process.

Specification Preparation

Once you have collected all the information you can about the current system and future objectives, you must use this information to answer the following questions:

- Are there deficiencies in the current system?

- Could the current system be improved?

- Is there a need for a completely new system?

- Is the task suitable for a computer?

If you decide a new computer system is the solution, the next step is to create the functional specification. If this system is for your own needs at home, the functional specification may be little more than a general idea with a few scribbled notes. Professionally, the functional specification may be a formal multivolume document defining the system to be implemented. This document will define the constraints of the new system along with expected accomplishments. It will describe equipment, staff, schedules, quantities, controls, the general approach, and the general results. From this document, which will be used as the guide for further development, the system specification will be designed.

The system specification is often divided into two parts: the internal specifications and the external specifications. The internal specifications define how the system will be built from the programmer's point of view. It is an intermediate-level document in that it will describe how the overall system will function as well as describe the different modules that will make up the system and the interfaces between those modules. The external specifications will describe the external view of the system. The aspects of the new system that will be visible to the users — input data and screens along with output reports and screen displays — will be defined here. Finally, the program specifications, or detail design, are the designs of each module given in sufficient detail to allow coding.

The names for these documents vary from organization to organization. Sometimes more emphasis is placed on one level of document than another, but the following is a summary of the levels of programming documents produced by the analyst:

- **Functional specifications**

  General description and scope of intended system

- **System specifications**

  Intermediate overview of system functions
  - Internal system specifications
    - Describes what each module is to do and how all modules relate to each other
  - External system specifications
    - Describes input/output operations
    - Describes system as seen by users

- **Program specifications**

  Detailed description of each program function or module
  Describes how each module is to work
  Includes flowcharts, or pseudocode algorithms

- **Test specifications**

PROGRAM DESIGN

If you studied the problem, you should have a clear understanding of the task and know all the pertinent facts. You should also have the functional and system specifications. Now, you need to produce the detail design of the different modules or functions to be used in the system. How do you figure out a way for the program module to accomplish the task? You must design an approach that will allow the computer to produce the result. In other words, you must come up with an algorithm to give the computer.

Algorithms

An **algorithm** is a step-by-step, never-fail procedure for accomplishing the goal in mind. An algorithm is not the program itself. It is the method or plan you choose to follow when writing the program. Consider an example. Earlier in this chapter, you were trying to program a computer to multiply. There was a flowchart of a procedure to accomplish this task. The approach used was repetitive addition. This approach was an algorithm.

Assume for a moment that you really want to program a computer so it will be able to multiply. You probably wouldn't choose an algorithm based on repetitive addition. It does work, but maybe there is a better way. In coming up with an algorithm, you must fully understand the task you want to accomplish; however, it is equally important to understand that it is the computer that should accomplish the task. Therefore, you must understand the computer and how it works.

First, you must think of a way to accomplish the task. There is already one method—repetitive addition. This is the way a human might approach the problem, but perhaps another method can be used. When you were a child, you used a multiplication table and memorized the answers. The same idea could be and has been used in the computer—a table lookup. The computer handles data well. Just build a table of multiplication results and save it in the computer. Now, all the computer must do is use the two numbers it wants to multiply together as pointers to look up the result in an array. You now have a second possible approach for building an algorithm. There are others as well.

Computers do not perform tasks the same way you would. What is the best way for a computer to multiply? This is a fundamental operation. You will be writing the program in a low-level language (machine or assembler), which means you will be working with binary numbers, the number system of the computer. In assemblers, there is the addition instruction, but there are also **shift instructions**. These shift instructions will shift all bits in a register to the right or left one bit and then zero-fill from the opposite end of the register. Suppose a register contained the binary number 00000101. A binary shift to the left one bit would give 00001010, whereas a binary shift to the right would give 00000010. Note that the right-most one was lost. (If you are not familiar with the binary number system, you should review Appendix A.)

Suppose you wanted to multiply 72 by 10 in base ten. This case is somewhat special. In this situation, you could get the correct result by just shifting the decimal point one place to the right to get 720, which is the same as shifting all the digits to the left one place and zero-filling on the right.

True, this approach only works when you want to multiply by 10, but this concept could be used for an algorithm. It also works for other cases, such as when you multiply by 100, 1000, or any multiple of 10. The reason this concept works is because you are using the base ten number system. If you had been working in the base five, it would work for 5, 25, and 125. In fact, if you look at base two (the number system of the computer), you will see that it works for 2, 4, 8, or any multiple of 2. Take the binary number that was shifted earlier, 00000101. This number is equal to the base ten value of 5. After shifting one bit to the left, the result is 00001010, which has a base ten value of 10. Shifting is the same as multiplying by 2. Shift two bits to the left, and you get 00010100, which has a value of 20 and is the same as multiplying 5 by 4. Shifting three places to the left gives 00101000, which is 40; this is the same as multiplying 5 by 8. The numbers 2, 4, and 8 are all multiples of the base two number system.

Suppose you want to multiply using shifting. Multiply the number 5 by the numbers 1 through 15 (see Figure 2.13):

Multiply	=	Binary equivalent				= Result
101* 1	=				+101	= 101
101* 10	=			+1010		= 1010
101* 11	=			+1010	+101	= 1111
101* 100	=		+10100			= 10100
101* 101	=		+10100		+101	= 11001
101* 110	=		+10100	+1010		= 11110
101* 111	=		+10100	+1010	+101	= 100011
101* 1000	=	101000				= 101000
101* 1001	=	101000			+101	= 101101
101* 1010	=	101000	+1010			= 110010
101* 1011	=	101000	+1010		+101	= 110111
101* 1100	=	101000	+10100			= 111100
101* 1101	=	101000	+10100		+101	= 1000001
101* 1110	=	101000	+10100	+1010		= 1000110
101* 1111	=	101000	+10100	+1010	+101	= 1001011

Figure 2.13 *Binary multiplication chart*

There is a pattern in the table that might help you develop an algorithm. Note the correlation between the one bits and the shifted values in the binary equivalent. Note the correlation between place value of the ones and the number of times a value was shifted. Perhaps there is a combination of shifting and addition that would be more suited to the computer than just repetitive addition or table lookup. Examine Figure 2.14:

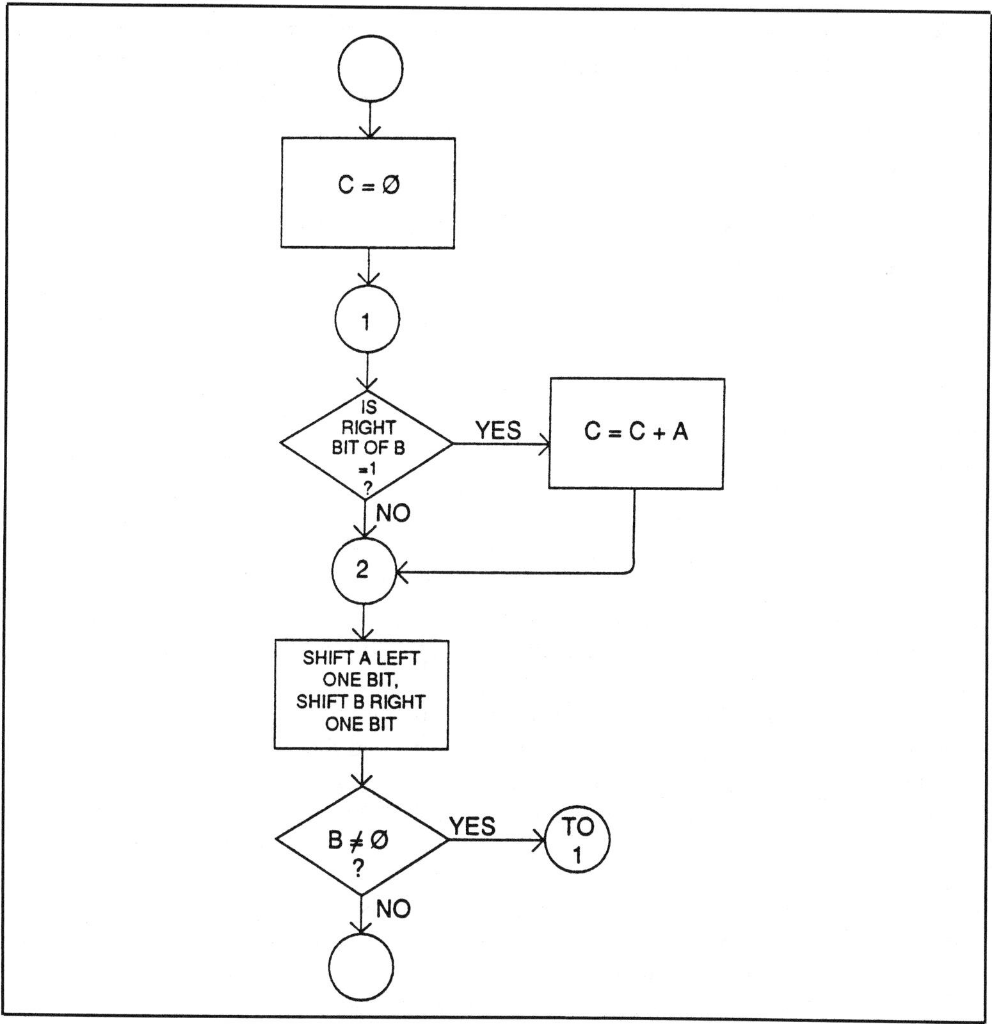

Figure 2.14 *Algorithm flowchart—multiply A and B by shifting*

If you don't fully understand how to program the operations in the flowchart in Figure 2.14, don't be overly concerned at this point. The explanation of bitwise operations in Chapter 6 should provide clarification. The important point here is the concept of the algorithm and the fact that three different algorithms have been posed for a simple problem.

It is doubtful that you will ever have a programming task for which there is only one possible algorithm. On the other hand, you might have many programming tasks in which you can only think of one algorithm. Once you come up with that first idea, it seems to block out all others. Try to keep an open mind. There may be a better idea.

Another important factor to remember when trying to come up with an algorithm is to consider all possible situations. The algorithm must work for all cases. Perhaps you have an algorithm that seems to work, but it must work every time. For example, will the algorithm in Figure 2.14 work for negative numbers or for zero?

Consider another example in which you are writing the code for an input screen. You know what input to expect, and you write your program to handle that input. But the user could by accident enter something you did not expect. Will your algorithm still work properly? Suppose you give the user four choices on an input screen: a, b, c, or d. What happens if the user has the Shift Lock key on and enters **B**? Would you be willing to accept this as valid input? Suppose you have an algorithm that requires the variable Y to be divided by the variable X. What would happen if X were somehow zero? Do you always check the divisor to make sure it is not zero before you divide? You must try to anticipate all possible situations.

This book has attempted to show you how an algorithm might be developed. Sometimes the task at hand will be so straightforward that there is no need for an algorithm, but other times one will be necessary. The process is one of discovery. You must first try to find some consistent pattern for obtaining the results you want. Then, this pattern must be converted to an algorithm that can itself be converted into a computer program. Remember, also, that there may be many different patterns that can achieve the same end result, but by different paths. There is no way that this book can give you a process that will always give you the best algorithm, or for that matter any algorithm, but this one example can be used as a guide for discovering your own algorithms when necessary.

Heuristics

It was said earlier that you may never have a task for which there is only one algorithm, but there are also many tasks out there for which no algorithm can be devised. In part, this statement is one of semantics. Take another look at the definition of an algorithm. "An algorithm is a step-by-step, never-fail procedure for accomplishing the goal in mind." Note the term "never-fail." If an algorithm doesn't work for all cases, by definition it is not an algorithm. There are tasks that can have no algorithm. For example, you could never write an algorithm to anticipate which key will be typed next by a chimpanzee sitting at a keyboard. It is doubtful if an algorithm could be devised to play the perfect game of chess. However, you could still write a program to attempt to perform either of these tasks. Instead of using an algorithm, you would probably use what's called a heuristic.

The word **heuristic** means self-discovery. When you program a computer by using a heuristic, you give the computer a general rule of thumb rather than a never-fail algorithm. This rule of thumb will allow the computer to perhaps discover a solution to the problem.

Suppose, for example, you must explain how to find the moon in the night sky. An algorithm would give specific instructions on how to use the exact time, a sextant, a compass, and a celestial almanac to locate where in the sky the moon will be found at any given moment. On the other hand, a heuristic might be as follows: "Look for the brightest object in the night sky." This rule of thumb will generally allow you to find the moon, but it is obvious that there are times when the heuristic will lead to incorrect conclusions. On a night when the moon has not yet risen or is obscured by a cloud, some other object will be chosen and called the moon.

It is not uncommon for a heuristic to incorporate a method of learning from past experience. Suppose the heuristic included instructions to remember the brightest objects found on past nights, and compare them to the brightest object found tonight before calling tonight's object the moon. Again, there is the possibility of error, but eventually the moon could be identified with a high degree of success.

How could you come up with a heuristic that would predict the keys that were going to be typed by that chimpanzee? Obviously, there is nothing that can be done to predict the next key with 100% accuracy. However, there may be a heuristic that would allow you to improve the probability of predicting the next keystroke. It is very difficult for a human to generate a true random response even when trying. The chimpanzee would not even be trying, so there may be some patterns that occur.

Suppose you devised a plan that would save all previous keystrokes in order. Now, analyze them before making a prediction. Suppose you found that the last three keystrokes had each been **j**. What would your prediction for the next keystroke be? Or, suppose that you found that out of the last 100 keystrokes, one character appeared 37 times. Suppose that the keys **u**, **i**, and **o** have appeared six times together and in that order, and the last two keys typed were **u** and **i**. You could make a prediction and have a good chance of being right. The challenge is in designing the heuristic that can recognize these patterns when they appear. No heuristic could ever predict with perfect accuracy, but you could design one to greatly increase the probability of a correct prediction.

ESTABLISHING STANDARDS AND CONVENTIONS

There is one other element that should be discussed when examining program development techniques. This has to do with the way you choose to do a task. In today's large professional programming shops, standards and conventions are almost always established for the staff to follow. The standards and conventions are often set up by a committee made up of both management and staff and can be changed if there is a valid reason for doing so. The actual standards will vary from place to place because there is no "correct" set of conventions to follow. Although standards vary, their simple existence—regardless of what they are—has value. The reason for their existence goes back to the need for code that is easy to understand and change quickly.

If everyone performs tasks the same way, it is easy for anyone on the staff to follow and understand the work of a fellow programmer. It also makes the code maintainable with a minimum of effort. The job of the manager is reduced because the staff knows what is expected of them.

There are programmers who resent the need to follow standards or conventions in their programming. They feel that doing so limits the creative process. In general, this should not be the case. The conventions simply standardize the form that is used in programming, not the logic you follow to solve the task at hand. In fact, these standards can be of great help to the programmer who is new to the staff. They can be used to guide and show the newcomer what is needed and expected to complete that first programming task. For this reason, it is a good idea for the newcomer to request and study any formal or informal standards that exist. If the standards are informal, then word of mouth and looking at work done by different programmers in the past will give you some indication as to what standards exist.

Some areas in which you might expect to find standards are as follows:

- comments in code and program documentation
- the physical appearance of the program (indentation, use of uppercase and lowercase, approximate size of module, etc.)
- terms used to describe the system to users on screens and reports
- layout of output screens and printer reports to give a unified appearance
- method of interface between program modules in the system
- naming of program labels and global variables
- controlling and documenting changes made to completed code

The more people there are working on a development project, the more need there is for standards and conventions; but even if you are the only one involved, establishing your own conventions will save you time in the long run. It is surprising how soon you forget a detail in a program that you wrote. If you always use the same conventions, it is easy to pick up a program written long ago and interface or modify it because you are familiar with the naming conventions, the general form of the code, and the interface procedure.

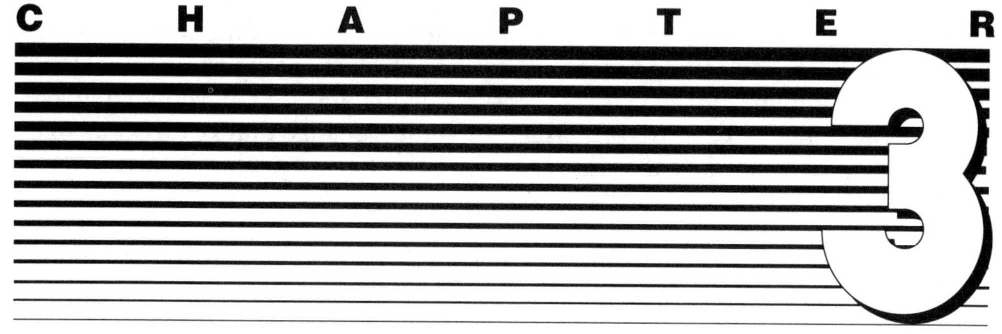

STARTING UP C

Just in case this is your first attempt at programming outside the world of interpretive BASIC, here are a few words of caution to ease the shock. You may not agree at the moment, but BASIC is a very forgiving and user-friendly language. It is especially so when compared with C. You must realize that BASIC was written to make programming easy, whereas C was written by a professional programmer for his own and a few associates' use.

C is a strong but unforgiving language. It was written to get the job done—not to be concerned about the programmer's comfort along the way; however, this is not to say that C is difficult to learn. As you will soon discover, it is reasonably easy to learn enough about C to be writing your own programs. It might take a little longer to become an expert. The difficulty stems from C's programming environment, which can be a shock when experienced for the first time—somewhat like swimming in the rapids of a glacier-fed river after learning to swim in a heated pool. In many ways, C is a more structured and rigid language, with a place for everything and everything in its place. For example, it will not check everything you enter for correctness. In some cases, C takes no responsibility and assumes you know how to create a program statement correctly. C will not always bother to tell you about a mistake.

C also allows a programmer to produce fast and efficient code. C code will often rival assembler code in efficiency while giving the programmer the ease of coding in a high-level language. C allows access to parts of the computer that BASIC protects you from. Programming in BASIC is like riding a bicycle with training wheels. With C, the training wheels are gone. A bug in your program can bring the system down. Make a mistake, and your program can crash and burn, often giving you little clue as to why.

WHAT YOU NEED TO START PROGRAMMING IN C

Now that you have been warned, it is time to prepare to write your first C program. With BASIC, all you had to do was load BASIC, type in your program, and then type **RUN**. Programming in C involves a few more steps. You will need a text editor so you can create your source program (the editor is not part of C), a C compiler to create the object code for you, and a link utility to create your executable code. Then, you can type in the name of your program and it will run. (Turbo C's Integrated Environment will make that icewater swim just a little less of a shock. It includes an editor, compiler, and link utility all in one package. If you are using Turbo C, the last part of this chapter is dedicated to getting you started with Turbo C.)

Editor

First, you will need a text editor so you can type in the source program and have it saved on the disk. Unfortunately, you cannot use BASIC as an editor for C. C does not use line numbers, and BASIC will not save anything without a BASIC line number. If you have a word processor with a mode for creating source files, you can use it. Otherwise, if you have nothing else you prefer, you can use the MS-DOS line editor EDLIN. Refer to the manual for the editor you choose and become familiar with it. Now you are ready to type in your program.

There is a legend that the first C program ever written said "Hello World." Now it has become a tradition. The first C program most programmers write does the same. Just so you won't break with tradition, bring up your editor and enter the following:

```
/* -------------------- PROG-1.C ---------------------- */
/* ------------- The first C program ----------------- */

void main()
{
     printf("Hello, world\n");
}
```

(You may need to remove the word **void** if your C version does not use the modern ANSI extensions.) Once the program has been entered into the computer, you must save it on the disk. When you save this source program, make sure the name has an extension **.C** as follows:

```
PROG-1.C
```

The extension identifies the file as a source program intended for a C compiler. This corresponds to the **.BAS** extension your BASIC programs have.

C Compiler

Next, you must have the C compiler loaded on the computer and ready to go. Refer to the user's guide or installation guide that came with your version of C. Compile the program; the compile will convert your source code into a machine language translation that the computer can understand. This machine language is called the object code. It will also contain the object code for the C library functions that you call with your program. Now, check the disk directory. You should find a file on the disk called PROG-1.OBJ. This is the object or machine language copy of the program you typed into the editor, but it is not quite ready to run at this point.

Link Utility

The next step is to run your link utility. If no link utility came with your version of C, then you can use the MS-DOS LINK utility. The link utility links all the different object modules you have created and any C run-time modules that are necessary to make your program operate properly. In interpretive BASIC, BASIC is always available and running; you are always operating under the BASIC umbrella of protection. When your program is running, it is being monitored; if something goes wrong, you get an error message. In C, once your program is running, C is gone. The only help C can give you at that time is from the C run-time modules that were included with your program, so you must link all the necessary parts of your program together.

After learning about and running your link utility, you should find at least one more new file in your directory, PROG-1.EXE. This file contains your object code linked to those C modules your program needs to run.

From MS-DOS, enter the name of the program, **PROG-1**. MS-DOS will look for a file called PROG-1 with an **.EXE** extension and, after locating it, will run your program. If the program does not run successfully, you have the frustrating task of getting your particular C environment under control before you can learn C. The rest of this chapter provides assistance for Turbo C users.

TURBO C STARTUP

The rest of this chapter is intended to give you a jump start on Turbo C. Only a subset of the total system will be covered, but this subset should get you off to a running start. The discussion is intended to supplement, not replace, the user's guide you received with Turbo C.

When you purchase Turbo C, you receive several diskettes. They contain a large number of files that will allow you to build 12 different versions of Turbo C, and you can add a graphics package to these if you want. The purpose of this chapter is not to cover all the different versions, but to assist you in getting one version operating. The first one always seems to be the hardest. Once you become familiar with this version of Turbo C, you can then branch out and try some of the others on your own. The version you will be working on is the Integrated Environment (TC), using the small memory model on an IBM personal computer or one that is compatible with MS-DOS.

Call up MS-DOS and enter the following command (**Note:** press the Return key after all commands):

`VERIFY ON`	(MS-DOS will verify all disk writes.)

Using the DISKCOPY command, make a copy of each of the Turbo C master diskettes, and then store the originals in a safe place.

Loading TC on a Hard Disk System

The following file configuration is the one recommended by your Turbo C manual. You may vary it if you want to, but it might be worthwhile to stick with this configuration until you get the Turbo C system running. You can customize your disk arrangement later. If you are using the recommended configuration and your hard disk drive is C, create the following directories:

`MKDIR C:\TURBOC`	(On drive C, make a directory called **TURBOC**.)

`MKDIR C:\TURBOC\INCLUDE`	(Within the TURBOC directory, make a directory called **INCLUDE**.)
`MKDIR C:\TURBOC\INCLUDE\SYS`	(Within the INCLUDE directory, make a directory called **SYS**.)
`MKDIR C:\TURBOC\LIB`	(Within the TURBOC directory, make a directory called **LIB**.)

Once these directories have been created, insert the Turbo C diskettes into diskette drive A, one at a time, entering the following command each time:

`COPY A:*.*  C:\TURBOC\*.*`	(Copy all files from diskette to the TURBOC directory.)

The command above is not enough when you come to the Turbo C diskette that contains the SYS directory (use the DIR command to list the contents of a diskette). In addition, use the following command to get the STAT.H file:

```
COPY A:\SYS\STAT.H  C:\TURBOC\INCLUDE\SYS\*.*
```

After you have transferred all the files to the TURBOC directory on disk C, you will need to redistribute some of them. First, move all the remaining .H files to the INCLUDE directory, using the following command:

```
COPY C:\TURBOC\*.H  C:\TURBOC\INCLUDE\*.*
```

Now, erase those files from the TURBOC directory. Enter

```
ERASE C:\TURBOC\*.H
```

Next, copy all the .OBJ files to the LIB directory, and then erase the originals from the TURBOC directory:

```
COPY C:\TURBOC\*.OBJ  C:\TURBOC\LIB\*.*
ERASE C:\TURBOC\*.OBJ
```

Do the same for the .LIB files:

```
COPY C:\TURBOC\*.LIB  C:\TURBOC\LIB\*.*
ERASE C:\TURBOC\*.LIB
```

The files are now in the appropriate positions, and you are ready to create the configuration file.

Creating the TC Configuration File for the Hard Disk

The configuration file TCCONFIG.TC must be created. This file shows TC where all the different files you just loaded can be found and which model system to use. The configuration file will be written automatically to the disk by TC, but you must first tell TC what the conditions are. Assuming you followed the suggestions above in building the different directories and placing the files in them, the following instructions will create the TCCONFIG.TC file. If you deviated from the suggestions above, make sure you change the instructions to reflect the differences.

The first step is to get Turbo C running. Enter the following:

`CHDIR C:\TURBOC`	(This will change your working directory to TURBOC on disk C.)
`TC`	(This will cause MS-DOS to look for the program TC.EXE in your current working directory. Once TC.EXE is found, MS-DOS will load and execute the program.)

You should follow the above procedure anytime you want to program using TC. This will ensure that you are in the correct working directory, and TC will be able to find the files that it requires in this directory.

The Turbo C Integrated Environment screen should then appear. The top line of the screen is the main menu, and should appear as follows:

```
File  Edit  Run  Compile  Project  Options  Debug
```

You are at the main menu level with the **File** option highlighted. Use the right arrow key to move the highlighted area to the right. When **Options** becomes highlighted, stop and press the Return key. This activates the options portion of TC, and a window will appear with the following:

```
Compiler
Linker
Environment
Args
Retrieve options
Store    options
```

Compiler should be highlighted. Again press the Return key. This time, a second window appears with another menu. The first option should be highlighted and should read as follows:

```
Model          Small
```

If it does not, press the Return key. Still another pop-up window will display the following options:

```
Tiny
Small
Medium
Large
Huge
```

Use the arrow keys to move the highlighted area to **Small**. Press Return. That window should disappear, and the first line of the previous window should change to the following:

```
Model            Small
```

You have just indicated to TC which of the memory models you chose for your system. At this point, that window will also disappear if you press the Esc key. You will have backed up one level and again be at the Options menu. Use the down arrow key to highlight the word **Environment**. Press Return again, and a new window menu will appear. The first four options are as follows:

```
Include directories:
Library directory:
Output directory:
Turbo C directory:
```

Highlight **Include directories** and press Return. A pop-up window prompt will appear. Here, you enter the path required to find the header (.H) files as follows:

```
C:\TURBOC\INCLUDE
```

Highlight **Library** to get the prompt for the Library directory. Now, enter

```
C:\TURBOC\LIB
```

This is the path to the library files and object modules that will be loaded with your C code. Press Return, move the highlight to **Output directory**, and press Return again. This time you must give the following path to your scratch work area:

```
C:\TURBOC
```

Finally, for the Turbo C directory, enter

```
C:\TURBOC
```

After you have pressed Return, the first four lines of the Options-Environment window should appear as follows:

```
Include directories:        C:\TURBOC\INCLUDE
Library directory:          C:\TURBOC\LIB
Output directory:           C:\TURBOC
Turbo C directory:          C:\TURBOC
```

You have indicated to TC all the conditions that it needs to find the appropriate files. Have TC save this file. Use the Esc key to back up to the Options menu again. Use the arrow keys to highlight **Store options**, and then press Return. A prompt window named **Config File** will appear. Make sure the window contains the following:

```
C:\TURBOC\TCCONFIG.TC
```

Press Return, and TC will now write the TCCONFIG.TC file to the TURBOC directory on disk C. (If you already have a configuration file, TC will ask you to confirm the overwrite.) Later, you may want to add to or change the configuration file. For now, this setup should get you running. Pressing the F10 key will return you to the main menu. You are now ready to create your first C program.

Loading TC on a Two-Diskette System

Turbo C has become so large that it is difficult to fit the entire program on two 5-1/4" double-density diskettes. If you have been using a two-diskette system, you may not have needed to work with directories on your diskettes. If this is true, you may want to look at your MS-DOS manual and become familiar with directories and path notations. With version 1.5 of Turbo C, it is necessary to do some selective loading in order to have a workable Turbo C system. The following is a suggested approach.

With MS-DOS in drive A and running, put a blank diskette in drive B (this will be referred to as diskette B). Enter the following:

`FORMAT B:`	(Format diskette.)
`MKDIR B:\LIB`	(Make a directory called LIB on diskette B. **Note:** the path requires a backslash.)

With your new diskette still in drive B, insert a Turbo C diskette in drive A. Using the DIR command on drive A, look for the files listed in the following commands. Keep trying the different Turbo C diskettes until you find all the files. When each is found, COPY the file to diskette B with the appropriate COPY command, as follows:

`COPY A:FP87.LIB  B:\LIB\*.*`
`COPY A:EMU.LIB  B:\LIB\*.*`
`COPY A:GRAPHICS.LIB  B:\LIB\*.*`
	(Copy files from disk A to the LIB directory on drive B.)

`COPY A:COS.OBJ  B:\LIB\*.*`
`COPY A:MATHS.LIB  B:\LIB\*.*`
`COPY A:CS.LIB  B:\LIB\*.*`
	(See **Note** that follows.)

Note: the last three filenames each end with the letter **S**, which stands for Small memory model. There are six different memory models you can build, ranging from Tiny to Huge. The Large one would have each file ending with the letter L. These files are called C0L.OBJ, MATHL.LIB, and CL.LIB, and would be loaded in place of the files shown above. If at all possible, stay with the Small notation while working through the examples in this book.

Locate the next group of files listed in the following commands and copy them as shown:

```
COPY A:CGA.BGI  B:*.*
COPY A:ATT.BGI  B:*.*
COPY A:EGAVGA.BGI  B:*.*
COPY A:HERC.BGI  B:*.*
COPY A:IBM8514.BGI  B:*.*
COPY A:PC3270.BGI  B:*.*

COPY A:GOTH.CHR  B:*.*
COPY A:LITT.CHR  B:*.*
COPY A:SANS.CHR  B:*.*
COPY A:TRIP.CHR  B:*.*
```

These files are used by graphics enhancements. You can save some space on the diskette by determining which file with the .BGI extension is appropriate for your computer system and loading only that particular one. Check the Turbo C manual on graphics enhancements to determine which file to use. For example, if you load the CGA.BGI file, Turbo C assumes you have a color graphics adapter on your PC.

Remove diskette B from drive B. Mark the label to identify it as the diskette intended to be in drive B when you turn your computer on. It also contains the scratch work area for your C programs.

Now insert a second blank diskette in drive B (this will be referred to as diskette A). Put the MS-DOS diskette back in drive A, and enter the following:

`FORMAT B:/S` (Format second diskette, and load MS-DOS onto diskette.)

`MKDIR B:\INCLUDE` (Create INCLUDE directory. The *Turbo C User's Guide* suggests this directory be on the same drive as the \LIB directory, but putting it here makes a larger scratch area for your programs.)

`MKDIR B:\INCLUDE\SYS` (Create SYS directory inside the INCLUDE directory. If you are familiar with XCOPY, you could combine this step with the next one.)

Again, locate the correct Turbo C diskettes and place them in drive A so you can copy the following files to the diskette currently in drive B.

`COPY A:\SYS\STAT.H  B:\INCLUDE\SYS\*.*`

(Copy STAT.H from SYS to the SYS directory.)

`COPY A:*.H  B:\INCLUDE\*.*` (Copy all remaining files with .H extension into the INCLUDE directory. Make sure GRAPHICS.H is included if you want to create graphics.)

`COPY A:TC.EXE  B:*.*` (Copy the Turbo C executable program to drive B.)

If your PC has the 5-1/4" double-density diskette drives, remove the diskette from drive B and label it. This diskette is intended to reside on drive A and contains the executable code that you will call to initiate the running of Turbo C.

Now insert the MS-DOS diskette in drive A and a third blank diskette into drive B. Enter

```
FORMAT B:
```

Finally, locate the diskette that contains the TCHELP.TCH file and insert it in drive A. Enter

```
COPY A:TCHELP.TCH  B:*.*
```

Remove and label the diskette from drive B. This diskette contains the help comments for Turbo C's Integrated Environment (TC). Once TC is running, you must remove the diskette from drive B and replace it with this third diskette before you can request on-line help from TC. This inconvenience is due to the size of the files involved and limited disk space available on two 5-1/4" diskettes.

Laptops and Other Special Hardware Considerations

Some PCs use the small 3-1/2" diskette drives, which actually hold twice as much as the 5-1/4" double-density diskettes. If you use the 3-1/2" diskettes or the high density 5-1/4" diskettes, you have enough space on your second diskette to include the TCHELP.TCH file with the TC.EXE file. You won't need to create the third diskette and switch diskettes to activate the on-line help.

If you are using other special hardware, you should check the *Turbo C User's Guide* for special considerations for your particular equipment. Also, be sure to read the .DOC and README files on the diskettes you received. For example, the manual suggests that you place MS-DOS in 80-column black-and-white mode before entering TC if you have a plasma or LCD display screen.

Creating the TC Configuration File for Two Diskettes

The configuration file TCCONFIG.TC must be created. This file shows TC where all the different files you just loaded can be found and which model system to use. The configuration file will be written automatically on the diskette by TC, but you must first tell TC what the conditions are. Place diskettes A and B into their appropriate drives. MS-DOS should be running with the A prompt displayed. Change the default disk to drive B by entering

```
B:
```

Make sure that you are pointing to disk B and have not changed directories. The system must look at disk B for certain files. Enter

`A:TC`	(This will cause MS-DOS to find and run a program called TC.EXE on disk A. Your default disk is still B.)

The Turbo C Integrated Environment screen will appear. When it does, follow the directions described in the "Creating the TC Configuration File for the Hard Disk" section earlier in this chapter. The only difference is that the paths to the different files must reflect their location in your system. The first four lines of the Options-Environment window should display the following when you are ready to store the configuration file:

```
Include directories:     A:\INCLUDE
Library directory:       B:\LIB
Output directory:        B:
Turbo C directory:       A:
```

By now, you have indicated to TC all the conditions that it needs to find the appropriate files. Save the information. Use the Esc key to back up to the Options menu again. Use the arrow keys to highlight **Store options**, and then press Return. A prompt window called **Config File** will appear. Make sure the window contains the following:

```
B:\TCCONFIG.TC
```

Press Return, and TC will now write out the TCCONFIG.TC file to disk B. Press the F10 key to return to the main menu.

Loading TC on a One-Diskette System

If you have a single double-density diskette drive system, you can still use Turbo C, but it will be slightly more inconvenient, and you will have a smaller scratch work area for your programs. This last factor will require you to keep the scratch area cleaned up so you will have enough room for new programs.

You will need to create three diskettes similar to the three created in the previous section; however, their contents will vary slightly.

As before, the first diskette must contain the \LIB directory and all the .OBJ and .LIB files that were placed in it for a two-diskette drive system. This diskette must still include the appropriate .BGI file as well as all the .CHR files. In addition, it will be necessary to add some items from diskette A in the two-diskette system. These items are the \INCLUDE\SYS directories along with all the .H files. This diskette should still have enough room for a small scratch work area for your programs. Label this first diskette as your **work** disk.

The second diskette you create will be similar to diskette A in the two-drive system. It will contain the MS-DOS COMMAND.COM file and TC.EXE file. It will not include the \INCLUDE\SYS directories or any .H files. Label this diskette as your **system** disk.

The third diskette will be exactly the same as the third diskette on the two-drive system. You can label this diskette as your **help** disk because it contains the help comments for TC.

When you are using Turbo C, you will turn on the computer while the system diskette is in the drive. Once MS-DOS is downloaded and running, enter **TC**. This system diskette also contains the Turbo C executable code. The TC program will be loaded into memory and started. At this point, remove the system diskette and place the work diskette in the drive. If you want to activate the on-line help functions, remove the work diskette and insert the help diskette before pressing the F1 key. Then, when you are through with the help functions, you must reinsert the work diskette before going on. In general, once the TC program is running, the work diskette will be the one in the drive.

Creating the TC Configuration File for One Diskette

When creating the TC configuration file for a one-drive system, leave the system diskette in the drive after you bring up TC. Then, follow the procedure described in the "Creating the TC Configuration File for the Hard Disk" section earlier in this chapter; however, because there is only the one diskette drive, make the changes necessary to reflect this difference. When you are ready to save the configuration file, the first four entries of the Options-Environment window should read as follows:

```
Include directories:      A:\INCLUDE
Library directory:        A:\LIB
Output directory:         A:
Turbo C directory:        A:
```

The TCCONFIG.TC file will be saved on the system diskette so it will be available when you bring up TC. This means that any time you want to choose Store options in the Options windows, you must first make sure the system diskette is loaded in the drive.

CREATING A C SOURCE PROGRAM WITH THE TC EDITOR

From the TC main menu, move the highlight, using the arrow keys until the **Edit** option is highlighted. Then, press Return. Now you are in the TC line editor, and you can create your first C source code. You can now copy the "Hello, World" program mentioned earlier in this chapter.

While you are in the editor, there are a few items you should notice. First, note the edit status line, which informs you about a number of conditions that currently exist for the editor. For example, you should see a default file name, **NONAME.C**, which you will change shortly. You will also see the word **insert**, which informs you that you are in insert mode. After you have entered some text, you can move the cursor back through the existing text, using the arrow keys. Anything you enter will be inserted into the text at that point. You can toggle in and out of this mode by pressing the Insert key. You can delete text by using the Delete and Backspace keys. Being able to insert and delete text provides sufficient editing capability to create your first program. (You might spend some time with the Turbo C manuals to learn additional editing features.)

Naming and Saving the Source File in TC

Once you have completed the source code, you must change the default filename. Pressing the F10 key will take you to the main menu option line with the Edit option highlighted. Your program is still visible in the edit window, but you are out of the editor and in the main menu. Move the highlight to the File option, and press Return. A window will appear with the following options:

```
Load       F3
Pick       Alt-F3
New
Save       F2
Write to
Directory
Change dir
OS shell
Quit       Alt-x
```

The **Load** option will be highlighted. Move the highlight to **Write to**, and press Return. A prompt window will appear, asking for the name of the new file. Call this program **PROG-1.C**. The **.C** extension identifies this file as a C source file. Even if you forget to include this extension in the filename, TC will insert it for you. After you enter the name and press Return, the prompt window will disappear, and you will be back in the File window menu. Move the highlight to **Save**, and press Return again. The source file will now be saved on the disk under this new name. Although you are still in the File window menu, you should be able to see some of your text in the Edit area behind the window. Note that the edit status line now contains the new filename instead of the default name that appeared previously. Because you have saved this file, in the future you can start up TC, retrieve the PROG-1.C program from the disk, and load it into the TC editor simply by going to the File window menu and using the Load option.

HOT KEYS IN TC

While in the File window menu, note that some of the options have special key notations next to them. For example,

```
Save        F2
Quit        Alt-x
```

These are TC **hot keys**. There are a number of these hot keys. You can use them from anyplace in TC to avoid moving through the menus. In fact, you have already used two hot keys—Esc and F10. The Esc key will exit the current window and return you to the last active window. You also used the F10 key to return to the main menu line at the top of the screen. F2, a hot key you see in the current menu, will save the edit file on the disk, using the name that appears on the edit status line. Pressing the [Alt/X] key combination will allow you to exit TC and return to MS-DOS. You could, of course, accomplish the same task by highlighting the **Quit** option on the current screen and pressing Return. At the bottom line of the screen are some additional hot keys that are appropriate for your current position in TC. For now, press the F10 hot key to return to the main menu.

RUNNING YOUR PROGRAM IN TC

To try your first program, move the main menu highlight to the **Run** option, and press Return. This will cause TC to initiate a string of actions. A new window will appear, and TC will take the source file in the edit buffer and compile an object program. Then, TC will link that object or machine language code with the C library functions necessary for your program. This will be the executable version of your program. Finally, the TC screen will disappear, and your old MS-DOS screen will reappear; then, your program will run. After your program runs, you will see a prompt at the bottom of the screen. Pressing any key will then return you to TC.

If you look at a directory of your scratch work area of the disk at this time, you should find the following files included:

PROG-1.C	The source file that you created and saved.
PROG-1.OBJ	The machine language object file created and saved by the C compiler.
PROG-1.EXE	The executable file that links your object file with the C object modules and library functions. This file is created and saved by the TC linker.

ERROR MESSAGES IN TC

In this section, errors will purposely be introduced to generate some error messages so you can experience the situation and the message part of the screen can be explained.

Return to the editor. You are going to modify your PROG-1.C program and intentionally introduce some errors. Change your program to appear exactly as follows:

```
main()
{
     printf("Intentional Error one"\n);
     printf("Intentional Error two\n")
     printf("Hello, World\n");
}
```

Exit the editor and run the program again, but don't change the filename.

Another window will appear. If you watch closely, you will see that you are being given a dynamic step-by-step account of the progress that TC is making in trying to run your program.

The first message you might see is a statement about "checking dependencies." TC checks the edit buffer and compares it against the source file (PROG-1.C) that is on disk. TC is also looking at the creation date and time of the object file (PROG-1.OBJ) and the executable file (PROG-1.EXE), comparing them to the most recent source file. If the executable file has a more recent date and time than the source, TC will not recompile and relink your source program. Instead, it will just execute the current executable file because later on, when you get some experience with C, you will be wanting to link a number of your source files together to create one program. You will have written, compiled, and tested each of the source modules separately. When you put them all together, you may want to change one of the modules. C knows, by checking the creation date and time attached to each of the files, that there is no need to recompile anything except the one source module that was changed.

For this reason, it is important for you to always enter the correct date and time when you bring up MS-DOS. If you accept the default date or type in a wrong date, at some time you may find any new changes that you make to your source file will be ignored. The old executable file will be run as is because it has the most recent creation date and time.

Examine the window again, and you will see a number of important facts pertaining to your program, the most devastating of which are called **errors**. By now, you should see that two errors have occurred, the process has stopped, and you are being prompted to press any key. Press the space bar. The window will disappear, and the first intentional error line will be highlighted in the edit area. You will also see some text in the message area of the screen, and one of these lines will also be highlighted. The message is telling you that in line 3 of the source file called PROG-1.C there is an error in the form of an illegal character.

TC highlights line 3 for you in an attempt to show you where the error occurred. Press the down arrow key. Note that the second error in the message window is highlighted and that line 5 of the text is also highlighted. TC is telling you that there is a statement missing in line 5. (Appendix B of the *Turbo C Reference Guide* has a more complete description of these error messages.) Actually, it is line 4 that has caused the problem: line 4 does not end with a semicolon. To correct this error, you must move to the editor.

It may not be immediately apparent, but you are in the Message area. You can tell you are there because nothing is highlighted on the top main menu line, and there is a double bar on each side of the title **Message**. Examine the bottom line of the screen. Some hot keys are listed there. F6 says **Edit**, so press F6. Observe that the highlighted lines are now gone, but the error message still stands out. Look closer. The double bars are now surrounding the title **Edit** instead of **Message**. Also notice that the cursor is now on line 5 of the text in the edit area and that F6 on the bottom line now says **Message**. If you had a long list of errors, you could use the F6 key to move back to the message area and scroll through the remainder of the messages after you corrected this one.

Correct this error by moving up to line 4 and placing a semicolon at the end of the line.

Take another look at the hot keys on the bottom line of the screen:

```
F7/F8-Prev/Next error
```

The F7 and F8 keys will allow you to stay in the editor and move through the remaining errors. Press F7. The previous error now stands out, and the message is duplicated and highlighted in the edit status line. It says that the backslash (\) is an illegal character. It is not. It is just illegal where it happens to be placed at the moment. **\n** means to print a carriage return and linefeed. The problem is that it should be included inside the quotation marks, so move over and change the line to read as follows:

```
Printf("Intentional Error one\n");
```

After correcting the errors, press the F10 key to return to the main menu. Run the program again.

You will notice that, in addition to the errors, the window displays references called **warnings**. These are potential problems. Unlike the way it handles errors, TC will continue to try to run your program if there are warnings. If you are concerned about warnings that are accumulating in the window, you can stop the compile and link process by entering the [Ctrl/Break] combination. It is then possible to look at the warnings in the same way you did the errors.

WORKING WITH PROJECTS

You may want to read this section again after you have read Chapters 4 and 5 and are well into reading Chapter 6. It deals with projects or full systems that require many separate functions or parts to be combined in order to create a total system. Turbo C refers to a system as a project.

Go to the main menu and move the cursor until the **Project** option is highlighted. Press Return. A window will appear with the following options:

```
Project name
Break make on  Errors
Clear project
```

The Project name option may or may not have a name following it. If it is not highlighted, use the up arrow to move the cursor until you highlight the Project name option. Now, press Return. Another window will appear. This time, it is a prompt asking for a path and filename. This filename will be the name of your project. Your executable code will end up having this name followed by a .EXE extension.

If a path and project name were

```
C:\TURBOC\SYSTEM5.PRJ
```

then the executable module would be

```
SYSTEM5.EXE
```

The project filename must have the extension **.PRJ**, and it must be the name of a file on the disk indicated by the path. The contents of this file will contain all the module filenames you want to be linked together to create the program called **SYSTEM5**. A sample file might contain the following:

```
c:\turboc\mod5.c
c:\turboc\mod17.c
c:\turboc\mine\mylib2.c
c:\turboc\mod21.c
```

This file can be created using the TC editor. Go back to the main menu; highlight the **Run** option, and press Return. The TC operating system will go to the project name area. Finding a filename there, TC will take the contents of that file, look up each file in the list, and compile each file if a current compile does not exist. After compiling, TC will link the object modules MOD5.OBJ, MOD17.OBJ, MYLIB2.OBJ, and MOD21.OBJ into one executable file named after the project file, and run it.

If you will be working on this project for a long time, you may want the Project name field to contain this project file when you bring the system up. To do this, set the project name as you would like it. Then, go to the main menu option called Options and press Return. The screen should display the following:

```
Compiler
Linker
Environment
Directories
Args
Retrieve options
Store options
```

Highlight **Store options** and press Return. TC will save the current option settings as well as the current setting for the project in the TCCONFIG.TC file. This file is read by TC at startup, and all settings are restored according to the state of the TCCONFIG.TC file.

If you want to work on some other code, you must remove the project name from the field. As long as the project name is there, it will take precedence over the source file in the editor. To remove this project setting, go to the project window and choose the Clear project option. If you want a cleared project option to be the default, store the TCCONFIG.TC file where there is no project filename.

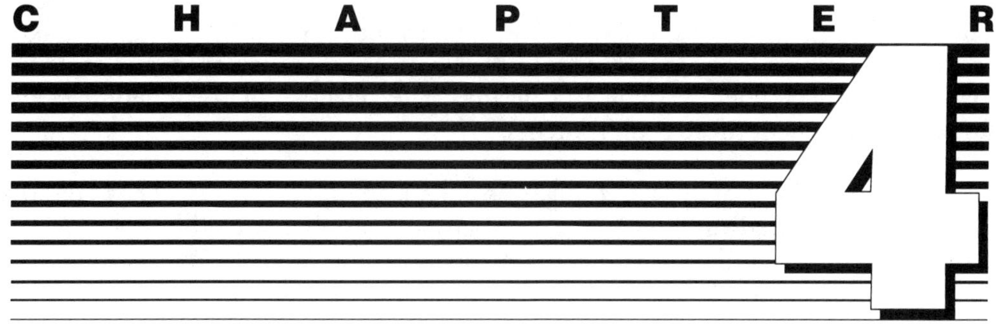

THE C PROGRAM TAKES FORM

The first step in getting started with C is to learn the form of the language. Like most programming languages, C requires that you use a particular format and follow certain rules when writing a program. The purpose of this chapter is to familiarize you with these requirements.

A C program is built out of what might be called C building blocks. These building blocks are called **functions**. You are already familiar with the functions of BASIC. They are similar to C functions. For example, in BASIC you would call the following function to get the square root of the variable A:

```
100 B = SQR(A)
```

The result (the square root of A) will be placed in the variable B. In C, you can accomplish the same task by also calling a function:

```
b = sgrt(a);
```

In both cases, the argument inside parentheses was passed to the function, and in both cases, the result was transferred back to the program by assignment to a variable. You have observed some differences, no doubt. BASIC has line numbers. The fact that C is without line numbers tells you that it is up to you to create the correct order in your program with the editor. You see that BASIC has uppercase letters and C has lowercase letters. The function names are spelled differently, and the C statement ends with a semicolon (;). All things considered, the two functions appear to be quite similar; however, the big difference is not apparent. In C, you can create your own functions as well as call existing library functions. In other words, these C functions are something like the subroutines you create in BASIC and then call using a GOSUB.

There is a significant difference between a subroutine and a function, however. In BASIC, all variables known to the program are known to the subroutine and vice versa. This is not necessarily true of a function. The function is like a black box. When you call the BASIC function SQR, you don't know or care how the function does the job. You don't worry about which variables the function uses to compute the square root. You aren't concerned that your program might be using the same variables as the function or that the function will change the values of your variables. The variables used by your program and the function are hidden from each other and have no effect on one another. In other words, the **scope** of the variables is **local**. This is also true of the functions you create in C. The variables of the main program and the variables of the function are hidden from each other and have no effect on each other even though they may have the same name. It takes an overt action to change the scope of a variable so that it is known to both the main program and the function.

To create a C function, you need to take two steps. First, you declare the function; then, you define the function. **Declaring** a function amounts to naming the function and declaring types of data that are passed to and from the function. **Defining** the function is the C code that you write. First, look at declaring a C function.

DECLARING A C FUNCTION

Declaring a C function lets the rest of the program know that the function exists; it also tells the program what type of data is passed to the function and what type of data is returned by the function. You must declare any function you intend to call or define in your C program.

Currently, there are two different methods for declaring a function: the traditional approach and the new approach that was defined in the ANSI C standard draft. (ANSI, the American National Standards Institute, is an organization that establishes standards for such things as computer languages.) The traditional function declaration takes the following form:

```
type name();
```

The word *type* indicates the specific kind of information returned to the program by the function, and *name* is the name given to the function. The form of the new method is as follows:

```
type name(type varname, type varname,...);
```

Here, the *type varname* that appears inside the parentheses refers to a variable type and the variable name that are passed to the function from the calling program (see "Declaring C Variables and Arrays" in this chapter). These are the variables that will accept and hold the data that is passed to the function when the function is called. The name given to this modern method of declaring a variable is **function prototype**. (Don't confuse this term with the prototype development process.) The new approach allows for more error checking by the C compiler. This book will, for the most part, use the new method that is compatible with Turbo C.

The *type* preceding the function name defines the type of variable that the function will return to the calling program. The types possible are the same as those used in declaring all variables, with one exception: the **void** type. The new ANSI extensions to C have defined this type to mean the function will not return a value to the calling program. Any function that performs a task, such as clearing the screen or displaying a message on the screen, would fall into this category. The C data types that are introduced here are as follows (see Appendix C for a complete list):

Type	**Meaning**
void	No data is returned to calling program.
int	An integer is returned.
float	A floating-point number is returned.
char	A character or string is returned.

Both the traditional and the new way of declaring a function end with a semicolon (;). With this exception, they are the same as the line that names a function when the function is being defined. The next step is to define the function.

DEFINING A C FUNCTION

When you define a function, you are writing the C code that makes up the function. In other words, you are writing the program. To give you some idea of the form a C function takes, examine the following:

```
type name()                  /* "type" shows type of value
                                that the function returns.
                                "name" is function's name. */
{                            /* Begin function             */
        statements;          /* Function code              */
}                            /* End function               */
```

Does this remind you of the "Hello, World" sample program you wrote earlier? It should because it is also a classic.

A function definition starts with the same line of code that was used to declare the function, except there is no ending semicolon. The type of data returned is specified, followed by the name of the function and the function prototypes enclosed between parentheses. The function prototypes tell the type and name of variables that will accept and hold data that is passed to the function from the calling program. The calling program does not know or care what these variables are called. It only needs to know the type, order, and number of data elements the function requires to be passed. If no data is passed to the function from the calling program, no variables will be declared between the parentheses, but the parentheses must still be there. See the following samples:

```
void funct1(int var)         /* An integer called "var" is
                                passed to the function.
                                Nothing is returned.        */

char funct2()                /* Nothing passed to function.
                                A character or string is
                                returned from the function. */
```

In the PROG-1 program, the name was **main**. C appropriately requires the main program to always be called **main**. This tells C where to start when it is asked to run the program. Even the main program is constructed like a function, but it does not need to be declared. The only way C can tell the difference between it and some other function in the program is by its name. The main function may be and often is the first function in the program, but it does not need to be at the beginning. It could appear anywhere, even at the end.

Something should be said about the comments. In C, a comment starts with /* and ends with */. Some versions of C will allow comments to continue over multiple lines. Comments are ignored by the C compiler and have no effect on the object code created.

Also note the use of braces. The code of a function definition is always enclosed between a left brace ({) and a right brace (}).

As mentioned earlier, the statements that make up the function are terminated by a semicolon (;).

Finally, white space (whilch includes spaces, tabs, and blank lines) is generally optional and used for cosmetic purposes. (Different versions of C vary somewhat.) There are conventions to make it easier to understand the code. An example is the indentation of the statements in the function, but the function will work with or without the indentation.

When you create a C function, you should first declare the function and then define the function. Following is a sample form of how to declare and define a function:

```
int fname();            /* Declare function "fname" */

void main()
{
     statements;
     statements;
}

int fname()             /* Define function "fname"  */
{
     statements;
}
```

In this form, the main program is defined as type **void**. It will call the function *fname* and receive an integer from the function.

return Statement

When a function that has been called by another function reaches the closing brace (}) and has nothing else to do, it will return to the calling program. It will automatically return a value of zero. Unless declared void, all functions return a value. The calling program can ignore the return value. It doesn't even need to assign the return value to a variable, but a value is returned. If you want to return something other than a zero, you must use the **return** statement. The following are examples:

```
return x;       /* Returns the value of variable x */

return 3*a;     /* Returns 3 times the value of variable a */

return ;        /* Returns a zero value */

return 5;       /* Returns the value 5 */
```

The return statement can be located anywhere in the function. Executing a return will cause the function to be exited immediately. Although a function can have multiple return statements, care should be taken not to create confusing code.

Blocks

Within a function, it is possible to combine a group of statements into what is called a **block**. This block of code will be treated as a single unit. For example, blocks are used to combine all the code that is to be executed within an iterative **for** loop or in the conditional **if** statement. A block of code is identified by left and right braces, as is a function. Following is an example of a block form:

```
type name()
{                              /* Beginning of function */
     statements;
     {                         /* Beginning of block    */
          statements;
     }                         /* End of block          */
     statements;
}                              /* End of function       */
```

Again, the convention is to indent to show relationships and make it easy to visually isolate the blocks from the functions.

DECLARING C VARIABLES AND ARRAYS

Variables are somewhat more involved in C than in BASIC. In C, a variable must be declared before it is used. This requirement is similar to the DIM or dimension statement in BASIC. In BASIC, you must dimension an array of more than ten elements. You are telling BASIC to reserve enough space in memory for the array. C requires you to declare all variables and arrays so it can reserve the necessary space in memory. C reserves a different number of bytes (eight bits) of memory for each different type of variable.

Character (**char**)	1 byte
Integer (**int**)	2 bytes
Floating-point (**float**)	4 bytes
Double-precision (**double**)	8 bytes

A variable is declared by stating the type of variable and the variable name, for example:

```
int x;
```

In this case, the variable *x* is declared an integer. In addition to reserving space for the variable in memory, the declaration also tells C what type of variable is involved. C needs this information to know what format to use when it is required to compute with or display the variable. In BASIC, you perform the same task in a somewhat different way. You designate an integer with the percent sign and a string with the dollar sign. *A%* means the variable is an integer, and *A$* means the variable is a string. This chapter will introduce you to five of the different types of C variables (see Appendix C for a complete list):

Variable Data Types:

Keyword	**Description**
int *x*	*x* is a signed integer from -32768 to +32767.
float *x*	*x* is a signed floating-point variable.
double *x*	*x* is a signed double-precision floating-point variable.
char *x*	*x* is a single-character variable.
char *x*[*n*]	*x* is a string variable (where *n* is a number, and the string has *n*-1 characters).

You may also come across what is called a **type modifier**. Following are examples of type modifiers:

- signed
- unsigned
- long
- short

These modifiers precede the type when a variable is declared and inform C that you want this variable to have different characteristics, as in the following example:

```
unsigned int x;
```

In this case, the variable could hold a number from 0 to 65535 rather than from -32768 to 32767 as a normal signed integer. A **normal** integer is both signed and short. If you were to declare the following variable, it would use four bytes in memory instead of two:

```
unsigned long int x;
```

In this situation, the variable could hold a number from 0 to +4294967295 rather than 0 to 65535.

The type **char** that declares a string is a good example of C's unforgiving nature. In declaring a string, the amenities of error checking are minimal, and C even expects you to do its job. When C stores a string variable, it puts the characters in consecutive memory locations and then places a null character in the next memory location so that it can find the end of the string in the future. You are expected to reserve that extra position in memory for this null character that C uses. If you forget, C will still place a null character in the next memory location regardless of the fact that no space was reserved for it.

In addition, C makes no effort to verify that you don't exceed the space you reserved for your variable. For example, if you reserve space for seven characters and then assign 15 characters to the string variable, C will not truncate or give an error message. It will just store the 15 characters starting in the correct position. C will fill up the seven reserved locations and then continue storing the remaining characters, ending up with the null character in the 16th location. These additional characters are stored right on top of whatever is next in memory. These locations could hold other variables or even program code, and this could crash the system.

In defense of C, there is a reason for this lack of limit checking. Because a string that is going to be placed in the variable could come from the keyboard or some other outside source, C has no way of knowing how large the string will be at compile time. To check the limit, C would need to check it during run time. This and other run-time checks would slow down program execution. Speed is probably one of the reasons you are interested in C in the first place. It works faster than BASIC, so you must pay a price. It is up to you to take care of any limit checking in your own C code.

Actually, the string variable that you have been reading about here is a special case of a C array. You could reserve multiple locations for any type variables, not just char types. Examine the following variable declaration:

```
int var[4];
```

This declares an array of four integers. These integers are called *var[0]*, *var[1]*, *var[2]*, and *var[3]*. Note that the first index is 0, not 1. The integers will be stored in eight consecutive bytes of memory, each integer requiring two bytes. Because this is not a string of undetermined length and the size of an integer is set, no null character is required to terminate the array. However, C still does not check limits. If you choose to store seven integers in this array, C will oblige by destroying the contents of adjacent memory.

Multidimensional arrays are also acceptable in C; however, each subscript or dimension must be enclosed within its own brackets. If you are used to the BASIC array notation, be very careful not to confuse it with C array notation. C array subscripts are indicated as in the following example:

```
int junk[8][32];
```

This is a two-dimensional integer array of size 8 by 32. The actual amount of memory required to store this array can be figured by multiplying the dimensions and the number of bytes the type requires—which, in this case, would be 8 * 32 * 2, or 512 bytes.

When you declare a variable, you have the option of initializing it. The following is an example of variable declaration and initialization:

```
int x=64;
```

Here, the variable *x* is declared an integer and initialized to the value of 64.

You can also initialize arrays when they are declared, as in the following examples:

```
int a[6]={0,0,0,1,1,1};

char color[7] = "YELLOW";
```

In the first example, the array *a* is declared, and the elements of the array will be initialized as follows: *a[0]* = 0, *a[1]* = 0, *a[2]* = 0, *a[3]* = 1, *a[4]* = 1, and *a[5]* = 1. The second example declares the variable *color* as a string array of seven elements, one of which is reserved for a null character. The array was then initialized and contains the word "YELLOW" followed by the null character.

Something else takes place when you declare a variable. The scope of the variable is determined by the placement of the variable declaration within the C program. The **scope** of a variable is the portion of the program that can use the variable. In other words, by the position of the variable declaration you can hide a variable and limit its scope to just a block, or you can declare it in another place in the program and expand its scope to as much of the program as you want. Note the following variable declarations:

```
int a;                   /* a - scope total program    */
main()
{
    int b;               /* b - scope main only        */
    statements;
    {
        int c;           /* c - scope block only       */
        statements;
    }
}
int d;                   /* d - scope all below        */
funct(int e)             /* e - scope function only    */
{
    int f;               /* f - scope function only    */
    statements;
}
```

In general, a variable is usable by only the block or function it is declared within. If it is declared outside a function, the scope of the variable is any function defined after the variable is declared. Any variable declared at the beginning of the program, before the first function is defined, will be usable by the entire program.

In the previous example, the variables *b* and *f* could be called with the same name, for example, *x*. C will reserve space for two different variables and will not confuse the two. Using *x* in the function will not affect the value of variable x used in main. Their scopes do not overlap, and you do not need to be quite so concerned about keeping track of which variables you have used before.

Global Variables and extern

Variables that are declared outside of a function and have a scope that encompasses the whole program are called **global variables**. They can be used by any function in the program, whether or not the functions are compiled in the same object code that the variable is declared within. The separate object modules must be linked together to create the executable code.

Although a variable has been declared global and is usable by any function in the program, it is not accessible until the function that wants to use it declares that variable an **extern**. Assume that the variable *a_globe_var* was declared global and defined in some object module:

```
int a_globe_var = 1492;
```

Then a function that is in a completely separate object module may access *a_globe_var* by including the following extern declaration in the function:

```
void a_function()
{
     extern int a_globe_var;
     ...
}
```

So, even though the scope of a variable is global, it must be declared extern before a function can use it.

Pointers

Pointers are one of C's strongest features. They allow C to compete with assembler-level coding; however, they are both a blessing and a curse. Pointers can be confusing. If used incorrectly, they cause disastrous bugs. Pointers point to locations in which other variables are stored. In other words, **pointers** are variables that hold the memory addresses of other variables. (Actually, pointers can be used to point anywhere in memory, but for now they will be used to point to variables only.) If you have a large block of data (for example, 2,000 characters), it is much easier and faster to physically move the pointer or address of the data than to move the data itself. Once you become used to pointers, you will be surprised at how handy they can be. At the moment, however, the task is to understand them. In the following example,

```
char ch = 'E';
```

the variable *ch* was declared a character variable and initialized to contain the letter E. If you could look in memory, you might find something like the following simulation:

Memory Address	Memory Contents
5300	-
5301	E
5302	-

The character E is stored in memory location 5301. In other words, the address of the variable *ch* is 5301. C will give you the address of the variable if you make use of the unary pointer operator—the ampersand (&). In the situation described above,

ch indicates the contents of the variable, or E.

&ch indicates the address of the variable, or the address where the E is stored (5301).

Now you need a way to store this address. To do that, you must declare a pointer variable, as in the following example:

```
char *pt;
```

The asterisk (*) tells C that this is not a character variable but a pointer to a character variable. The variable *pt* is intended to hold an address, not a character; however, it is intended to hold only addresses of character variables. Now you have a way to store that address. You would define the pointer variable *pt* in this way:

```
pt = &ch;
```

This definition says assign the pointer *pt* the address of the variable *ch*. If you could look into the computer's memory, you would see something resembling the following:

Memory Address	Memory Contents
5300	-
5301	E
5302	-
5303	-
5304	5301

As before, the variable *ch* still contains an E and is located in address 5301, but now there is the number 5301 located in address 5304. The variable *pt* was given the memory location 5304 when it was declared. Then, when *pt* was assigned the address of the variable *ch*, 5301 was put in location 5304, so the variable *pt* now holds the address of the variable *ch* and, therefore, points to it.

The asterisk (*) is also used as a unary pointer operator. It performs the opposite operation of the ampersand (&). The asterisk returns the contents of the variable located at the address pointed to. Consider the following values associated with the example variables you have been examining:

ch indicates the variable, E.

&ch indicates the address of the variable, 5301.

pt indicates the address of the variable, 5301.

**pt* indicates the variable at the address pointed to, E.

A pointer variable has a number of unique features that make it different from a regular variable. Earlier, it was said that the pointer *pt* could only point at character variables because it was declared as type **char**. Actually, as you might expect, C doesn't bother to check to make sure the pointer is not used to point to something other than a character. The program will just not work right if it is.

Assume that you had a number of integer variables stored in consecutive locations in memory. If you have a pointer called *numpoint* pointing at the first integer, and you want to make it point to the second one, you could increment or add one (1) to the pointer:

numpoint = *numpoint* + 1

This technique would also work if *numpoint* had been declared an int pointer. When you tell C to add one (1), it interprets that to mean one char, one int, or one float, depending on what type the pointer was declared. Remember that each different type of variable (char, int, or float) takes up a different number of bytes when stored. If *numpoint* had been declared an int pointer, C would add two to the address in *numpoint* to correctly get to the next integer; but if *numpoint* had been declared a float pointer, C would add four to the address in *numpoint*, thinking that is where to find the next floating-point number. So it is necessary to declare the pointer the same type as the variable you want to point to.

Because of this issue, pointer arithmetic is limited to increasing or decreasing the address. Actually, you can add and subtract integers to or from the pointer, but you can't perform any other operations—no multiplication or division.

Functions, Variables, and Label Names

The names used for functions, variables, and labels are referred to as identifiers in C. (**Labels** are the names used to identify a line of code.) **Identifiers** may start with either a letter or an underscore. After the first character, an identifier may contain any letter, any numeric digit, or an underscore. Only the first 32 characters are used by C to distinguish between identifiers, which means that if you make an identifier longer than 32 characters, C will confuse it with another identifier if the first 32 characters are the same. Having the capability for such a large field of characters for naming purposes means that you can make the names very descriptive and self-documenting.

Unlike BASIC, C distinguishes between uppercase and lowercase characters, which means that var, Var, and VAR are three different and distinct names as far as C is concerned.

Types of Constants

C has as many different types of constants as it has variable types. This chapter has introduced only five of the different types. To distinguish between the different types of constants, C requires you to follow certain formats when defining them. For example, a **string constant** is enclosed in double quotation marks, and a **character constant** is set off with single quotation marks as follows:

```
char y[7] = "string"
char x = 'a'
```

There are some characters that cannot be enclosed between any type of quotation marks, such as the bell and carriage return characters. These are defined in what are called **escape sequence character constants**. Some of these character constants are listed here (see Appendix C for a complete list):

Escape Sequence Character Constants:

Code	Constant Represented
\n	newline (carriage return and line feed)
\f	form feed
\a	alert (bell)
\"	double quote
\\	backslash

Assignment Operator

You will often see the following type of assignment when programming:

```
x = x + 1
```

You might even interpret the previous assignment as

x equals *x* plus one

But *x* cannot really equal itself plus one more. What the assignment really means is

assign to *x* the existing value of *x* plus one

The symbol = is not an equal sign here; it is an **assignment** symbol. In BASIC, the same symbol is used to mean both equal and assignment. This is not true in C. In C, the = symbol only means assignment. The symbol = = is used in C for the relational operator that means "equals."

Compiler Control Lines

One more type of statement must be explained before concluding this discussion on the form of a C program. These statements are called **compiler control lines**, or **preprocessor directives**. They cause the source program to be changed before the compile takes place. These statements can be identified because they always start with a pound, or number, sign (#), and they do not end with a semicolon. (Some C compilers require the pound sign to be in the first column of the line.) The two types of C compiler control lines introduced in this chapter are **#include** and **#define**.

The #include line takes one of the following forms:

```
#include <file.h>
#include "file.h"
```

Placing one of these lines in your program will cause the contents of the file called **file.h** to be inserted in your program before the compile takes place. The use of the angle brackets tells the compiler to look for the header file in the INCLUDE directory you specified for Turbo C. The use of the quotation marks tells the compiler to first look for the file in your current working directory. Consider the following example:

```
#include <math.h>

void main()
{
     int x;
     x = sqrt(64);
     ...
}
```

Your main function declares an integer variable *x* and then calls the square root function to take the square root of 64. The function then returns the result to variable *x*. Remember, when you use a function, you should first declare the function. Has the sqrt() function been declared? The file math.h contains the declarations and compiler control lines necessary for all the math library functions that came with your C compiler. Because the math.h file was included and loaded with your program before it was compiled, the square root function was declared along with many other math library functions you did not use. Anytime you want to call one of the C library functions supplied with your compiler, you should include the appropriate header (or .h) file. Refer to your C program reference guide to determine which header file should be included with each of the library functions you use.

Header files serve other purposes in addition to declaring functions. They can also declare variables and define constants that you might need in your program. It is possible for you to create header files for your own library functions. You might find it valuable to print and examine some of the header files.

Sometimes, you can get by without including the header file for some functions. At other times, leaving them out will cause problems. Turbo C automatically includes some header files when you compile a program. Until you become more familiar with these header files, it would be a good idea to always include the header file listed for each function.

The second compiler control line is the **#define**. It is used to define a **symbolic constant**. This symbolic constant may take a surprising variety of forms. Consider the following example:

```
#define PI 3.14159
```

The convention is to use capital letters to designate symbolic constants. Now, the constant PI can be used in a program instead of typing in the actual value. Any time C finds the constant PI in the program, it will make the substitution before it compiles your code. You could enter the following C program statement:

```
cir = PI * dia;
```

Before compiling, C would change the statement to

```
cir = 3.14159 * dia;
```

Following is another example. Assume you have a program that prints out the name of the current president of your company numerous times. When the president is replaced with a new president, you must change the name wherever it is used—unless, of course, you used a symbolic constant. Then it would only be necessary to make one change to the program. Examine the following:

```
#define PRES "Robert Redman"
```

If each reference in the program uses the constant **PRES**, the only place you need to change the code is in the **#define** line.

The symbolic constant does not have to be a true constant. It could be an often-used C statement that you are just tired of typing over and over. Examine the following:

```
#define ERRMES printf("Error on input.  Please retype.\n")
```

Now, whenever you enter

```
ERRMES;
```

in your program, C will substitute the following line of code before it compiles:

```
printf("Error on input.  Please retype.\n");
```

The compiler control lines, or preprocessor directives, can be placed anywhere in the program; however, they will only affect the code that appears after them. For this reason, you will usually want to place them at the beginning of the program.

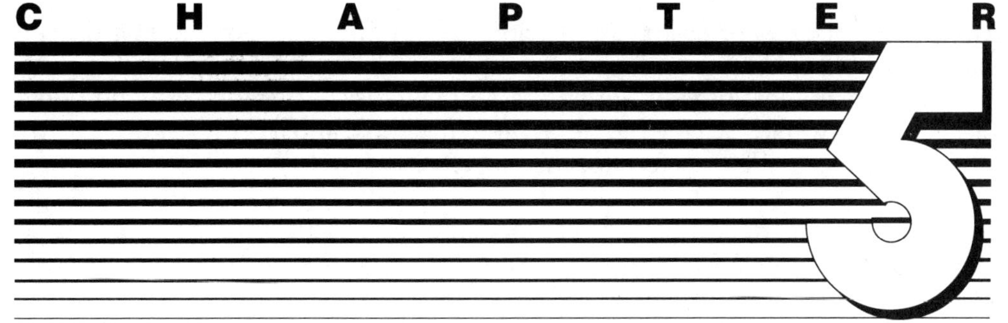

WRITING C CODE

This chapter covers programming (writing code) in C; however, only a limited subset of C will be discussed. This subset will provide enough background to allow you to perform most of your early programming tasks. For the rest, additional programming topics are covered throughout the book, and it is suggested that you keep a C user's guide or reference manual close at hand.

For such a strong language, C is comprised of surprisingly few program statements. The proposed ANSI standard for C lists only 32 keywords, and obviously not all keywords are program statements. In contrast, BASIC has well over 100 commands or statements. The reason C has so few statements is that many of the operations accomplished with program statements in other languages are handled by calling library functions in C. This characteristic is what gives C some of its transportability between computers. When you want to transport a C program from one computer to another, you simply recompile on the new computer. This recompile will call library functions that are designed for the new computer. These new functions usually give the same results and have the same name as the functions used on the old computer, but they generate the machine language object code of the new computer.

Because of this, much learning in C revolves around the C library functions rather than C program statements. To prove the point, the first topic you will explore is input/output (I/O), which is accomplished using C library functions.

INITIAL KEYBOARD AND SCREEN INPUT/OUTPUT FUNCTIONS

This section is limited to the rudimentary input from keyboard and screen output. When you learn a new language, it is important to get control of at least one method of output early in the learning process. Until you have a method of output, you cannot be sure that the results you expect are actually happening. It is for this reason that the **printf()** function is discussed first.

printf()

You can see the printf() function in operation in your first C program (Chapter 3), but explanation of how to use it has been delayed until this time. The printf() function is used to send formatted output to the screen. It varies from the conventional C function in that it allows for a variable number of arguments. An example of its general form follows:

```
printf("format-string",argument,argument...);
```

The **format string** (or control string, as it is sometimes called) is made up of conventional characters, escape-sequence character constants, and conversion specifications. The conventional characters are reproduced exactly as they appear. The escape-sequence character constants all start with a backslash (\); they cause control characters to be printed. The conversion specifications all start with a percent sign (%) and indicate how and where the arguments are to be inserted in the output.

Consider the following example, where the variables *spd* and *nam* have been declared **integer** and **string**, respectively:

```
printf("A track record, %d mph, was set by %s.\n",spd,nam);
```

The format string is included between the quotation marks. The **%d** and **%s** are conversion specifications, and they indicate where the arguments will be inserted and what type of format will be used when the arguments are printed. The **%d** means a decimal integer, and the **%s** means a character string. In this case, the arguments they refer to are the variables *spd* and *nam* that follow the format string. Make sure that the number of conversion specifications included in the format string is the same as the number of variables listed as arguments; C expects you to do this correctly and will not check for errors. If these numbers don't match, strange results can occur, and you will receive no indication of what went wrong.

The following is a partial table of conversion specifications for the printf() function (a complete table can be found in Appendix C).

printf() Conversion Specifications:

Conversion Specification	**Output Description**
%d	signed decimal integer
%f	signed floating-point
%c	single character
%s	string of characters

The **\n** is the escape sequence character constant, indicating a new line. A new line will be printed where this constant is inserted in the text. Unlike the BASIC PRINT statement, in C, a single printf() function can be made to produce multiple new lines simply by including the escape sequence \n multiple times in the format string. See Appendix C for a complete list of these escape sequence character constants.

All other characters in the sample format string are conventional characters, which are reproduced on the screen as they appear in the string.

Enter the following program:

```
/* -------------------- PROG-2.C ---------------------- */
/* ----------------- Outputting data ------------------ */

#include <stdio.h>

void main()
{
     /* ------ Declare and initialize variables ---- */
     int spd=132;
     char nam[9]="Jim Ford";

     /* ------ Display line of text on screen ------ */
     printf("A track record, %d mph, was set by %s.\n"
          ,spd,nam);
}
```

The C compiler will allow you to continue a line from one line to the next. The semicolon indicates when the line is complete, not the carriage return. In this example, there is a print statement that appears as follows:

```
printf("A track record, %d mph, was set by %s.\n"
       ,spd,nam);
```

This is just one line continued on to the next line. It could be written as one line:

```
printf("A track record, %d mph, was set by %s.\n",spd,nam);
```

Whenever you want to continue a line, just break it where white space could be inserted without changing the meaning; however, you cannot continue the line by breaking it between the quotation marks of a printf() function.

Whenever you are going to call a C library function, it is important to check your program reference guide to find which header file, if any, should be included. Failure to include proper header files will give unpredictable results. In some cases, the header file can be omitted without an apparent problem; however, until you become familiar with header files, it is best to include the appropriate header file for any given library function. According to the *Turbo C Reference Guide*, the prototype for the printf() function is contained in the **stdio.h** header file and therefore is appropriate to include with the code.

When run, the previous program should cause the following line of text to be displayed on your screen:

```
A track record, 132 mph, was set by Jim Ford.
```

scanf()

Now you can send information to the screen. The next step is to be able to receive information from the keyboard. One way you can accomplish this task is by calling the **scanf**() function. An example of the general form for the scanf() function follows:

```
scanf("format-string",argument,argument...);
```

The characters included in the format or control string are made up of format specifiers, white space, and nonwhite space characters. The format specifiers all start with a percent sign (%) and are similar to those used in the printf() function. As in the printf() function, there should be a matching variable argument for each format specifier in the format string. White space in the format string will be ignored by scanf(). Any nonwhite space character in the format string will be expected from the keyboard, but once received will be discarded. scanf() will terminate if the nonwhite space character that is expected is not found.

Consider the following example:

```
scanf("%s%d",&nam,&spd);
```

In this example, scanf() will expect a string because of the **%s** format specifier. After input, the string will be terminated by the first white space received from the keyboard. The string will be given the variable name *nam*. Then, scanf() will expect a decimal integer as a result of the **%d**. scanf() will give the integer the variable named *spd* after input of the integer is terminated. The last input data will be terminated and execution continued when a new line character or carriage return is sent from the keyboard. Again, there is no error checking. If the number of arguments does not match the number of format specifiers, your program could crash, and C would give no warning or clue about why it happened.

The only thing left to be explained is the ampersand (&) preceding the arguments, but you know from Chapter 4 that & means the address of the variable. scanf() needs to know the address in which to store the variable, not the current contents of the variable. If you forget to indicate the address, strange results can occur.

Following is a partial table of conversion specifications for the scanf() function (a complete table can be found in Appendix C).

scanf() Conversion Specifications:

Conversion Specification	**Input Description**
%d	decimal integer
%f	floating-point
%c	single character
%s	string of characters

Try scanf() now. Modify your PROG-2.C source program to read as follows:

```
/* --------------------- PROG-3.C --------------------- */
/* ----------------- Inputting data ------------------- */

#include <stdio.h>

void main()
{
     /* ------ Declare and initialize variables ---- */
     int spd=132;
     char nam[9]="Jim Ford";

     /* ------ Accept new variables from keyboard -- */
     printf("Type your first name and the speed.\n");
     scanf("%s%d",&nam,&spd);

     /* ------ Display line of text on screen ------ */
     printf("A track record, %d mph, was set by %s.\n"
          ,spd,nam);
}
```

Once again, a new library function was added to the program. A check of your C programming reference will show that the header file **stdio.h** should be included in your program when you call scanf(), but because it was already included once, it wasn't necessary to include it again.

Remember that because a white space terminates the input string, you will only be able to input one name here. You should also remember that the string variable is declared to reserve only nine memory locations; if your name is longer than eight characters, you could have trouble.

PROGRAM BRANCHING

Now that you have the beginning of I/O under control, you can study C programming and test the results at will. You should find that many of C's programming instructions are similar to BASIC's. A good example of this is the **if** statement.

if else Statement

C's if statement is a conditional branching instruction that has the following general format:

```
if(condition) statement1;
else statement2;
```

The specified condition is tested. If the condition is true or nonzero, **statement1** will be executed. If the condition is false or zero, then **statement2** will be executed. Under no condition will both statements execute. Once the appropriate statement has been executed, unless redirected in that statement, program control will continue with the next statement in line.

Blocks may be created following the **if** or the **else** keywords if more than one statement is necessary for either condition. See the following form:

```
if(condition) {
      statement1;
      statement2;
      statement3;
}
else statement4;
```

In this case, **statement1**, **statement2**, and **statement3** will be executed as a block if the condition is true.

The else portion of the if statement is optional. When you are nesting if statements, there can be some confusion about which if statement the else applies to. The rule is that the else applies to the nearest preceding if statement that does not have an else associated with it.

The condition test may use any or none of the following relational operators:

Relational Operators:

Operator	**Test For**
= =	equal
<	less than
>	greater than
! =	not equal
> =	greater than or equal
< =	less than or equal

You can see that, except for equal and not equal, these are the same relational operators you used in the BASIC IF statement. Remember that the single equal sign in C means assignment. It will not work in the if statement to test the condition. Consider the following examples:

Example 1:

```
if(var==5) printf("EQUAL/n");
else {
     printf("var IS ");
     printf("NOT EQUAL");
     printf(" TO 5.\n");
}
```

Example 2:

```
if(var2) printf("var2 is non-zero\n")
```

In the first example, the word **EQUAL** will be printed if *var* has a value of 5. If it doesn't, the block of statements will be executed, and **var IS NOT EQUAL TO 5.** will be printed.

Note in the second example that there is no actual comparison to be made; this is fine with C. The if statement sends the comparisons away to another function for evaluation. The results of the evaluation are returned to the if statement in the following way: when the comparison proves true, a one is returned; when the comparison is false, a zero is returned. Then, the if statement chooses an option, depending on whether the result returned is zero or nonzero. The fact that there is no comparison to be made in the second example does not matter to the if statement. It simply looks at the value of *var2*. Any nonzero value will cause the true option to be taken. If the value is zero, the else option will be executed; however, because there is no else option in this example, nothing will happen.

It is also possible to use logical operators with the if statement. The logical operators are as follows:

Operator	**Meaning**	
&&	A && B	indicates both A and B
||	A || B	either A or B
!	! A	indicates not A

These logical operators are used in C the same way they are used in the BASIC IF statement. Consider the following examples:

```
if(ch = 'q' && ch = 'Q') printf("This will never print");

if(ch = 'q' || ch = 'Q') printf("This will print");
```

In the first case, with &&, the printf() function will execute only when both conditions are true. It is impossible for a type char variable to be equal to both q and Q at the same time; therefore, the statement will never be printed. In the second example, on the other hand, the printf() will execute whenever the variable *ch* is equal to q or it is equal to Q.

switch case Statement

In BASIC, you have an instruction called the ON GOSUB. The **switch** statement is the equivalent instruction in C. This statement will allow you to take different actions depending on the value of a variable. The switch statement takes the following form:

```
switch(variable){
     case constant1:
          statement;
          statement;
          break;
     case constant2:
          statement;
          break;
     case constant3:
          statement;
          break;
     default :
          statement;
}
```

The variable will be tested against the constants in each case. When the variable is equal to the constant, the statements following that case will be executed until a break statement is encountered. If the variable is equal to none of the constants, the statements following the default will be executed. The default is optional, and if it is not included, nothing will happen if a match is not found. Notice the punctuation. Each constant and the default are followed by a colon, and all of the case statements are set off as one group, using braces.

goto Statement

Although C is a structured language in which it is seldom necessary to use the notorious **goto**, the instruction set does include it. The C goto is very similar to the BASIC GOTO, but, because there are no line numbers in C, you must give the line to which you want to go an identifier called a **line label**. This identifier is a conventional C identifier that is placed at the beginning of the line and followed by a colon (:). The following endless loop demonstrates the form of the goto statement.

```
rut:        printf("I am in a rut.\n");
            goto rut;
```

The label must be in the same function as the goto. Also note that the colon is not part of the label. It is simply the way that C identifies a label when it appears in a line of code. Don't forget it.

PROGRAM LOOPS

It is often necessary to go through multiple iterations of some action in order to complete a task. This process is referred to as **looping**. C has three different types of loop statements: **for**, **while**, and **do while**.

for Statement

Although it appears quite similar to the BASIC FOR statement, the C **for** statement is considerably more versatile. Consider the general form of the C for statement:

```
for(initialize; test; increment) statement;
```

Or, if a block is used, the statement can take the following form:

```
for(initialize; test; increment) {
     statement;
     statement;
     statement;
}
```

Note that there are three separate sections inside the parentheses, separated by semicolons. Although you have a wide latitude for what you can legitimately put in each of these sections, the fundamental action intended for each is described as follows:

initialize Initialize variable(s).

test Repeat loop until test on variable(s) fails.

increment Cause some change on variable(s) after each iteration of loop.

Make sure you use the relational operators (= =, etc.) in the test section the same as you would in an if statement. The initialize and increment sections would normally have the assignment operator (=).

Observe the implied plural on variables. C's for statement is not limited to a single variable to control the loop. (Just separate each initialization and increment with a comma.) Nor is it necessary to use the same variables in each of the three sections. Each section can be acting on entirely different variables. In fact, you can even leave any or all of the sections blank, and the loop will still function. The trick is to make sure it functions the way you intend. Begin with the following rather conventional example:

```
for(x=1; x<=16; x=x+1) printf(" value is %d\n",x);
```

If you assume that the other required parts of the function are there, the preceding loop will initialize *x* to 1 and then test *x*. If *x* is less than or equal to 16, it will execute the printf() function. Finally, it will increment *x* by 1. The comparison will again be tried, and the process will continue until the test fails. This loop will print the following:

```
value is 1
value is 2
value is 3
...
value is 15
value is 16
```

With C's for statement, you need not limit the increment to addition or subtraction as you do in BASIC. Suppose you change the above example to a geometric progression with the following:

```
for(x=1; x<=16; x=x*2) printf(" value is %d\n",x);
```

This time, the results would appear as follows:

```
value is 1
value is 2
value is 4
value is 8
value is 16
```

If you choose to experiment and leave some of the sections blank, you will find that leaving the test section blank creates a true condition, which means that any time you leave the test section blank, you create an infinite loop—one that will run forever.

Now try out some of the concepts you have been reading about. Enter the following example program:

```
/* -------------------- PROG-4.C ---------------------- */
/* ---- Examples of for loop and switch statements ---- */

#include <stdio.h>

void main()
{
     /* ----------- Initialize variables ----------- */
     int tally, input_no;

     /* -------------- Sample for loop ------------- */
     for (tally = 1; tally <= 5; tally++) {
         printf("\nType a one-digit number\n");
         scanf("%d",&input_no);

         /* -------- Sample switch statement ------- */
         switch (input_no) {
           case 3:
               printf("You picked case three.\n");
               break;
           case 2:
               printf("You picked case two.\n");
               break;
           case 5:
               printf("You picked case five.\n");
               break;
           default:
               printf("There is no case %d.\n"
                    ,input_no);
         }
         /* -------- End of switch statement ------- */

     }
     /* ----------- End of for loop block ---------- */
     printf ("That's all folks.\n");

}
/* ------------------- End of main ------------------- */
```

The increment section of the for loop has the expression **tally++**. The same result could be obtained by using **tally=tally+1**. Note that in the case statement, the constants are **3**, **2**, and **5**. They don't start with 1. They are not consecutive. You have a fairly free hand in choosing the constants you want.

Instead of the **printf("You picked ..."** statement in each of the cases, you could call one or more functions to process a keyboard request. The previous sample program could be expanded to handle the keyboard input for a menu screen. In that situation, the cases might resemble the following:

```
case 3:
     process_orders();
     break;
case 2:
     send_statements();
     break;
case 5:
     make_corrections();
     break;
```

while Statement

The second loop statement of C is the **while** statement. Its general form is as follows:

```
while(test) statement;
```

Or using a block, it could appear as follows:

```
while(test){
      statement;
      statement;
      statement;
}
```

The loop statement(s) within the while statement will continue to execute as long as the test proves true. Note that the while loop instruction does not include an initialization or any sort of increment as part of the instruction. This means you must initialize the test variable before entering the while loop and then make sure there is some mechanism for changing the test variable within the loop.

The while statement, like the for statement, executes the test before it executes the statements that follow. This means that the statements in the loop may never execute if the test proves false the first time the test is made, which is the primary difference between while and do while statements.

do while Statement

The **do while** statement will execute the test after the first iteration of the loop. If you always want the loop to execute at least once, then you should use the do while statement. The general form of the do while is as follows:

```
do {
     statements;
} while(test);
```

Again, it is up to the programmer to initialize and modify the test variable to control the number of iterations the loop makes. If the test proves true and there is no way to change the test variable within the loop, an infinite loop has been created, in which case you may need to use a **break** statement.

break Statement

Recall that the **break** statement was used in the switch statement to terminate each case. It can also be used to terminate a loop. Consider the following example:

```
/* -------------------- PROG-5.C --------------------- */
/* --------------- Example of a break ---------------- */

#include<stdio.h>

void main()
{
     int x,y=0;

     /* -------- The for loop has no test ---------- */
     /* --- It would be infinite if not for break -- */
     for(x=1; ; x=x*2) {
          y=y+1;
          printf(" x=%d  y=%d\n",x,y);
          if (y>4) break;
     }

     printf("  All done. ");
}
```

Without a test in the test section, this for loop has no way of stopping itself; however, it can still be stopped with the break statement. Note that unlike the variable *x*, the variable *y* has no relationship to the for statement; it is simply part of the block of code being executed inside the for statement. Yet when the break statement is used, the variable *y* can be used to terminate the for loop.

continue Statement

The **continue** statement is used in the same manner as the break statement but with almost opposite results. When the continue statement is encountered as part of a loop, it immediately forces the next iteration of the loop. Any code that follows the continue statement will be skipped on that iteration. Consider the following example:

```
for(record=1; record<=500; record=record+1) {
     /* --- Read name, address, and zip code -- */
     ...

     /* ---- Print all with a 97201 zip code -- */
     if (zip != "97201") continue;

     printf("s% s% s%\n",name,address,zip);
}
```

In this example, the loop will execute 500 times; however, the printf() function will be skipped anytime the zip code is not equal to **97201**.

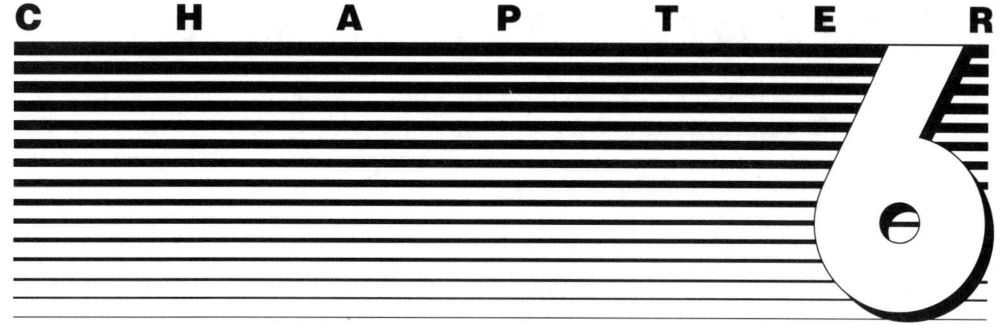

MASTERING COMPUTERIZED DATA

UNDERSTANDING THE VARIETY OF NUMBER TYPES

The first step in understanding and mastering numeric data is to realize that the computer has a variety of ways to handle numbers. This is because the computer is asked to do many things for many different people. Each person needs a different type of number:

Occupation	Sample Number	Type Needed
Engineer	233.927630228	double-precision
Politician	457000000.00	floating-point
Accountant	5430.98	floating-point
Stock boy	179	integer
Scientist	9.7668×10^{-18}	scientific notation
Programmer	35FA	hexadecimal
The computer	101011	binary

There are times when one person might use all these different types of numbers, depending on the task. The point is that different needs require different types of numbers.

If the computer had only one way of handling numbers, it would, of course, have to be the binary number system, which is not particularly convenient for humans. When working with humans, the computer needs at least two different ways of handling numbers: one for itself and one for humans. Because humans have such diverse needs, any method of working with numbers that would give the accuracy needed for all the different groups would be so slow and cumbersome that its value would be limited. The original BASIC tried to do this to a degree, but it had severe limitations. Many people could not use it in their work, so BASIC was soon changed to accommodate a wider variety of users. You can still use BASIC as it was originally designed, and it will try to convert to an appropriate type of number, depending on the size of number that it finds you using; however, if you want dollars and cents in columns, more speed, or more accuracy, you will want to use some of the added features.

There are three factors that affect the type of number you might use:

- the number base needed
- the size of the number (or the range of digits needed before and/or after the decimal point)
- the accuracy of the number (or the significant digits needed)

The fact that the computer uses one base and humans use another causes base to become a factor any time you work with numbers. The other two factors of size and accuracy are a different matter. Most languages give three fundamental types of options: **integer**, **floating-point**, and **double-precision**.

Integers are used when you are only concerned about whole or counting numbers (1, 2, 3, 4, etc.). They usually have a size limit of about positive or negative 32,000. In this case, the number is stored as a binary integer.

The next choice, floating-point numbers, relates to the ability to handle decimal fractions. They take the form 173.26 or 1.7326E+2, in which the number following the E is referred to as the exponent. These numbers are often stored as binary coded decimals (BCD), in which each decimal digit is converted to a binary code and the decimal point is stored separately. As you can imagine, computing with this cross between a binary and decimal number can be a cumbersome process for the computer. Depending on the space allowed for each, you have a limit on the number of significant digits and a separate limit on the exponent or number of decimal places that can be kept track of.

If either the number of significant digits or the exponent is too small for your needs, you will usually find that there is a double-precision floating-point option available in which both the significant digits and the exponent capability are increased.

Octal and Hexadecimal Numbers

First, consider the number base. All numbers stored and used in the computer are in some form of binary or bit notation. Only in the very last stage does the computer convert numbers to digits that are acceptable to human conventions. As the number is being put on the screen or on the printer, it is converted to a special symbol so you can read it. Everything is in some binary notation in the computer. If you want to actually see what is in different registers or memory locations, you will be looking at base two. For convenience, memory dumps will usually be given in octal (base 8) or hex (base 6), which are easily converted to or from binary. (See Appendix A for an explanation of base two.)

BASIC has a limited ability to work with octal and hex numbers (the OCT$ and HEX$ functions). In contrast, the C language was designed with such activities in mind. The following are C examples. Assume for a moment that you want to look at a location in memory that contains an integer variable. While you're at it, you also want to look at the address of that location. Consider the following code:

```
/* --------------------- PROG-6.C --------------------- */
/* -------- Print types of numbers and addresses ------ */

#include <stdio.h>

void main()
{
     int x=21;

     /* -- Print values of x in base 10, 8, and 16 - */
     printf("Value of x is:\n");
     printf("%o in octal\n%x in hex\n%d in decimal\n"
          ,x,x,x);

     /* ---------- Print the address of x ---------- */
     printf("\nAddress of x is:\n");
     printf("%o in octal\n%X in hex\n%d in decimal\n"
          ,&x,&x,&x);
}
```

Note that the variable *x* was defined as 21 base ten. The first section of code prints *x* in octal, hex, and decimal. Note also the new printf() specification codes. **%o** indicates octal. **%x** and **%X** indicate hex values, with the characters for 10 through 15 being printed in either lowercase or uppercase, respectively. (See the complete list of specification codes in Appendix C.) In the second section of code, you are printing the address of the variable *x* in the three different number bases, yielding the following results on the screen:

```
Value of x is:
 25 in octal
 15 in hex
 21 in decimal

Address of x is:
 177754 in octal
 FFEC in hex
 -20 in decimal
```

The values for the variable are as expected, but printing the addresses has produced some strange results. (The address you get when you run this program on your computer will probably vary from that of the example.) All three results are the computer's correct conversion of the same binary notation for a number.

The octal value is reasonable, and it is the address, but perhaps it is a little long for convenience. Converting to binary is easy. Just convert each digit into its binary value to get the binary number:

octal	1	7	7	7	5	4
binary	1	111	111	111	101	100

As for hex, trying to remember that the letters A through F stand for the digits ten through fifteen might be a little confusing at first. The hex conversion of the address has two advantages: first, it is short; second, it groups well with the 16 bits of the address. The octal conversion had one bit left over. Look at the hex conversion:

hex	F	F	E	C
binary	1111	1111	1110	1100

You, the programmer, will be using octal and hex numbers in order to see what is inside that computer you're working on. In fact, some of the examples in this book will be doing just that, letting you look inside the computer by using octal or hex numbers.

The next section will discuss the rather confusing decimal address of -20.

Integers

To understand integers, look at that decimal address, a negative twenty. It obviously doesn't make much sense as an address. An address takes 16 bits, and this address is 1111111111101100 in binary. When C was instructed to print that number, using the %d (decimal integer printf() conversion specification), it did just that. It considered this number a signed integer and converted it as such. A signed integer has 16 bits, but the left-most bit indicates the sign of the number. Zero means positive, and one means negative. This binary number is a two's complementary negative number. So C interpreted the first one in the binary address as the sign and then converted according to **two's complementary arithmetic**. Without going into a complete explanation of two's complementary arithmetic here, just think of a negative number as something that will give a zero result when added to its positive counterpart. Negative five added to positive five equals zero. Add a positive binary twenty to our negative binary twenty and see what happens. Remember that in binary 1+1=10, 1+0=1, 0+0=0, and 1+1+1=11; don't forget to carry. The following example is grouped in fours for visual clarity only:

Binary		Decimal
1111 1111 1110 1100	=	-20
0000 0000 0001 0100	=	+20
1 0000 0000 0000 0000	=	0

Now you might say, "That's not zero. There's a 1 in the left-most position." Remember that the computer performs arithmetic in a **register**. For integers, that register is 16 bits wide. The 1 you see on the left was a carry to the 17th position. If you look at the 16 positions of the register, you will see only zeros. To the computer, that is a zero and it forgets about the extra 1 that was carried out of the register. (This is the reason that computers are often not wired to subtract. There is no need for it; the addition capability will produce results for both addition and subtraction if you just use the right numbers.)

In C, dropping the carry bit or carrying into the 16th position can cause problems. If you are adding positive integers and exceed the limit of a register, you could get a negative or zero result. If you don't check for this possiblity, your answers could be in error. Here, you must put in some type of limit check to ensure that your program does not produce an inaccurate answer. In this particular situation, a partial solution could be to tell C to consider this a positive number, including the sign bit. This is accomplished by declaring the variable a type int with an unsigned modifier (**unsigned int**). This tells C to consider this variable a positive integer, so C doubles the possible size of an integer. The range changes from 32768 to +32767 and becomes 0 to 65535. This is only a partial solution, of course, because that number could also be exceeded. Once again, you must put in the run-time limit check yourself. C will not check it for you. BASIC is another matter. If you designate an integer, BASIC performs the runtime limit check; if it exceeds the integer register limit, it will print **overflow** and stop. BASIC makes things easy for the programmer, but remember—BASIC is slower.

If you return to the addresses that were printed out, you'll see that the -20 may not be much of an address, but that binary address happened to be the two's complement of a -20. Because a %d conversion was asked for, that's just what C converted it into—a decimal integer. At least now it's understandable why the -20 was printed.

Floating-Point Numbers

If you need an inventory of automobiles on a car lot, an integer would work. You don't need to count fractional parts of cars. On the other hand, the accountant inside the office of that same car lot needs dollars and cents figures, which means two digits to the right of a decimal point. This would require a floating-point number (a number that can keep track of fractional parts, using decimals). To keep track of both the significant digits and the fractional part, C needs more space to store the number. C will take twice as many bits for a floating-point number as it does for an integer—in other words, 32 bits.

This additional space allows numbers to be handled in the following form:

3.689024
1145.67
78926.3
0.0003572

Numbers stored as floating-point can be output as shown above, using the %f conversion specification, or they can be displayed to you in a notation that is referred to as exponential format, or scientific notation, using the %e conversion specification. These notations appear as follows:

Usual Format (%f)	Exponential Format (%e)
126.3333	1.263333E + 002
0.00000000327	3.270000E - 009
54927000.0	5.492700E + 007

In exponential format, the number following the E represents the power of ten by which you multiply the number to the left of the E. Or you can just think of it as the number of positions to the right or left that you move the decimal point.

Remember that using a floating-point instead of an integer takes twice as much memory to hold the number and slows down computation time.

Double-Precision and Floating-Point Numbers

There are times when more accuracy is necessary or when you must work with extremely small or large numbers. What this means is that there are more significant digits of accuracy required or that the significant digits are farther from the decimal point. For politicians working with budgets of billions of dollars of tax money, what's a few thousand more or less? In other words, they work with big numbers but not very accurate ones. They could probably get by with 4 or 5 significant digits. A number such as $483,600,000 would be fine. The digits 4, 8, and 3 are accurate. The 6 is probably approximate in that all smaller digits were rounded off to generate the 6. A single-precision floating-point number would work. On the other hand, scientists and engineers usually need more accuracy or precision in their numbers. Numbers such as 3.14159265 or 0.0000000021057424 or even more accurate might be necessary. For accuracy such as this, they would need double-precision floating-point numbers and perhaps scientific notation for their work.

Both BASIC and C offer the option of double-precision numbers, which will allow a larger number of significant digits as well as a greater exponent in exponential format. Remember that you pay a price for this precision. Computation speed slows down still more, and more storage locations are required to store the number. It is usually double the amount of space a single-precision floating-point number requires for storage. In C, 64 bits, or eight bytes, are needed to store a double-precision number.

UNDERSTANDING MATHEMATICAL OPERATIONS

You may feel you are familiar with the usual mathematical operations and rightly feel that you already understand this topic; however, you saw from the discussion on integers that computers perform arithmetic differently from the way humans do. At times, this different approach can cause some problems if you are not aware of the conditions—for example, a positive mathematical computation could exceed the limit of an integer register and become a negative integer.

Arithmetic Operators

The arithmetic operators used in C are as follows:

Arithmetic Operators:

Operator	**Operation**
+	addition
-	subtraction
*	multiplication
/	division
-	unary minus
%	modulo
++	increment
--	decrement
()	ordering
=	assignment

The first four operators should be self-explanatory. You may or may not be familiar with the last six.

The unary minus (-) will transform the number to the negative of the number, and you are now aware that this could be a different form of number from the positive value. An integer would create the two's complement.

Just think of modulo (%) as the remainder of a division. See the following examples:

8 % 3 = 2	8 divided by 3 leaves a remainder of 2.
15 % 5 = 0	15 divided by 5 leaves a remainder of 0.
11 % 6 = 5	11 divided by 6 leaves a remainder of 5.

The increment (++) and decrement (--) do not appear in this form in most other languages. In BASIC, an increment is accomplished as follows:

```
100 X = X + 1
```

The same task can be accomplished in C with either of the following methods:

```
x = x + 1;

x++;
```

Both of these examples will increment *x* by the value of one. You must be careful with the last method of increment, however. Examine the following code:

```
x = 5;
a = 0;
b = 0;
                    /* After execution values are */
a = x++;            /*   a = 5, b = 0, and x = 6   */
b = ++x;            /*   a = 5, b = 7, and x = 7   */
```

In the first case, *a* was assigned the value of *x* before the increment took place. In the second case, *b* was assigned the value of *x* after the increment was performed. The difference relates to the ++ (increment) following or preceding the *x*. In both cases, *x* was incremented. The -- (decrement) functions in the same way except, of course, it subtracts one from the value of the variable. (This is an exception to the normal order of precedence explained in the next section.)

The last two symbols, () (parentheses) and = (assign), are also considered arithmetic operators in C. The parentheses are used to control the order of operation and to clarify an expression. You have already read about the assign symbol and how it should not be confused with the concept of equality. Remember, in C, the symbol = means **assign**, and the symbol == means **equal**.

As you study C further, you will see that some symbols, such as the following, have multiple meanings:

```
*  %  &   |  -  =  /
```

You can only determine the correct meaning of each of these symbols by examining the context in which it is used.

Order of Precedence

In any programming language, it is important to be aware of the order in which mathematical operations will be performed. Rules of algebra are not necessarily followed. What is the value of the following expression?

```
2 + 3 * 5
```

The result might be 25 or 17, depending on which operation takes precedence. In this case, the answer is as you probably expected. C gives precedence to multiplication, so the answer is 17. If addition had precedence or operations were taken from left to right, the result would be 25. If you ever have a question about how C will generate a result, you can always force the desired result by using parentheses. Anything inside parentheses is given precedence:

```
(2 + 3) * 5
```

This would force the result to be 25, whereas the following would leave no question that the answer is to be 17:

```
2 + (3 * 5)
```

The following list shows which operations take precedence for C arithmetic operations:

1. ordering	()
2. unary operators	-- ++ -
3. multiplication and division	* / %
4. addition and subtraction	+ -
5. assignment	=

Computation with Mixed Types

Another area that can cause a result to vary from what you might expect is that of operating on different type variables or constants. The general rule of thumb is that C will convert different types up to a common type before computation. Type char becomes type int. Type float becomes type double. This means that a type float multiplied by a type int would result in their both becoming type double for the computation.

MATHEMATICAL FUNCTIONS

Some mathematical operations are accomplished by calling C library functions. C, of course, has library functions for trigonometric and logarithmic operations. It even has a function to find the hypotenuse of a right triangle, which is a geometric operation. However, there are a few mathematical operations that have more general value. This section discusses these operations along with some other commonly used math operations.

You should keep two things in mind when working with these functions. First, remember to include the appropriate header file for any function you use. Second, C has a variety of number types. In some cases, there are different functions for different number types. To obtain the absolute value of a number, you are required to call the function that works with the type numbers you are using.

abs()	Calculate absolute value of an integer.
labs()	Calculate absolute value of a long integer (where **long** is a type modifier).
fabs()	Calculate absolute value of type double.
cabs()	Calculate absolute value of a complex number.

This section will cover the uses of different functions. You should consult the reference guide for your version of C to determine which version of a given function to use in any particular case and which header (.H) file to include with your code.

abs()

Finding the absolute value of a number is simply taking the value of the number without regard to its sign. The absolute value of -7 is 7; the absolute value of +7 is 7. This will, of course, convert the negative two's complementary integers discussed earlier to positive integers.

There are times when you need a positive value. You don't want to first test the number to see if it is negative and if it is negative, multiply by a negative value to make it positive. So you use the abs() function. Assume for a moment that you are writing a computer game. There are two objects on the screen, and their horizontal positions on the screen are x1 and x2. You want to know if they are within five positions of each other. The following if statement would accomplish that task:

```
if( abs(x1-x2) <= 5 ) { ...
```

To calculate the distance between them, you can subtract one coordinate from the other without regard for their relative size. You don't care if the result is positive or negative. You only want to know if the absolute value is less than or equal to 5.

floor() and ceil()

There are times when you want to round off a number to an approximate value. The **floor()** and **ceil()** functions are designed to help do that; however, they do not round to the nearest integer. The floor() function produces the largest integer that is not greater than your number; ceil() gives the smallest integer that is not less than your number. For example,

```
floor(7.89)     produces 7
ceil(5.13)      produces 6
```

Although the result is an integer value, it is returned as type double.

pow()

The function **pow()** lets you raise a number to some power. It takes the following form:

```
ans = pow( num, exp );
```

where the variable *num* is raised to the power *exp*.

rand() and srand()

The **rand**() function is used to produce a pseudo-random number. The function produces random numbers in the range of 0 to 32767. These numbers are generated in such a way that the same sequence of random numbers is always generated each time the program is run. This can be helpful in debugging code. You can always reproduce the same conditions while testing.

Once the testing is done, you would like the random numbers to be unpredictable. This is where the **srand**() function is used. Calling srand() with a new "seed" number will cause the sequence of random numbers to change. It is quite common to use the **time**() function as a seed. This way, you are always giving it a different seed to start with, and thus a different, and unpredictable, sequence of pseudo-random numbers will be produced. See the following example:

```
time(&t);
srand(t);
```

There are times when you would like to limit the range of random numbers. The following formula will allow you to generate the range you want:

```
rand() % n      /* Produce integers from zero to n-1 */
```

To simulate the roll of a single die, you would want the random numbers generated to be from 1 to 6; therefore, to generate only numbers from 1 to 6, you would use the following:

```
die = rand() % 6 + 1;
```

Whatever number rand() produces will be converted to a number from 0 to 5 when you divide six into it and take the remainder. That, of course, is what the modulo 6 (% 6) does. Now, add one to that result, and you have numbers from 1 to 6 only. How could you produce integers from a -6 to +6?

sqrt()

This function finds the square root of a number. It works just as you would expect:

```
x = sqrt(y);
```

In the previous expression, *x* will contain the square root of *y* when control is returned from the function.

UNDERSTANDING BITWISE OPERATIONS

When using an assembler, you are required to work with individual bits. Because C was written as a transportable substitute for assembler languages, it can also work with individual bits. These bitwise operations fall into two categories: **logical** operations and **shifting** operations. The bitwise operations will work on the types int and char only. Remember that floating-point and double-precision numbers are stored in a BCD format, and bit operations on these numbers would only confuse C and produce some very confusing results.

Logical Operations

This section covers four logical operations: AND, OR, XOR, and NOT. In each case, the operations are bit by bit. There is no condition that causes the result of one operation to affect the results of an adjacent bit as the carry operation does in normal addition.

In C, the bitwise operator for the logical AND is &. The following is a table of all possible AND operations:

Logical AND

```
1  & 1  = 1
1  & 0  = 0
0  & 1  = 0
0  & 0  = 0
```

To produce a 1, the logical AND operation requires both bits to be a 1.

The bitwise operator for the logical OR is |. To produce a 0 (zero), the OR requires both bits to be a 0 (zero).

Logical OR

```
1  |  1  = 1
1  |  0  = 1
0  |  1  = 1
0  |  0  = 0
```

The logical XOR is indicated by the caret symbol (^). XOR is the abbreviation commonly used for the term **exclusive or**. The XOR operation produces a 1 when the first bit or the second bit is a 1 but not when both of them are 1s.

Logical XOR

```
1  ^  1  = 0
1  ^  0  = 1
0  ^  1  = 1
0  ^  0  = 0
```

The symbol used to indicate NOT is the tilde (~). The logical NOT simply reverses the bits.

Logical NOT

~ 1 = 0
~ 0 = 1

NOT is used to mean the one's complement and should not be confused with the two's complement (or negative of the number) that was spoken of earlier. If you want to take the integer five and create both its one's complement and two's complement in binary, you can do so by running the following program and converting the hex to binary:

```
/* -------------------- PROG-7.C ---------------------- */
/* --- Print hex values of 5, NOT 5, and negative 5 --- */

#include<stdio.h>

void main()
{

    printf("%X,  %X,  %X\n",5,~5,-5);

}
```

This will give you the following hex numbers: 5, FFFA, and FFFB. Converting to binary would result in the following:

	Hex	Binary	
5 =	5	0000 0000 0000 0101	integer five
~ 5 =	FFFA	1111 1111 1111 1010	one's complement
- 5 =	FFFB	1111 1111 1111 1011	two's complement

Now you can make a few observations. The one's complement simply reversed the bits. The two's complement is just the one's complement with a 1 bit added to it. This is exactly the way that a negative two's complement is created by the computer: reverse the bits, and then add a 1. Note that if you add the one's complement to the original binary 5, you get 1s in all 16 register positions. On the other hand, adding the two's complement to the original binary 5 gives you 16 zero bits in the register and a lost carry bit. So, in a sense, both the one's and two's complements complement the original number 5, but the two's complement will function as a negative of the original.

The purpose of this discussion and the one in the section on integers in this chapter is to give you a glimpse of the internal architecture of a digital computer and how it works. By branching into C programming, you are working closer to the internals of the computer. From time to time, you might need that understanding to figure out what is happening in your program, or it may give you insight on how to accomplish a new programming task.

The AND operation can be used to turn bits off. Any bit you AND to a zero will become zero. On the other hand, the OR can be used to turn bits on. Any bit you OR with a 1 will be forced on. Suppose you were accepting input from the keyboard and you had to determine which alpha characters were being chosen as options on a menu with 25 choices. Each choice is represented by a different letter of the alphabet, and you want to accept either the uppercase or lowercase character for each option. Instead of 50 different tests, one for uppercase and one for lowercase for each character, you could add this one line of code and cut the number of tests down to 25:

```
ch = ch | \x20;            /* Force ch to lowercase */
```

This assumes that *ch* is a type **char** variable and contains the alpha character in question. If you look at Appendix B, you will see that the uppercase and lowercase hex codes of the alpha characters are similar. Remember, an ASCII character takes eight bits. The lowercase characters all have one more bit set than the uppercase characters—0010 0000.

Char	Hex	Binary
a	61	0110 0001
A	41	0100 0001
b	62	0110 0010
B	42	0100 0010
...		
z	7A	0111 1010
Z	5A	0101 1010

In hex, a binary 0010 0000 is a 20. The character constant, **\x20**, in the previous line of code is a constant that produces a hex code of 20, and the | ORs that hex 20 to the character. So with the one line of code, you forced that additional 0010 0000 bit in each character on and left all other bits unchanged. The lowercase characters are unchanged because the sixth bit was already set for them. All uppercase characters would have that sixth bit set in them, thus changing them to lowercase characters. You only need to test the lowercase characters, which cuts the work in half. If you want the characters all to be uppercase, you would force the 0010 0000 bit to zero in all cases.

Shifting Operations

There are two more bitwise operations in C that should be discussed: the **shift left** and **shift right** operations:

>>	shift right
<<	shift left

The shift left will zero **backfill** (add characters to fill in the space left by the shift) on the right. Any bits that are shifted off the left end are lost. The shift right is different. It will backfill on the left with the **sign bit**, or left-most bit. This means that if the sign bit is 1, the right shift will backfill with ones, keeping the sign bit 1. If the sign bit is a zero, the right shift will backfill with zeroes, keeping the sign bit zero (positive). Examples:

0000 0000 0111 1000 < < 1 gives 0000 0000 1111 000**0**

1111 1000 0101 0000 > > 3 gives **111**1 1111 0000 1010

0000 0000 1101 0111 > > 4 gives **0000** 0000 0000 1101

The backfills have been printed in bold. Any bits shifted off the end are lost, as seen in the third example.

In Chapter 2, you read about how shifting a binary number one place to the left is equivalent to multiplying by two.

0000 0000 0000 0101 = five
0000 0000 0000 1010 = ten

Logically, that means shifting a binary number back again to the right is equivalent to dividing by two. There are other tasks the shift operators can perform as well. For example, you have examined a number of computer outputs in octal and hex. Each time, you had to convert output to binary by hand when you wanted to see the individual bits. You could make the computer do that for you.

To write a function that will print out the hex and binary values of a 16-bit variable, you first need what is called a **mask**. Declare an integer variable, and call it mask. Initialize it as shown:

```
int mask = 0x8000;
```

This initialization uses a hex value to place a 1 in the left-most position of 16 bits. If you could look at this integer variable in memory, you would see the following:

mask = 1000 0000 0000 0000

By the nature of the logical AND operation, any integer you AND to this mask would have all bits forced to zero except the left-most bit. This left-most bit would keep its original value—either zero or 1—so this mask will allow you to examine the left-most bit all by itself. If you shifted the mask so that the 1 was in some other position, you could examine any bit in the variable and know if it is a 1 or a zero; however, remember that a right shift backfills with the sign, so it might be better just to shift the variable left one bit to look at the next bit in line. To print out the binary representation of a variable, you can examine each bit individually and print a zero or 1 depending on what value the bit contains. Study and then enter the following C function:

```
/* -------------------- HEX_BIN.C --------------------- */
/* -- Displays the hex and binary values of integer --- */

#include<stdio.h>

void hex_bin(int input)
{
     int t1, t2, bit, mask = 0x8000;

     /* ------------- Display hex value ------------ */
     printf("%X  ",input);

     /* ------------ Display binary value ---------- */
     for(t1=1; t1<=4; t1++) {

         /* --- Divide in groups of 4 bits each ---- */
         for(t2=1; t2<=4; t2++) {

             /* --------- AND mask to input -------- */
             /* - to isolate current left-most bit - */
             bit = input & mask;
```

continued...

...from previous page

```
                /* ---------- Display 1 or 0 ---------- */
                if (bit) printf("1");
                else printf("0");

                /* - To get next bit to left position - */
                /* -- Shift input to the left one bit - */
                input = input << 1;
            }
            /*  --- Insert space after four bits ------ */
            printf(" ");
        }
        printf("\n");
        return ;

}
```

This function, called hex_bin(), will produce a hexadecimal and binary display of any integer passed to it. Whenever you want the hex and binary value of an integer, just compile this function with your code. Note that the variable *input* will contain the integer value of what is sent to the function. The first time through the loop, the left-most bit is checked, and a zero or 1 is printed. Then, the contents of *input* are shifted to the left one bit. This way, the next bit is now in the left-most position. Using the logical AND and the same mask, you can look at this next bit in line. This function can be put in your personal library and then compiled with any program for which you want to have the hex and binary values. To test the function, take the following sample program and compile it with the function hex_bin():

```
/* -------------------- PROG-8.C ---------------------- */
/* ------------- Calls hex_bin() function ------------- */
/* --------- With int, char, and pointer values ------- */

void hex_bin(int input);

void main()
{
     int t = 21;
     char ch = 'a';
     int *pt;

     /* ------------- Test integer ----------------- */
     hex_bin(t);

     /* ------------- Test character --------------- */
     hex_bin(ch);

     /* ------------- Test pointer ----------------- */
     pt=&t;
     t=pt;
     hex_bin(t);
}
```

Note that this code calls the function three times. The first time it is called with an integer and the second time with a character. You can see that the function calls for an integer to be passed, but it accepts the character and converts the ASCII character code to an integer with the same bit pattern. In the third call, a pointer is passed. If you try to pass a pointer directly to the function, C will object. Remember, pointers are special, and there are many restrictions on how you can use them. First, convert the pointer to an integer in the line that reads

```
t = pt;
```

C really doesn't like you to do this either. Turbo C will give a warning but will allow you to do it. Now that you have converted the pointer to a type integer, send the integer to the function.

To get these two separate pieces of code to work together, you must link together the object code for both. Do whatever your C system calls for to get the two modules linked together.

In the Turbo C (TC) system, you should create a project file indicating the paths and filenames of all the source code to be linked (see "Working with Projects" in Chapter 3). For example, if the source modules resided on diskette drive B, the following could be the contents of your project file:

```
b:hex_bin.c
b:prog-8.c
```

You could create the project file with the editor and save it as JOB-8.PRJ. Then, go to the TC main menu Project option. Enter the path and name of the project file into the Project name prompt so that it reads

```
Project name    B:JOB-8.PRJ
```

Now run the program. The project file will be checked to find which source code to compile and link.

After the program runs, your screen output should resemble the following:

```
   15  0000 0000 0001 0101
   61  0000 0000 0110 0001
   FFE8  1111 1111 1110 1000
```

The pointer address will most likely be different from the one shown above. However, the binary value should match the hex address that was passed to the function. The 15 is the hex value for the decimal 21, and the 61 is the ASCII hex code for a.

The previous examples demonstrate the use of the bitwise operators on integers and characters. Although many professional programmers never need to worry about bits, some must work with them daily. The more you understand the total picture, the easier it will be for you to undertake any type of programming task.

UNDERSTANDING CHARACTERS

Most likely, you know what a character is; however, just in case a few readers would like a brief review, this section will start with the fundamentals. When you see the letters **F** and **A** on the screen, you can distinguish between them. They each have a different meaning to you. All numbers and letters of the alphabet have a distinct image that you can recognize.

Unfortunately, the computer does not see as you do. It can only distinguish between two items, a 0 bit and a 1 bit. To a computer, a bit is either on or off. When you press the A key, the image of an A is not sent to the computer. The computer would not understand it. Instead, an eight-bit binary code is transmitted (i.e., more ones and zeroes), which is a unique binary code that it can recognize as an A. It is that binary code that makes it possible for the computer to distinguish between the F and the A. Therefore, whenever a computer is working with a character or a string of characters, the characters must be in a binary code that it can recognize. When you want a character displayed on the screen, the computer will take that binary code that it recognizes and produce a visual symbol that you recognize. When you work with a computer, it's something like speaking a foreign language. Sometimes you speak in English, and sometimes you translate and speak in the foreign language. In this case, sometimes you translate and use the ASCII codes, or the language of the computer.

C has a special way of handling a single character; it has a special type for declaring a character variable:

```
char ch = 'e';
```

In the above example, the variable *ch* is declared a character variable. It is then initialized to hold the character **e**. Note that the constant **'e'** is set off by single quotation marks. This is C's way of identifying a character. The variable *ch* is assigned a single location in memory. C doesn't need the ending null location because it knows that there is only one character stored in a character variable.

You can use the assign operator at run time to change the value of a character variable, using either a character constant or a variable:

```
ch = 'b';    /* Contents of "ch" changed to "b" */

ch = ch2;    /* "ch" now has same contents as "ch2" */
```

Notice that there is a difference between a character and a string. You can't assign a string at run time. And, because a character variable can contain only one character, it is impossible to concatenate two characters and store the results in a character variable.

ASCII Codes

In the computer, each character is converted to ASCII (American Standard Code for Information Interchange). There are some computers that use other codes, but virtually all personal computers use ASCII. There is an ASCII conversion table in Appendix B. ASCII is a seven-bit code used to represent 128 different characters including the null code.

Actually, eight bits are normally used to store or transmit an ASCII character. The contents of the eighth or left-most bit varies depending on how that bit is put to use. In a computer, this bit is often set to zero and not used. Sometimes when transmitting data it is used as a **parity** bit. Before you transmit the character, you count the number of ones in the seven-bit code. If the sum is even, you leave the eighth or parity bit as zero. If the sum is odd, you make the parity bit a 1. This way, the count of 1 bits is always even when you count all eight bits, and it is said to have even parity. Now the character is transmitted with the parity bit. The receiving device counts the 1 bits, and if it does not get an even count, it knows that there has been an error in transmission. Perhaps a bit was dropped or a voltage spike on the line changed a zero to a 1. The receiving device can request the character to be transmitted again. Both odd and even parity systems are used. It just depends on your equipment and what it is designed to do.

Computers use the eighth bit in a different way: to extend the number of characters that can be represented. This one additional bit doubles the number of characters that can be stored in eight bits from 128 to 256.

UNDERSTANDING STRINGS

A string is a series of characters grouped for use in a computer. Of the following two options, try to choose the one that is a string.

```
FACE
1052
```

You were supposed to choose FACE, but actually you can't tell. Either choice could be an integer or a string. Whether a variable is a string depends on how it is presented to the computer and how the computer stores the data. FACE could be a hex value, with the **F** meaning fifteen, **A** meaning ten, etc. It could then be saved as a two's complementary integer in memory, which would have a signed decimal integer value of -1330. On the other hand, it could be a string and be saved as ASCII character codes to represent the word **FACE**:

```
int num = 0xFACE;   /* FACE is hex integer stored in num */

char str[5] = "FACE";   /* FACE is a string stored in str */
```

The same is true with the value 1052, except that it has a number of other options. 1052 could be a decimal integer, an octal integer, a hex integer, a floating-point number, or a character string; each option would be saved in memory in a different way. The decimal, octal, and hex integers would each convert to a different binary value when stored as a two's complementary integer. The floating-point value would be converted to a binary-coded decimal, and, finally, the string would be stored as ASCII character codes with a null at the end.

```
int num = 1052;   /* saved as decimal in variable num */

char str[5] = "1052";   /* saved as string in str */
```

When 1052 is saved as a string, it is treated as if it were a word. You cannot perform any arithmetic operations on it while it is a string.

Strings are declared as shown in the previous examples. They are declared as type **char** in the same way that a character is, but the variable is an array. The array is C's clue that you are declaring a string instead of a character. Once again, remember that when declaring the size of the string array, C requires an additional location in memory for the "null" character. This is the way C locates the end of the string. You can also initialize a string as you declare it:

```
char gg[5] = "book";    /* variable "gg" contains "book" */

char hh[9] = "B";  /* variable "hh" contains string, "B" */
```

Note that strings are set off with double quotation marks. Even though the **"B"** in the second example is a single character, it is stored as a string and has a null character following it. You can also see that the string variable has nine locations reserved even though only two were used.

Once the variable has been declared, it is no longer possible to use the assign operator (=) to change the value of a string variable. You might wonder why you can use the assign operator when you declare the string but cannot use it later in the program.

Declaration takes place at compile time, not when you run your program. At compile time, the whole C compiler is there to do the work, and C is not concerned about speed at that time. So at compile time, C reserves the space in memory for the string and then stores the characters right out of your source program into that string space; however, any attempt to assign a new value to the string variable later in the program means that you want to assign the string during run time. The full strength of the C compiler is not around to do the work, and remember C keeps run-time modules to a minimum to increase the speed of your program.

Also, the source code is not available at run time. Those characters you typed in with the source are not with you, which means that in order to store them in the string during run time, they must be saved somewhere in memory so they will be available during run time. This is true even of string constants. If the constant is to be used during run time, it must be assigned a memory location in the object code the same as a variable, which means the contents of some locations in memory must be moved into other memory locations. C's run-time modules will not do this. If you want to move a string in memory, you must write a small program or function to move the string. Actually, this step is done so often that someone has saved you the time and already written a special library function to do just that. However, the inability to move strings during run-time is another example of the limitations C has that enable it to execute programs faster.

strcpy()

The function **strcpy**() is used to copy the contents of a string from one location in memory to another during run time. Its general form is as follows:

```
strcpy( to_string_pointer, from_string_pointer );
```

The contents of the *from_string_pointer* will be moved into the *to_string_pointer*. Note that the function strcpy() requires pointers to the string, not to the name of the string. This is true of the whole family of string library functions that start with the letters **str**. Note the following examples:

```
strcpy( &str2, &str1);

strcpy( str3, "Hello");
```

The second example uses a string constant, not a string variable. This constant is actually stored as part of your object code in memory in much the same way that the variable is stored, except C does not give you the address of the constant's location in memory as it does for a variable.

You may have noticed something else in this second example. The ampersand is missing on the first argument, and the function requires a pointer to a string. There are three ways you can point to a string in the C language. First, you can use the unary operator & as a pointer to the address:

```
char strng[22];   /* declare the array, "strng", a string */
```

Now *strng* is the name of the string, but *&strng* is the address of the first location of the array or string. Therefore, *&strng* can be used as an address pointer to the string.

The second method of pointing is to use a type char pointer. Note the following example:

```
char str[15];     /* declare string "str" for 15 bytes     */
char *str_pnt;    /* declare "str_pnt" a char pointer      */
str_pnt=&str;     /* assign pointer the address of "str"   */
```

Now the string pointer *str_pnt* contains the address of the string "str" and can be used as a pointer to the string.

The third method of pointing to a string is possible because a string is just a special case of an array. In the previous array, *str[3]* is the fourth element of the array. The first is *str[0]*; but just plain *str* is not only the name of the string, it is also a pointer to the beginning of the array. In the previous example, the following all mean the same thing:

```
str
&str
str_pnt
```

Now the string pointer *str_pnt* contains the address of the string *str* and can be used as a pointer to the string.

strcat()

The library function **strcat**() allows you to join two strings. Consider the following example program:

```
/* ------------------- PROG-9.C ----------------------- */
/* ---------------- Using strings --------------------- */

#include <stdio.h>
#include <string.h>

void main()
{
     char heading[50]="Dear Ms. ";
     char name[10]="Hampton";

     /* --------- Append name to heading ----------- */
     strcat( &heading, name);

     /* ------------- Display heading -------------- */
     printf(heading);
}
```

This function appends the second string to the first. Note that the ampersand is used to indicate an address pointer in the first argument to **strcat**(), and just the name of the string array is used for an address pointer in the second argument. They both work. When you enter and run this code, you should receive the following output on the screen:

```
Dear Ms. Hampton
```

You may have noticed another shortcut here. In the print() function, you can simply put the name of the string in parentheses and omit the format argument if you are only printing a string.

There are many other members of this family of string library functions. In addition to copying and joining strings, you can perform any number of other operations. This includes searching one string for the first occurrence of a character or substring.

strstr()

The function **strstr**() allows you to search a large string for the first occurrence of a substring. Its general form is as follows:

```
strstr( str_pointer, sub_str_pointer);
```

This function returns an address pointer showing where the *sub_str* appears in the *str_pointer*. If the substring is not found, a null is returned. See the following example program:

```
/* -------------------- PROG-10.C --------------------- */
/* --------- Strings pointers and addresses ----------- */

#include"stdio.h"
#include"string.h"

void main()
{
    /* -------------- Declare variables --------------- */
    char s[80]="Now is the time to learn about strings.";
    char s2[5]="time";
    char *p;

    /* ------------- Find substring s2 in s ----------- */
    p=strstr(s,s2);

    /* --------------- Print results ------------------ */
    printf("%x is starting address of string s\n",s);
    printf("%x is where \"time\" starts in string s.",p);
}
```

Your screen output should resemble the following when you run this program:

```
ff96 is starting address of string s
ffa1 is where "time" starts in string s
```

If you count the characters in string *s* up to the **t** in "time," you will see that the function did, in fact, return the address of that **t**.

There are many other string functions besides those in the str family. Some of these functions will allow you to convert to and from strings.

atof() and atoi()

At times, you may want to take a string that contains numeric digits and convert them to a number type that can be used for computational purposes. Two of these functions are as follows:

atof() Convert an ASCII string of numeric digits to a floating-point number.

atoi() Convert an ASCII string of numeric digits to an integer.

Both functions use the same general form:

```
num = atoi( pointer );
```

The return value is the converted number and will be put in variable *num*. The argument sent to the function is a pointer to the ASCII string that contains the numbers you want converted. The functions recognize both leading white space and a leading sign. In addition, atof() will recognize a decimal point or the exponential (E) format. Both functions will terminate upon finding an unrecognizable non-numeric character in the string. Enter and run the following sample program:

```
/* -------------------- PROG-11.C --------------------- */
/* ------------- Converting strings ------------------- */

#include"stdio.h"
#include"stdlib.h"

void main()
{
     /* ------------ Declare variables ------------ */
     char s[32]="     +752.397 This is the string.";
     float f;

     /* --- Convert string s to a float variable --- */
     f=atof(s);

     /* ------------ Print both results ------------ */
     printf("%s \n %f is the converted number.\n",s,f);

}
```

It is possible to convert any type of number to a null-terminated string as well.

itoa()

The library function **itoa**() converts an integer to a string, and there are other library functions for converting the other types of numbers to strings. The itoa() function is just an example of those available. The general form of the itoa() function is as follows:

```
itoa( num, pointer, base);
```

The *num* is the integer you want converted, and *pointer* contains the beginning address of the location in memory that is to hold the new string. The *base* is the number base to which you want the integer converted before it is saved in the string. With the following lines of code, you could convert the number 56 to a string representing the binary value of 56 and display it on your screen:

```
char str[17];         /* Declare blank string.     */
itoa( 56, &str, 2);   /* Convert 56 to a string    */
                      /* representing binary value */
                      /* of 56; put in "str".      */
printf("%s",str );    /* Print string "str".       */
```

If the above code were made into a function, the output would resemble the following:

```
111000
```

When you are declaring a string to hold the output of the function itoa(), make sure that the string is long enough to hold the converted value. The string can be as many as 17 bytes, when you consider converting to binary. Remember, you cannot use this string for computational purposes.

Using Array Subscripts or Pointers

You can access the individual elements of a string array using array subscripts. For example, *str[3]* refers to the fourth element of the array. You can also access each element of an array using address pointers. Even though pointers are a little more difficult to use, there is an advantage at times to using them. They can be much faster than subscripts. The following sample program demonstrates the use of both pointers and subscripts:

```
/* -------------------- PROG-12.C --------------------- */
/* ------- Address pointers and array subscripts ------- */

#include"stdio.h"

void main()
{
    /* -------------- Declare variables --------------- */
    char s[40]="Now is the time to learn about strings.";
    char *p;
    int i;

    /* ------ Print every other character with -------- */
    /* -------------- Array subscripts ---------------- */
    for (i=0; i<40; i=i+2) printf("%c ",s[i]);

    printf("\n ");

    /* ------- Print all others with a pointer -------- */
    p=&s;
    for (i=1; i<40; i=i+2) printf("%c ",*(p+i));
}
```

This program will first print every other character of the string **s** by using array subscripts. Note the increment of **i=i+2**. This increment will cause the subscript to skip every other character. Also take note of the printf() specification, %c. Even though you are taking this character from a string, it is only a character you want to print, so use the character specification.

The second part of the program will print the remaining characters, using an address pointer. First, the pointer is assigned the address of the string:

```
p=&s;
```

Note the printf() function in the loop. Again, a character is specified, but examine the argument that is to be printed:

```
*(p+i)
```

The address contained in **p** is incremented by the current value of **i** so you will get an address somewhere in the string. Also, the asterisk (*) says take the contents of that address. The end result is the following two lines of characters:

```
N w i   h   i e t   e r   b u   t i g .
 o   s t e t m   o l a n a o t s r n s
```

You can see that both methods can access any element of the string, and when programming, you can choose the approach that best serves your need at the time.

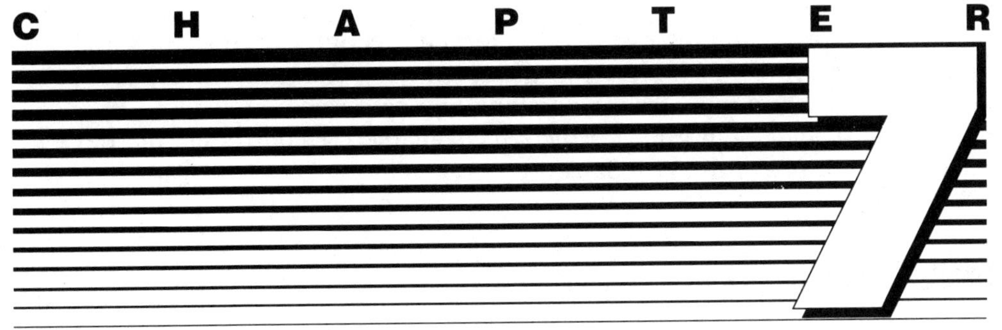

MASTERING THE KEYBOARD

To master the programming of any peripheral device interfaced to the CPU, or Central Processing Unit (the heart of the computer), you must understand how the CPU works. You must also understand how to service the device. In addition, you must understand the instructions available for controlling the device. Consider the nature of the keyboard.

UNDERSTANDING THE KEYBOARD

The keyboard is an input device. For the most part, it uses the QWERTY arrangement of keys, as does the standard typewriter. The name QWERTY comes from the top row of alphabetic letters on the keyboard. The QWERTY arrangement was designed when the typewriter was first developed to slow people down when typing. At that time, typewriters were slow mechanical devices that could not keep up with the speed of human fingers, and now the human race is still hobbled by QWERTY in the age of electronics. No doubt this is because people are familiar with it. Regardless, the keyboard allows a user to electronically send data to the computer's CPU by pressing a key or a combination of keys on the keyboard.

Key Codes

From the discussion in Chapter 6 (in the section "Understanding Characters"), you know that pressing the A key doesn't send an A to the CPU. Instead, it sends the hex number 41, which is the ASCII code for an A. Most of the keys on the keyboard have a unique ASCII code that is electronically generated whenever the key is pressed. There are a few keys, however, that have a different purpose. These special keys alter or change the code that the other keys send. An example you're familiar with is the Shift key. When held down, this key causes the code of another key that is pressed at the same time to shift from lowercase to uppercase. The other special code-changing keys are the Alt (alternate mode) key and the Ctrl (control) key.

The program you are about to examine explores what happens when a key is pressed and shows just what information was passed to the CPU. It will also display on the screen the symbol(s) that the code(s) represents. You may be surprised to find that two codes, or 16 bits, are passed. You are going to learn just what those codes are for.

Don't be overly concerned with understanding the program at this point; it will be discussed later in the chapter. Enter the following program:

```
/* -------------------- PROG-13.C -------------------- */
/* ------ Look at ASCII codes sent from keyboard ------ */

#include <stdio.h>
#include <bios.h>

void main()
{
     /* ------------ Declare variables ------------- */
     int key, ch1 = 0x0000, ch2;
     int mask_right=0x00ff;

     /* ------ Loop until "Q" or "q" is typed ------ */
     while (ch1 != 0x0051 && ch1 != 0x0071) {
          printf("Press a key (\"Q\" to Quit).");

          /* ------- Wait for key input --------- */
          while (bioskey(1)==0);

          /* ------------ Take input ------------ */
          key=bioskey(0);

          /* --- Split 16 bits into two bytes --- */
          ch1=key & mask_right;
          ch2=key >> 8;

          /* ---- Print both bytes of input ----- */
          printf("\n2-byte hex input is %x :\n",key);
          printf("left half  %x, is %c\n",ch2,ch2);
          printf("right half %x, is %c\n\n",ch1,ch1);
     }
}
```

A word of caution before you run this program: randomly typing different combinations of keys can cause unexpected results. Instead of getting a character, you may end up generating a nonprinting function such as a ring of the bell. Or you could hang the system by entering a [Ctrl/Break]. Just in case, make sure that you save your source code before you run the program. It is possible to get around this problem by outputting a printable character with each iteration of the loop. If the system hangs, restart either by using the power switch or pressing the Ctrl, Alt, and Del keys simultaneously, [Ctrl/Alt/Del].

Now run the program. Your screen's output should resemble the following:

```
Press a key ("Q" to Quit).
```

Press the f key. Then, hold down the Shift key and press the f key again, [Shift/f]. Your screen output should resemble the following:

```
Press a key ("Q" to Quit).
2-byte hex input is 2166 :
left half  21, is !
right half 66, is f

Press a key ("Q" to Quit).
2-byte hex input is 2146 :
left half  21, is !
right half 46, is F

Press a key ("Q" to Quit).
```

Both times that you entered a character, 16 bits were sent to the screen. When you entered the f, you received a code of 66 in the right byte and a code of 21 in the left byte. Entering the f gave a code of 46 in the right byte and 21 again in the left byte. At least as far as the right byte is concerned, that is exactly what the table of ASCII codes (see Appendix B) indicates should happen, but that is not all that happened. You can see that in addition to the letter you expected, a second code (a hex 21, which is the code for an exclamation point) was sent along with the expected one. You already know that you don't get an exclamation point along with every f you type. So you now know that the CPU is selective about which part of the code it will use.

This example also demonstrates that there is not an automatic or direct tie between the keyboard and the screen. The letter f was not the first item to appear on the screen. In fact, it was the last. If you leave the last printf() function call out of the program, the f will never appear.

If at times there appears to be a direct connection between the keyboard and the screen, don't be misled. Actually, it is C, BASIC, MS-DOS, or some other software that is displaying the character on the screen. Regardless of what is entered on the keyboard, you can control what appears on the screen. If you wanted, you could make the screen display the letter Z every time the user enters an f, or you could make the screen display a whole word when the user presses a given key. The point is that you can control what is to be displayed. It's not automatic. The hardware simply tells you what was entered. The rest is up to you.

Now, enter [Ctrl/f]. This time, your screen output should resemble the following:

```
Press a key ("Q" to Quit).
2-byte hex input is 2106 :
left half  21, is !
right half 6, is ♠
```

You received a new code. The left byte is the same, but the right byte is a 6. And MS-DOS translated this code to the playing card symbol for spades. The ASCII code table says that 6 is the code for **ACK**. (ACK, or acknowledge, is a nonprinting code—one that has no symbol. It is used to acknowledge the receipt of an electronic transmission of data.) The system, it seems, inserted a spade when it saw this code. There are other unusual symbols that can be generated from the keyboard of an IBM-PC or a compatible, but before you start experimenting, first look at a few more keys.

This time, enter [Alt/f]. The following appears:

```
Press a key ("Q" to Quit).
2-byte hex input is 2100 :
left half  21, is !
right half 0, is
```

The number of bytes received is still two. The right byte is zero, which is the null character. (When the code is zero, nothing is displayed, not even a blank space.) The left byte is still 21 hex, which is the code for an exclamation point (!), and that is exactly what is displayed on screen.

Scancodes

Just in case you think that the left byte is always a hex 21, press the g key. The following output should appear:

```
Press a key ("Q" to Quit).
2-byte hex input is 2267 :
left half  22, is "
right half 67, is g
```

In this case, the left byte is hex 22, so it is not always a 21. In fact, it's only a 21 for the f key. If you start at the upper left corner of the keyboard, you will find the left byte starts with a hex 1 and continues with 2, 3, 4, and so on as you move across the keyboard. This left byte is called the **scancode**. (See the table of scancodes in Appendix B.) Return to the f key example. By examining the codes in hex, you can more easily consider the bits involved. You might even want to convert them to binary.

Key	**Hex**	**Binary**
f	2166	0010 0001 0110 0110
[Shift/f]	2146	0010 0001 0100 0110
[Ctrl/f]	2106	0010 0001 0000 0110
[Alt/f]	2100	0010 0001 0000 0000

Notice what is happening. The codes for each are similar. The change-code keys simply suppress one or more bits from the right code. You already knew that about the Shift key. You wrote a program to force a bit on or off to get the uppercase or lowercase character.

But why do you need the left byte? The left byte is the scancode—also called the **extended keyboard code**—that tells which key was actually pressed. Without it, there are not enough bits to generate all the different combinations of keys. In Chapter 6, you learned that each character was represented by eight binary bits inside the computer. With eight binary bits, you can only get 256 different combinations, or codes. There are about 80 keys. Now, except for those keys that change the code of other keys, every key sends a unique ASCII code when pressed. If you include the Shift key in this count, you double the number of different codes you need. The Alt key triples and the Ctrl key quadruples the number of key codes needed. So four times 80, or about 320, separate codes are needed to represent all the different key combinations that might be generated from the keyboard. In other words, using just eight bits you have about 60 more key combinations than you have key codes. So how do you get these additional codes? The method used by the hardware is to send the scancode with each key that is pressed. This way, the number of possible codes that can be sent to the program is more than enough.

Remember that when you work with a character in the computer, you only use eight bits. When you print a character on the screen, you only send eight bits. So the extra eight bits (or scancode) are only there when a key is actually pressed. They are put there by the keyboard hardware and are usually dropped somewhere along the line. However, anytime the right byte is the null character, it is a clue that you must look at the scancode to determine which key was pressed. Many different keys and key combinations will send a null in the right half.

In fact, if you are working in BASIC, you never see the left byte except when the right byte is all zeros. The following BASIC program serves much the same purpose as PROG-13.C does in C.

```
1  '* -------------- PROG-14.BAS ------------------ *
10 '* --- Look at ASCII codes sent from keyboard -- *
20 CLS
30 PRINT
32 PRINT "Press a key (";CHR$(34);"Q";CHR$(34);
34 PRINT " to quit)."
39 '* --- See if a key was pressed if not wait ---- *
40 A$ = INKEY$  :  IF A$ = "" THEN 40
49 '* ------ See how many bytes were sent --------- *
50 PRINT "Number of bytes received ";LEN(A$)
59 '* ------ Print codes and characters sent ------ *
60 PRINT "First code is "; HEX$(ASC(A$))
70 IF LEN(A$) > 1 THEN 72 ELSE 80
72 PRINT "Second code is "; HEX$(ASC(MID$(A$,2,1)))
80 PRINT "Character is ";A$
89 '* ------- Loop until "Q" or "q" is typed ------ *
90 IF A$="q" OR A$="Q" THEN END ELSE GOTO 30
```

If you were to run this BASIC program and type in the same keys you did for the C program, you would find that the only time you get two bytes sent to the program is when the first one is null. All other times, BASIC drops the scancode, and you never see it. You only work with the right byte.

What are all these special extra codes used for? Most of them are undefined and unused, and you are free to define and use them however you choose. (A few of these codes have been reserved for special uses, such as the [Ctrl/Break] for an interrupt; this key combination is trapped by MS-DOS,and will hang the PROG-13.C program.) Generally speaking, if the code is passed on to your program, that code is free to use. There are a few keys that have no printable character associated with them, such as the cursor movement keys.

Run PROG-13.C again and press the up arrow key. The screen output should resemble the following:

```
Press a key ("Q" to Quit).
2-byte hex input is 4800 :
left half  48, is H
right half 0, is
```

You pressed only one key. The code sent to the program consisted of a right byte of all zeros, or a null. The left half or scancode is a hex 48, or an H. You now know that anytime your program receives a null with an H scancode, the user has pressed the up arrow key. You know the user wants the cursor on the screen to move up, and it is your program's responsibility to move it up for the user.

If you are curious about the other codes and symbols generated by your PC and by MS-DOS, check in your programming manual for the extended ASCII codes. You can also experiment with the program that you now have running. (Don't forget [Ctrl/Break] will hang the program.)

Program Function Keys

The keys marked F1, F2, and F3 are called program function (PF) keys, and their function can be set by the programmer. For C, these keys work much the same way as any other nonprinting undefined key. (BASIC has given them special functions, however, that will tend to restrict the programmer.) Using the C version of the previous program will yield the following results when you press the F1 and F2 keys.

```
Press a key ("Q" to Quit).
2-byte hex input is 3b00 :
left half  3b, is ;
right half 0, is

Press a key ("Q" to Quit).
2-byte hex input is 3c00 :
left half  3c, is <
right half 0, is
```

It is up to you to recognize when any given key is pressed (including the PF keys) and to program the desired response for that particular key. This response is not necessarily putting some symbol on the screen. Pressing a particular key might activate a whole system of programs that does something such as control the security of a building, or a single key code might delete the line that is currently being typed by the user in a word processor system you are writing.

SERVICING THE KEYBOARD

Peripheral devices—such as a printer, disk, screen, and keyboard—are connected to the central processing unit, but they are not an integral part of it. Data must be transferred between the CPU and the peripheral device. Because the CPU is more "intelligent" and faster, it is responsible for pacing itself and matching the speed of the slower peripheral device. In other words, it is up to the CPU to "service" the peripheral device. In the case of the keyboard, failure to service the device in time would mean the loss of user keystrokes.

It is somewhat easier to service a device in BASIC than it is to service it directly using an assembler. This is because both MS-DOS and BASIC perform the initial servicing for you automatically. With C, you have a choice. You can work on a high level and let the operating system handle part of the device servicing, as it does for BASIC, or you can write code that works by itself and does not need the operating system. In the case of the keyboard, MS-DOS accepts the 16-bit code generated by the keystroke and places it in the keyboard **input buffer**. Then, when C and BASIC get a request for keyboard input from your program, they look in the input buffer to see if there is anything waiting. If there is, they take the input and pass the scancode and/or ASCII key code to your program when you request it. Depending on how you request it, they may also display the symbol on the screen.

This keyboard input buffer that MS-DOS uses to hold the input data is referred to as a **stream** in C. It is this input buffer that allows users to type ahead when they know what the computer is going to ask for next. This is possible even though the program has not yet requested the data. When the program is ready, it can request the codes from the buffer.

The input buffer has a limited size. If your program waits too long to request keyboard input, the buffer could overflow and data would be lost. You will know this is happening when there is an insistent beeping as you type. MS-DOS, BASIC, and even C's I/O functions have given you a little more leeway and your timing doesn't have to be quite so accurate, but it is still necessary for your program to service the keyboard. You must request keyboard input often enough that data vital to the program is not lost.

Three methods are available for servicing the keyboard:

- The first and most often used method for application programming is **wait-for-input**. With this method you process each input of data when the code reaches that point in the program. If the user has not yet entered a response, the program simply stops and waits until the user does enter one. No processing in your program will take place during the wait. This method assumes, with some limitations, that users will type only when you want them to and that they will not overflow the keyboard input buffer. In some cases, it is not possible to make those assumptions. If so, one of the other two methods should be used.

- The second method is **polling**. With this method you give users freedom to type whenever they want; however, the program has other tasks to accomplish, so it can't simply wait around for a keystroke. Your program cycles through the tasks it has, giving them all its attention. When the program gets to the task of servicing the keyboard, it can query or poll the device to see if there has been a keystroke since the last time it was polled.

- In the third method, called **interrupt traps**, you again give users the ability to type whenever they want while the computer goes about taking care of all its other tasks; however, you must first set an interrupt trap that will interrupt whatever is currently being worked on and go to (trap) the keyboard service routine as soon as a key is pressed.

These three methods are discussed in more detail in the following sections.

Wait-for-Input

The INPUT instruction in BASIC and the scanf() function in C are good examples of the wait-for-input type of keyboard service instructions. When the program is ready for input, it simply calls the keyboard and asks for input that is in the keyboard input buffer. If the expected input is not there, the program stops and waits until it arrives. However, this explanation is really an oversimplification from two points of view.

First, you are not really servicing the keyboard, or device. The critical or initial servicing of the device was taken care of by the operating system or special run-time I/O service routines. These routines accept the input from the keyboard hardware and place it in an input buffer. Your instruction services the input buffer. It removes input data from the buffer so that the buffer will not overflow, which would cause input to be lost. That is exactly what the operating system did for the keyboard. A keystroke on the keyboard puts a code in a hardware buffer or register. If the operating system does not reach and remove the code from the hardware buffer before additional keystrokes are made, input will be lost. In a sense, both your program and the operating system are performing the same type of operation and servicing the keyboard—except your program is doing it at a more leisurely and lower-priority level.

The second oversimplification has to do with the idea of stopping and waiting. The computer does not really stop and wait. Once a processor has been started, it stops only when it is turned off; it is always doing something as long as it's on. What must be understood is that your program is not the only code that is running; other pieces of code are running at a higher priority than yours. Your program only gets part of the processor time and only when there is nothing more important to be done.

One of many tasks that must be performed is servicing the keyboard. Some program must run out and grab that key code before another keystroke comes along. Also, some types of screens need to be refreshed by the processor. Computers keep track of time as well, so some programs must service a "clock." That process may consist of no more than keeping track of each cycle of the alternating current in the AC power, but when it happens, the program that is running is interrupted, and the clock tick is recorded. Once that is done, control returns to the program that was running before.

There are times when the processor really has nothing to do, such as when your program isn't running and there is no device to service. In this case, the processor still keeps running. Sometimes, it just runs in a **noop** (no operation) loop, waiting for something to happen. Some computers have what is called the **null job**. When there is absolutely nothing else to do, control is passed to this special program. It is somewhat like one of your programs, except that it is always there and ready to run. It counts in binary — 1, 10, 11, 100, 101, 110. This program starts over each time it is called, so even when these keyboard input instructions appear to just wait, you can be sure that something is happening somewhere in the computer.

Besides scanf(), there are other wait-for-input functions in C:

getche()	Takes the first character out of the input buffer and returns it to the program. This function will echo the character to the screen. Where *ch* is a type char variable, this function takes the following form: *ch* = getche().
getch()	Takes the first character out of the input buffer and returns it to the program. This function does not echo or display the character that was typed. Where *ch* is a type char variable, this function takes the following form: *ch* = getch().

gets() Takes a string from the keyboard input buffer. It removes up to and including the first carriage return from the buffer and then places the character string in the designated string variable. The carriage return is replaced by a null at the end of the string. All characters are displayed on the screen. Assuming *str* is declared a string, this function takes the following form: gets(&str).

All of these functions will wait for the keyboard input expected before returning control to your program. This type of instruction is most commonly used for application programming. Again, care must be taken not to overflow the string array in the gets() function. If there is a concern, perhaps using a different function would be better.

Polling

Servicing a device (in this case, the keyboard) using the polling method lends itself to situations that are cyclical in nature. To ensure that no data is lost, the program must poll the device at regular intervals. The interval of time between pollings must be shorter than the time it takes a user to fill the input buffer by typing 16 characters. Consider for a moment the following cycle of tasks:

```
while( flag==1 ){
     service_keyboard();
     service_screen();
     get_record();
     process_record();
{
```

Think of this as a program that was created to perform some kind of task, accept keyboard input, and display something on the screen. Don't be concerned about exactly what the functions do or how they do it. This is just a loop that will continue until the variable *flag* is no longer a 1. The keyboard will be checked for input each time the loop takes place. If the time spent performing the other tasks is greater than the time it would take the user to type 16 or more characters on the keyboard, keystrokes could be lost. If it is critical that data is not lost, it would be necessary to reduce the time spent at other tasks, or service the keyboard more often. If it is not possible to reduce the time spent on the other operations, perhaps the following cycle of tasks would solve the problem:

```
while( flag==1 ){
      service_keyboard();
      service_screen();
      service_keyboard();
      get_record();
      service_keyboard()
      process_record();
{
```

Here, you service the keyboard more often, reducing the time between servicing without reducing the time spent on any other task; however, the same care must be taken to ensure that you don't spend too much time servicing a keystroke and, as a result, fail to service some other device properly. For example, assume that the service to the screen in the previous example amounts to graphically simulating the flight of a butterfly as it gently flutters from flower to flower. Imagine what happens to the effect when the butterfly suddenly stops flying and is suspended in midair because someone has pressed a key and your program is processing the keystroke. Considerations of this nature are referred to as **real-time programming** and are normally encountered in the development of system software. As you can see, however, they can be encountered anywhere.

Now you need an instruction that will let you check the keyboard to see if anything has been entered. If there has been input, process the input as you would normally. If there has been no keyboard input, then do something else, but don't wait. In other words, you need a method to service the keyboard by polling.

The BASIC instruction that allows the programmer to poll the keyboard is INKEY$. This instruction takes the following form:

```
A$ = INKEY$
```

When you execute this instruction, BASIC passes to the variable (*A$*) the first character code in the keyboard input buffer. Only the first character in the buffer is removed; all others remain in the buffer. The character will not be displayed. Responsibility for displaying the character on the screen is left to the program. Note the dollar sign in INKEY$. It tells you that all characters—even numbers—are passed as ASCII codes. If the buffer is empty, BASIC returns the null code. In BASIC, however, remember that if the character in the buffer requires an extended character code, two codes will be passed; the first is also a null, and the second is the scancode. BASIC passes all characters to the program except the following key combinations:

[Ctrl/Break]
[Ctrl/Num Lock]
[Ctrl/Alt/Del]
[Ctrl/PrtSc]
[PrtSc]

Now consider C. What function in C will accomplish the same task as the INKEY$ instruction in BASIC? Remember PROG-13.C. It is time to figure out just what that program does. First, the variables are declared:

```
int key, ch1 = 0x0000, ch2;
int mask_right=0x00ff;
```

The integer *key* will accept the direct input from the keyboard. The integers *ch1* and *ch2* will hold the right and left bytes of the 16-bit input. The integer *ch1* is initialized to something other than the code for a Q because it will be tested in the next line of code to see if the program is finished. Just for a moment, skip the next few lines of code. Go on to the following lines:

```
ch1=key & mask_right;
ch2=key >> 8;
```

At this point, *key* contains the 16 bits that were passed to the program from the keyboard input buffer. These two lines of code split the 16 bits into two 8-bit bytes and put them, right-justified, into *ch1* and *ch2*. Two different methods can be used. Note the way this is accomplished. In the variable *mask_right*, the left 8 bits are all zeros and the right 8 bits are all ones. That is why it was defined as a hex value of 00ff. When you use this mask with the logical AND operation, the left 8 bits become zeros and the right 8 bits stay as they are, which puts the right-hand byte in *ch1*.

Now for the second method. Take the original 16 bits again in *key* and shift them over 8 places to the right. You have shifted and dropped the right byte out of the register, and the left byte remains right-justified in *ch2*. You could use the mask again here if you were concerned about the fill from the left.

The remaining code in the program prints the results.

The two statements that you skipped earlier are the most important at the moment:

```
while (bioskey(1)==0);
key = bioskey(0);
```

The first statement is a while loop that apparently does nothing. There are no statements within the loop itself. There is only the test condition, which will be tested over and over again. This instruction calls the function bioskey(1) and tests the result. If the result is zero, the loop has nothing to do, so it loops and again calls the function to test the return for a zero. The function bioskey() with the argument of **1** checks the keyboard input buffer to see if anything has been entered. If nothing has been entered, a zero is returned. If something had been entered, a 1 would be returned, causing the while loop to break and execution to continue with the next statement in line. When you ran this program, it appeared to just stop and wait for input; however, you can see that the program did not stop. It was actually in a very tight, busy loop of testing the input buffer to see if a key had been pressed.

When those input functions stop and wait for input, they may impatiently wait, but they don't stop. If there are other tasks to perform, this is the point at which your program could branch out and perform a task before coming back to check the input buffer again.

Assuming a key was pressed, move on to the next line of code. The next statement in line also calls the same function, but with a different argument. When you call the function bioskey() with the argument of **0**, you will be returned an integer containing the first 16-bit keyboard code from the input buffer. The code is physically removed from the buffer. Any other key codes in the buffer will remain there. It is after this point in the program that the 16 bits are split into two bytes and then printed. (Note that the ASCII code is returned. If you were expecting a numeric value that you could use for computing, it would be necessary to convert from the ASCII code to the type of number you wanted.)

This bioskey() function will respond to a third possible argument. If the function is called with the argument of **2**, the current status of the code-changing keys will be reported. An 8-bit integer is returned, in which each bit set has the following meaning:

```
Bit Position                  Hex  Meaning
                              Bit
1111 1111
 \\\\ \\\\_____________  01   Right Shift key is down
  \\\\ \\\_____________  02   Left Shift key is down
   \\\\ \\_____________  04   Ctrl key is down
    \\\\ \_____________  08   Alt is down
     \\\\
      \\\\_____________  10   Scroll Lock is on
       \\\_____________  20   Num Lock is on
        \\_____________  40   Caps Lock is on
         \_____________  80   Insert is on
```

If you call bioskey(2) and a hex 40 is returned, you know that the Caps Lock key has been set. On the other hand, if an A2 is returned, you know that both the Insert and the Num Lock keys have been toggled, and the left Shift is being held down. If you're not sure about that, look at it in binary. A hex A2 in binary is 1010 0010. Check that number against the chart above.

If you needed to know when the Scroll Lock was on, you would use the logical AND with a binary mask of 0001 0000. All bits except the one you need would drop out, and you could test for a nonzero result.

You have accumulated a lot of information about how the keyboard works and also about how to program in C. To put this knowledge to work, assume that your boss asked you to write a function in C that would use the cursor keys to control the cursor movement on the screen. First, your function would have to accept characters from the keyboard. Then, it would determine which cursor key was pressed. Finally, you would actually move the cursor in the direction requested by the user. However, your boss did not give you sufficient information. There are other questions you must consider:

- Will this function require any data passed to it from the calling program?
- Will this function return any information to the calling program?
- What should the function do if a key other than a cursor key is pressed?

- Should you display the characters you accept from the keyboard on the screen?

- Should you wait for a character to be typed, or after seeing nothing was typed, return immediately to the calling program?

- What sort of cursor movement does your boss want?

Obviously, these and perhaps other questions must be answered. To answer them, you need more information about the application that will be calling your function. It is not only legitimate but mandatory that you return to your manager with such questions. If you are not supplied with the necessary specifications for your function, then you must act as an analyst and get the answers.

Suppose you determined that nothing would be passed to your function when called. If no input was waiting, the function would return immediately to the calling program and not wait for input. If a character was typed instead of a cursor key, that key code would be returned to the calling program. Otherwise, a zero would be returned. No key input is to be displayed on the screen, and the type of cursor movement cannot be determined at the moment (i.e., you haven't read the chapter on screens yet). With the information you do have, give this project a try. Then come back and see if your function resembles the following:

```
/* -------------------- CUR_CTRL.C -------------------- */
/* -- Move cursor as directed by cursor keys pressed -- */

#include <stdio.h>
#include <bios.h>

void cur_up();
void cur_rght();
void cur_down();
void cur_left();

int cur_ctrl()
{
     /* --------- Initialize variables ------------- */
     int key, sch, ch_mask = 0x00ff;
```

continued...

...from previous page

```
     /* --------- Any keyboard input? -------------- */
     if (bioskey(1) == 0) goto done;

     /* ---------- Yes, get the key codes ---------- */
     key = bioskey(0);

     /* --- Return if righthand byte not a null ---- */
     if ((key & ch_mask) > 0) goto done;

     /* ------- Isolate and find scancode ---------- */
     sch = key >> 8;

     switch (sch) {
          case 'H':
               cur_up();
               break;
          case 'M':
               cur_rght();
               break;
          case '\x50':
               cur_down();
               break;
          case 'K' :
               cur_left();
               break;
          default:
               printf("%c",'\07');
     }
     key = 0;
done:     return(key);

}
```

Start at the top. First, there is a description of the function. Then, you include the proper header files. Don't forget, there is a new library function you are going to call.

You may or may not have included the next group of lines. This example declares a group of four other functions that will in turn be called depending on which key is pressed. You may have decided to perform these operations within this function, and so would not have these lines, but remember to keep your functions small so they are easy to understand. Note that these additional functions are called without arguments and return nothing.

Next, this new function is defined. It is called without an argument but will return an integer to the calling program. The variables are declared and initialized. The variable *key* will hold the input keycode, and *sch* will hold the scancode character when it is extracted from *key*. The mask (*ch_mask*) contains all zeros in the left byte, and will be used to look at the right byte of *key*.

The next line of code calls the bioskey() function with an argument of **1**. This queries the keyboard input buffer to see if there is input waiting. If a zero is returned and no keystroke is waiting, the variable *key* is set to zero; then, there is a branch to the line label **done**. At **done**, you can see that the variable *key* is returned to the calling program. No doubt you noticed the use of the dastardly goto statement. You could have used a return statement instead of a goto, but that would necessitate having multiple exit points in the function. Remember the rule for structured coding: "Only one entry point and one exit point for each module." The question is which do you feel would be least confusing—the use of the goto or the multiple exit point? The decision is yours.

If the response was a 1 and there is keyboard input waiting, you ask for the keycode with the function bioskey() again. This time, use an argument of **0**. With the logical AND operation and the mask, you can check to make sure that the right bit of the keycode is a null. All the cursor arrow keys have a null right byte. If the right byte is other than a null, you again branch to **done**, this time returning whatever keycode was sent in the variable *key*. Assuming that the right byte is a null, the next step is to look at the left byte. This can be done by shifting the byte to the right eight positions and putting it into the variable *sch*. Using *sch* in a switch statement, you can determine which cursor key was pressed. Examine the scancodes of the cursor arrow keys for a moment:

Key	Scancode	Character
up arrow	48	H
right arrow	4D	M
down arrow	50	P
left arrow	4B	K

You can see from the case statements that either the hex code or the character represented by the ASCII code can be compared with the incoming code. Both will work. Can you think of other notations that could be used?

If there is a default situation, it means that there was a null byte in the right half, but there was not a cursor arrow key in the left half. If that happens, a character with an ASCII code 07 is printed. The variable *key* is then set to zero and returned to the calling program. If the default situation should happen, what would be printed on the screen?

You may recall that the key combination [Alt/f] produced a null right byte. Also, keys such as Home and End have a null byte. Those two could also be considered cursor movement keys. Perhaps your boss wanted those included. If you haven't already included them in your code, how would you do it?

Consider, again, the switch statement. It contains four function calls, and no one has told you how they should work, but a professional such as yourself could still build some stubs to test your function. It appears that you will need four stubs for the four cursor arrow keys plus, of course, those for the code you added for the Home and End keys and a main stub to call the cur_ctrl() function. They might resemble the following:

```
/* ------------------- PROG-15.C ---------------------- */
/* ---------- Calls cur_ctrl() to test code ----------- */

int cur_ctrl();

void main()
{
     int keyin = 0;

     /* ----------- Call cur_ctrl() until ---------- */
     /* -------- a noncursor key is pressed -------- */
     printf("Type a character.\n");
     while (keyin == 0) {
                keyin = cur_ctrl();
     }
     printf("%x",keyin);
}
```

This main stub must declare your function in order to call it and accept returns. Now you need the other stubs:

```
/* -------------------- CUR_UP.C --------------------- */
/* --------------- Stub for CUR_CTRL.C ---------------- */

void cur_up()
{
     printf("Cursor up key pressed.\n");
     return;
}
```

```
/* -------------------- CUR_RGHT.C -------------------- */
/* --------------- Stub for CUR_CTRL.C ---------------- */

void cur_rght()
{
     printf("Cursor right key pressed.\n");
     return;
}
```

```
/* ------------------- CUR_DOWN.C --------------------- */
/* --------------- Stub for CUR_CTRL.C ---------------- */

void cur_down()
{
     printf("Cursor down key pressed.\n");
     return;
}
```

```
/* ------------------- CUR_LEFT.C --------------------- */
/* ---------------- Stub for CUR_CTRL.C --------------- */

void cur_left()
{
     printf("Cursor left key pressed.\n");
     return;
}
```

You can see that these stubs simply identify themselves and then return to the calling program, which is sufficient to test your function. Once you have the information on how they are to work, you can fill in the stub with actual code.

To run the test, you must compile your function and each of the stubs, and then you must link them into a single executable program. If you are using Turbo C, your project file would have to contain the following filenames with their appropriate paths plus any others you may have added:

```
prog-15.c
cur_ctrl.c
cur_up.c
cur_rght.c
cur_down.c
cur_left.c
```

Testing of this type is called **unit** testing. You are testing only a single unit or self-contained part of the total system. It is only a small amount of code and can be tested thoroughly. Once debugged and tested, it can be considered clean unless a change is made in that code, so if you complete the other stubs and a problem occurs, you can assume it has occurred in the new code and not in cur_ctrl(), which you tested already. Try it.

You could also poll the keyboard using BASIC. The BASIC function you would use is INKEY$. The same program in BASIC might resemble the following:

```
1 '* --------------- PROG-16.BAS ----------------- *
2 '* ------ Calls subroutine at 2000 to test ----- *
10 PRINT " Type a character. "
20 WHILE KY$=""
30   GOSUB 2000
40 WEND
50 PRINT HEX$(ASC(KY$))
90 END
1999 '* - Move cursor as directed by key pressed - *
2000 KY$ = INKEY$                   'poll keyboard
2010 IF KY$ = "" THEN 2090          'buffer empty?
2020 IF LEN(KY$) = 1 THEN 2090
2030 SCH$ = MID$(KY$,2,1)           'get scancode
2040 IF SCH$ = "H" THEN GOSUB 3000 : GOTO 2080
2050 IF SCH$ = "M" THEN GOSUB 3100 : GOTO 2080
2060 IF SCH$ = "P" THEN GOSUB 3200 : GOTO 2080
2070 IF SCH$ = "K" THEN GOSUB 3300 : GOTO 2080
2072 PRINT CHR$(7);
2080 KY$ = ""
2090 RETURN
2999 '* ---------- Stub for cursor up ------------ *
3000 PRINT "Cursor up key pressed."
3090 RETURN
3099 '* ---------- Stub for cursor right --------- *
3100 PRINT "Cursor right key pressed."
3190 RETURN
3199 '* ---------- Stub for cursor down ---------- *
3200 PRINT "Cursor down key pressed."
3290 RETURN
3299 '* ---------- Stub for cursor left ---------- *
3300 PRINT "Cursor left key pressed."
3390 RETURN
```

PROG-16.BAS accomplishes the same task as the C program. The main C stub is duplicated by lines 1 through 90. The subroutine located at line 2000 is equivalent to the C cur_ctrl() function, and the cursor movement stubs are located at line 3000 and beyond.

Interrupt Traps

The third method of servicing a device is the interrupt. Some computers require the CPU to service peripheral hardware devices with the polling method; however, the polling method puts considerable overhead on the processor. It is much better if the device can just let the CPU know when it needs servicing. Most computers today function in just that way. The external device interrupts the CPU and lets it know when it needs some attention.

The family of INTEL-8086 microprocessors function in this way. These are the chips with which the IBM PC and IBM-compatible processors are built. You don't need to understand the way the chip is built in order to program it, and it is beyond the scope of this book to cover the topic of interrupt programming in detail. But it is to your advantage to have at least a general understanding of how your microprocessor chip handles device interrupts.

These chips have two **interrupt pins** that a peripheral device can use to signal the CPU when the device needs servicing. One of these pins is the **non-maskable interrupt** (NMI). It cannot be turned off and is used for only extreme emergencies. When the power voltage to the system suddenly starts to drop, a signal is placed on this pin to alert the CPU of the impending doom. The processor has time to save the contents of important registers before it goes down. Imagine what it would be like to have a critical system that required 37 hours to complete running, and after the system had been running for 34 hours, there was a power failure that required you to start the job over. With the NMI, the CPU can be alerted in time to save critical data and, with the right programming, could reload and start up where it left off when the power failed.

The second interrupt pin (**INTR**) is for normal device interrupts. This interrupt pin can be turned off (disabled) if you are doing something that is too important to be interrupted. There are many reasons why an interrupt can occur. A device such as the keyboard will interrupt for servicing when a key is pressed. Hardware failures and software errors will also cause interrupts. Operations such as division by zero or a memory write error will also cause an interrupt signal to be put on the INTR pin.

When the keyboard puts a signal on the INTR pin, indicating it is in need of attention, and assuming the INTR is enabled, the code that is currently running will be interrupted as soon as the current machine language instruction is complete. The CPU then saves the contents of some of the registers and requests a response from the device that did the interrupting. The response the CPU wants is a 12-bit code that indicates the reason for the interrupt. You might think of the code passed to the CPU as a pointer to a pointer. The 12-bit code points to a low address in memory, and the low address in memory points to the code that will service the device or the reason for the interrupt.

The hex addresses 0 through 3FF in memory are reserved as pointers for interrupts. There are 256 different types of interrupts possible. The CPU uses this 12-bit address to find the pointer to the particular interrupt service routine called for. After the interrupt is serviced, the CPU restores the few registers that it saved and then returns control back to the exact place in the program that was initially interrupted.

To service an interrupt with your own code, be sure you know where your code is located and then substitute the address of your code for the address of the normal interrupt service routine. After your code does what you want it to do for that situation, your routine must also restore all the registers that you used to their initial condition. If your routine doesn't do this, the program that was interrupted will start up again, thinking it has a particular item in a register when in fact you changed the contents of the register by servicing the interrupt. As you can imagine, this will cause strange results, and some other programmer will wonder what went wrong with his or her code, so in addition to servicing the interrupt, you must clean things up and leave everything as you found it. This must be done rapidly so that other devices are still being serviced within their time limits. Note that this explanation is what actually happens but is oversimplified in some ways and overly complicated in other ways.

How is it oversimplified? If you were writing your own interrupt handlers, you would also have to be concerned about when it is safe to enable and disable the INTR. You could not keep the INTR disabled so long that some other device would lose critical data because the device would not be able to cause an interrupt for its needs. Also, it was pointed out that your code must first save and then restore the contents of CPU registers that were not automatically saved and restored during the interrupt. There are four 16-bit general registers. Each one has additional special uses. There are also four pointer or index registers, four segment registers, one instruction pointer, and nine flags to be concerned about.

How is the previous explanation overly complicated? Both BASIC and C have done some of the work for you. Yes, even BASIC will allow you to perform some limited interrupt servicing, using the ON ERROR or ON KEY statements (see the sample program LOOKFOR.BAS in Chapter 12 as an example). You can service items such as hardware and software errors or user entries such as a [Ctrl/Break]. Actually, BASIC services the initial interrupt but then passes control on to you to handle as you choose. C also has some functions that will take some of the work out of handling an interrupt. The actual coding of interrupts is beyond the intended scope of this book, but one easy interrupt function handler will be covered next.

A function called **ctrlbrk()** will let your C program trap and service a [Ctrl/Break] interrupt. When you call this function, it will set up the address for your interrupt handler in vector 0x23. Whenever your program gets a [Ctrl/Break] interrupt, control will be passed to your handler. Your interrupt handler does not need to save all the registers and other items previously discussed because C performs the initial servicing and then transfers control to your interrupt handler when that work is done. Once your handler has completed its work, C will again clean up for you before returning to your regular code that was interrupted. Also, you do not need to be concerned about the length of time your interrupt handler takes. C will turn the INTR on again and peripheral devices will be allowed to interrupt your handler. So, you see, all the hard work has been done for you, but C will let you know whenever a [Ctrl/Break] is pressed.

You may wonder why you would want to know about this situation. Obviously, the user wants to stop the program from running. Why not let the operating system stop your program for the user? Suppose you have data in memory that should be put on the disk before you let the program stop. This gives you a chance to do that before you gracefully stop the program yourself. Then again, suppose you can't allow the user to stop for security purposes. Perhaps this is the only program that he or she is allowed to run. Once a program has terminated in this way, the user is normally left in the operating system, which means he or she is free to run any program or utility that is available.

Following are the steps necessary to use ctrlbrk() and to handle your own [Ctrl/Break] interrupt. First, include dos.h in the code:

```
#include <dos.h>
```

Next, declare and define your interrupt handler:

```
int my_handler(void)
{
     ...
     (Code to gracefully bring down your program.)
     ...
     return 0;
}
```

Your handler should return a 0 if you want to abort after the handler is finished. Any nonzero return will allow your code to continue from where it was interrupted. The final step is to insert your handler into the interrupt trap sequence by calling the function ctrlbrk() early in the main() program:

```
main()
{
ctrlbrk(my_handler);
...
}
```

When your program is terminated normally, either by completing its run or by a [Ctrl/Break], your handler will be automatically removed from the interrupt trap sequence. This is still one more task that you are not required to do when you use this function to set up the interrupt for you.

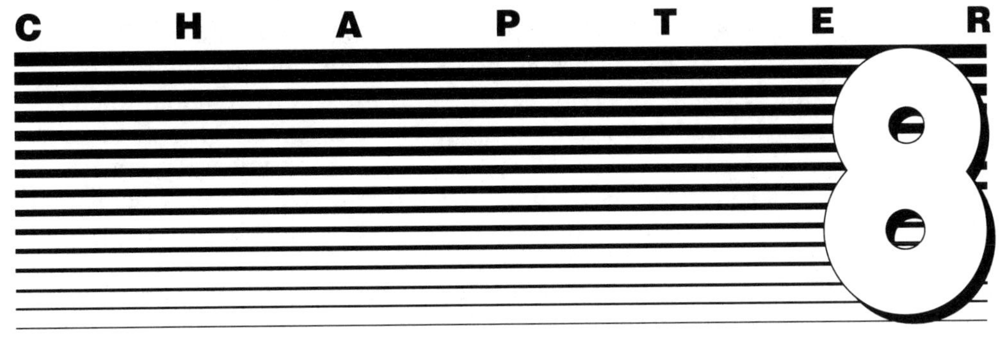

MASTERING GRAPHICS

So far, you have read about and used a variety of computer operations. You have learned how the computer works with numbers, and you have examined the way the computer handles alphanumeric text. The next topic you are about to tackle is graphics. In this chapter, you will examine how the computer graphically represents an image—how it can be made to draw pictures. In some ways, you could think of programming graphics as manipulating a new type of data. It requires a different way of displaying data on the screen. It also requires additional hardware. Your system must have some type of graphics adapter in order to program with graphics. Some PC systems come with a built-in graphics adapter. Others require that you purchase one separately. You can also purchase enhanced graphic adapters that will give better resolution and more color variations than were originally designed for the IBM-PCs and their compatibles; however, this book will confine itself to the standard graphic capability.

Although there were efforts to make the computer draw pictures before, it has only been since the introduction and almost universal use of a display screen as a computer output device that graphics have taken such a prominent position in professional programming. This chapter will cover the use of graphics on your IBM-PC's color graphics adapter (CGA) or compatible devices. The approach to producing graphics will vary somewhat, depending on the hardware design of the computer, screen, and graphics adapter and on the graphic software used. There are also other devices that can be used by the computer to produce a graphic image. Some examples are dot-matrix printers, laser printers, and plotters.

UNDERSTANDING PIXELS

An impressionist artist by the name of Georges Seurat started a new school of painting in the 1880s called pointillism. He felt that the way to produce a painting on canvas was to create the image out of individually colored dots (points). From a distance, the human eye would not see individual dots, but would fuse these dots into the intended image. On a computer, the dots are actually small rectangles, but the concept still works. Examine Figure 8.1:

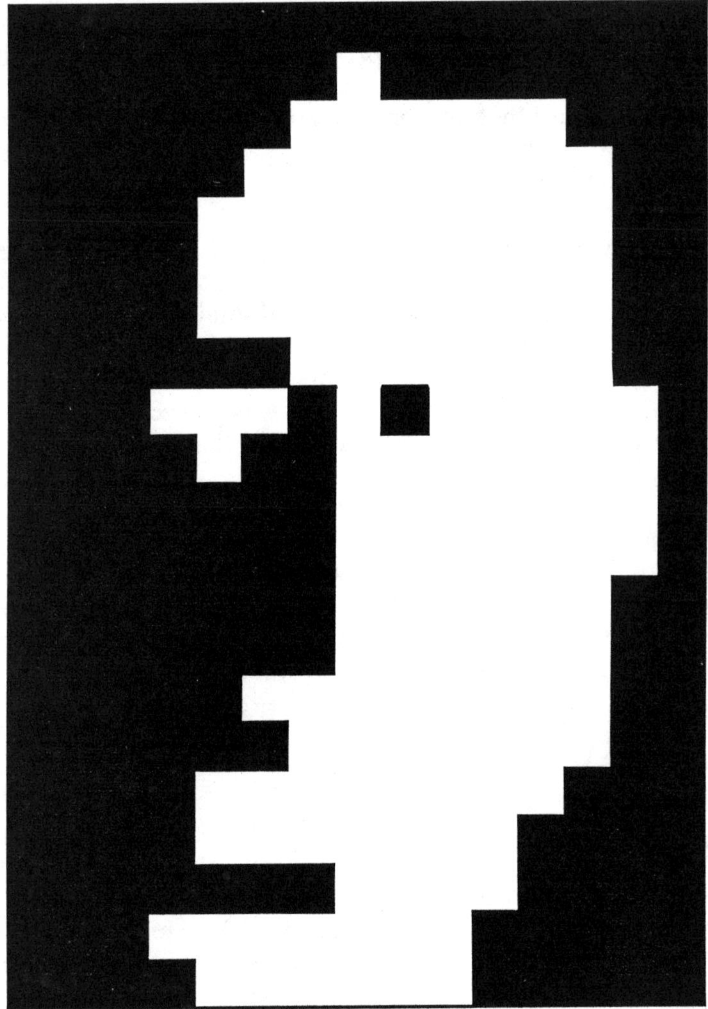

Figure 8.1 *Dots*

At this size, the image is crude and perhaps meaningless. You see the individual rectangles. Now, squint at the figure or prop the book up so you can still see the image as you walk away from it. Move back as far as you can. Does your eye transform this into an image that has some meaning? On a computer screen, each rectangle would appear as a small dot, and the eye would form those dots into the image of a face looking at you.

Seurat felt that not only would the human eye create and thus see the desired image, but it could also generate the full spectrum of colors out of just the colors blue, violet, red, orange, yellow, green, and white. If small dots of these pure colors were placed next to each other, the human eye would fuse the dots together to create all the other colors and shades of colors. The eye would "mix the paint." If a predominance of small yellow and blue dots was placed in one area, the eye would see varying shades of green when it looked at that area of the painting.

Pointillism is the principle behind computer graphics. The screen has been divided up into small dots. Each dot is called a **pixel**. An image is then created out of a grouping of dots on the screen. In some cases, only black and white dots are used to generate computer graphics. In other situations, colored pixels can be generated to represent the desired image. When in graphics mode, the screen has two resolutions: high resolution and low resolution.

High Resolution

In high resolution graphics mode, the screen is divided into 128,000 small rectangles. Each of these rectangles is a pixel and can be addressed or referenced by its horizontal and vertical coordinates—commonly referred to as the X and Y coordinates, respectively, and usually written as (X,Y). The X coordinate ranges from 0 to 639, and the Y coordinate ranges from 0 to 199. The pixel (0,0) is located in the upper left corner of the screen. Only two colors are possible in high resolution graphics: black and white. This means that a single bit can be used to represent each of the 128,000 pixels. If the bit is 1, the pixel is black; if the bit is zero, the pixel is white. Think of each pixel on the screen as having a bit in what is called a **screen buffer** (sometimes called the screen's **active page**). Examining how the bit is set in this buffer tells the hardware what color to set the pixel on the screen.

Low Resolution

In low resolution graphics mode, the screen contains only half as many pixels—64,000 to be exact. This means that each low-resolution pixel is twice as large as a high-resolution pixel. The X coordinate ranges from 0 to 319, and (as in high resolution) Y ranges from 0 to 199. So the little rectangles or pixels are wider but the same length as in high resolution. Assuming you have a color screen, you can now have four different colors on the screen at one time. In the screen buffer, four colors can be represented by two bits—00, 01, 10, and 11 (i.e., 0, 1, 2, and 3). So again the screen can be represented in the screen buffer by the same 128,000 bits, that is, 64,000 pixels at two bits each.

Colors

What are the four colors you can have on the screen? You have a limited selection and can choose only four at any given time. The screen is considered to have a background and a foreground. The background is like the white of this page you are reading. The foreground is the color of the letters that are printed on the white page. For the CGA, you can have one background color and three foreground colors at any given time. The background can be any one of the 16 background colors. But for the foreground, you must choose one of four preset groups of colors called **palettes**. Each palette has three predefined colors that are set. You do not have individual color choices for the three foreground colors. The palette is defined by the initialization mode you choose.

Background Colors:

Code	Color	Code	Color
0	black	8	darkgray
1	blue	9	lightblue
2	green	10	lightgreen
3	cyan	11	lightcyan
4	red	12	lightred
5	magenta	13	lightmagenta
6	brown	14	yellow
7	lightgray	15	white

Foreground Colors:

Pixel Code	Mode or Palette 0	Mode or Palette 1	Mode or Palette 2	Mode or Palette 3
1	lightgreen	lightcyan	green	cyan
2	lightred	lightmagenta	red	magenta
3	yellow	white	brown	lightgray

Each pixel is represented by a code of 0, 1, 2, or 3. In addition, one background color is defined for the whole screen, and one palette is initialized for the whole screen. Each dot or pixel that has a code of 0 in the screen buffer will be set to the active background color. Each pixel with a code of 1, 2, or 3 will be set to the corresponding color defined in the initialized palette. Without changing the codes for any given pixel, you could change the color of all the background pixels on the screen by selecting a new background color.

So far, everything discussed in this chapter is the same for either BASIC or C. Now it is time to examine how you use this information to produce a graphics program.

BRINGING UP A GRAPHICS SCREEN

When you turn on the computer, it comes up in character mode. There is nothing that must be done to make it understand the characters you are soon to display on the screen. This is not true of graphics. You must initialize your screen to work with the graphics adapter and load the appropriate graphics drivers with your program. When you are done with the graphics, you must return the screen to character mode (in other words, turn off the graphics).

In Turbo C, this process is accomplished with the following steps. The project file (.PRJ) must contain the name and path to your C file(s) and the GRAPHICS.LIB file. This last file should be in your \lib directory. The entry in your project file would resemble one of the following two examples, depending on your disk and directory configuration:

```
C:\turboc\lib\graphics.lib

B:\lib\graphics.lib
```

The next step is to include the appropriate header file for graphics:

```
#include <graphics.h>
```

Finally, you initialize the graphics. This is accomplished by first declaring and defining two integer variables:

```
int graph_driver = 1, graph_mode = 0;
```

You can use any variable names you want, but the values you define them equal to are a different matter. The variable called *graph_driver* must indicate the type of graphics adapter you have on your system. The 1 used in this case is for the CGA card. (If a 0 were used, the system would attempt to automatically detect the type of graphics adapter you have and then set the driver code accordingly.) The value that the *graph_mode* variable contains is the mode or palette code you choose. The palette codes were defined for you previously; however, this is the mode code that is also used to indicate high and low resolution. The codes 0 through 3 designate low resolution as well as the palette code. A mode code of 4 designates high resolution and, of course, only two colors—black and white.

The next step is to actually initialize the system to use graphics. This is done with the **initgraph**() function:

```
initgraph( &graph_driver, &graph_mode, "" );
```

Note the two &s. The initgraph() function expects address pointers to the variables, not the values of the variables. The third argument will contain the path to the graphics driver, which is the CGA.BGI file (or the .BGI file appropriate for your graphics adapter). The null character in this third argument indicates that the file is in the current directory. Once you are in graphics mode, you are free to create whatever graphics you choose; however, when you are done, remember to return to character mode by calling the following function:

```
closegraph();
```

Executing the **closegraph()** function clears the screen and erases any graphics.

DRAWING WITH PIXELS

Once you are in graphics mode, the next step is to understand how to plot one point or pixel on the screen. This is accomplished with the **putpixel()** function in C. BASIC has an instruction called PSET, which is used for the same purpose.

putpixel()

The putpixel() function has the following general form:

```
putpixel( x, y, color );
```

The *x* and *y* are the respective horizontal and vertical coordinates of the point, and *color* is the code (0 through 3) of the color you want the point to have. Try the following sample program.

```
/* ------------------- PROG-17.C ---------------------- */
/* ------ Demonstrate the putpixel() function --------- */

#include<graphics.h>
#include<conio.h>

void main()
{
     int graph_driver=1, graph_mode=0;
     int i;

     /* ---------- Initialize graphics ------------- */
     initgraph(&graph_driver, &graph_mode, "");

     /* ------ Draw a diagonal row of points ------- */
     for(i=1 ; i<190 ; i=i+3)
           putpixel(i,i,2);

     /* --- Wait for keyboard input - then go on --- */
     getch();

     /* -------- Erase every third point ----------- */
     for(i=1 ; i<190 ; i=i+9)
          putpixel(i,i,0);

     getch();

     /* ----------- Turn graphics off -------------- */
     closegraph();
}
```

When you run this program, a diagonal series of dots will appear on the screen. You must press a key to continue. The program uses the wait-for-input feature of the getch() function to temporarily "stop" processing while you look at the result. Note that the color code used in the first loop is 2. In the second loop, the color code is 0 — the background color. The second loop will erase every third dot in the line. To erase the pixel, you simply draw the point in the background color. Remember to press a key again when you have finished looking at the result.

You now have a graphics program. Incorporating this program into the program stub PROG-15.C from the last chapter may give you a way to control where you want the pixels drawn, using the cursor keys. Rename that program and modify the code to match the following:

```
/* ------------------- PROG-18.C --------------------- */
/* ---- Draw & change color with cursor & no. keys ---- */

#include<graphics.h>
#include<conio.h>

/* ------------ Declare global variables ------------- */
int pix_color=1, pix_x=159, pix_y=99;

/* --------- Declare function that is called --------- */
int pix_ctrl();

void main()
{
    int graph_driver=1, graph_mode=0;
    int endit = 0;

    printf("This program will let you draw using the\n");
    printf("cursor arrow keys.  Pressing keys 0 \n");
    printf("through 3 will change the color of pixel\n");
    printf("accordingly.  Pressing any other key will\n");
    printf("stop program. \n\n");
    printf("        PRESS ANY KEY TO START.   ");
    getch();
```

continued...

...from previous page

```
    /* ------------ Initialize graphics --------------- */
    initgraph(&graph_driver, &graph_mode, "");

    /* -------- Get a keystroke and draw point -------- */
    while (endit == 0){
     endit = pix_ctrl();
    }

    /* ------------- Turn graphics off ---------------- */
    closegraph();
}
```

Several changes were made. Graphics.h is included along with some variables declared outside the main() function. This means that the variables *pix_color*, *pix_x*, and *pix_y* are global variables and may be used by any function linked to this module. They will be used to represent the color, X coordinate, and Y coordinate for the pixel that is to be drawn on the screen. An explanation of what the user is to do and the initialization of graphics are also included as new code. It continues by calling a new function called pix_ctrl(). This is a modified version of the old cur_ctrl() function from Chapter 7. Note the changes:

```
/* -------------------- PIX_CTRL.C ------------------- */
/* ----- Display pixel as directed by cursor keys ----- */
/* ------ Set pixel color by numeric code pressed ----- */

#include <stdio.h>
#include <bios.h>

void pix_up();
void pix_rght();
void pix_down();
void pix_left();
```

continued...

...from previous page

```
int pix_ctrl()
{
     /* ----- Declare external global variables ---- */
     extern int pix_color;

     /* -- Declare and initialize local variables -- */
     int key, sch, ch, ch_mask = 0x00ff;

        /* ----------- Any keyboard input? ------------ */
     if (bioskey(1) == 0) goto done;

     /* ---------- Yes get the key codes ----------- */
        key = bioskey(0);

     /* --- Set color or return if code not null --- */
     ch = (key & ch_mask);
     if (ch >= '0' && ch <= '3') {
          pix_color = atoi(&ch);
          key = 0;
          goto done;
     }
     if (ch > 0) goto done;

     /* ------- Isolate and find scancode --------- */
     sch = key >> 8;

     /* ----- Call appropiate function for case ---- */
     switch (sch) {
          case 'H':
               pix_up();
               break;
          case 'M':
               pix_rght();
               break;
          case 'P':
               pix_down();
               break;
```

continued...

...from previous page

```
                case 'K' :
                     pix_left();
                     break;
                default:
                     printf("%c",'\07');
           }
           key = 0;
done:      return(key);

}
```

One of the important changes is the declaration of the variable *pix_color* as an extern. Because this code is compiled in a separate object module, you must let C know which globals you want to use here. You will see the code that takes the numeric key codes and uses them to change the value of pix_color. This function also calls some additional functions: pix_up(), pix_rght(), pix_down(), and pix_left(). These are the cur_up(), cur_rght(), cur_down(), and cur_left() stubs filled out with code. Although the current function might get a little long, you could put this additional code right here in this switch statement; however, a very important process should be emphasized and this situation provides an excellent opportunity to do so:

```
/* -------------------- PIX_UP.C ---------------------- */
/* ----------- Move pixel up and display it ----------- */

#include<graphics.h>

void pix_up()
{
     /* ------ Declare external globals used ------- */
     extern int pix_x, pix_y, pix_color;

     /* ----- Move y up but not off screen --------- */
     pix_y = pix_y - 1;
     if (pix_y < 0 )  pix_y = 0;

     /* ---------- Draw the point ---------------- */
     putpixel(pix_x, pix_y, pix_color);

     return;
}
```

Note that the header graphics.h is again included in this function. Even though the header was included with PROG-18.C, it must be included again in each of these functions that are compiled separately. Failure to do so can cause problems.

This program is a good example of the approach used to build a large system made up of many different functions and thousands of lines of code. You can see how all the functions are declared and called, how global variables are declared and used as externs, and how each separately compiled module must include its own header files.

Note the way the cursor key is processed once it has been pressed. If pix_up() had been called, the up arrow was pressed. You want to move the cursor up; therefore, only the vertical (or *pix_y*) coordinate is affected. The upper left corner of the screen was (0,0), and (0,199) is the lower left corner. That means you must make *pix_y* smaller (subtract from it) to move the cursor up. Once you have your new value for *pix_y*, you should also check to make sure it is still on the screen. If the value is off the screen, you could print an error message, wrap around, and bring it back on the bottom of the screen or, as in this case, just put it back on the top edge of the screen by giving it a value of 0. Remember, it is up to you and your code to perform the run-time checks. The remaining functions are as follows:

```
/* -------------------- PIX_RGHT.C -------------------- */
/* ---------- Move pixel right and display it --------- */

#include<graphics.h>

void pix_rght()
{
     /* ------ Declare external globals used ------- */
     extern int pix_x, pix_y, pix_color;

     /* ----- Move x right but not off screen ------ */
     pix_x = pix_x + 1;
     if (pix_x > 319 )  pix_x = 319;

     /* ---------- Draw the point ----------------- */
     putpixel(pix_x, pix_y, pix_color);

     return;
}
```

```
/* -------------------- PIX_DOWN.C -------------------- */
/* ----------- Move pixel down and display it --------- */

#include<graphics.h>

void pix_down()
{
     /* ------ Declare external globals used ------- */
     extern int pix_x, pix_y, pix_color;

     /* ----- Move y down but not off screen ------- */
     pix_y = pix_y + 1;
     if (pix_y > 199 )  pix_y = 199;

     /* ---------- Draw the point ----------------- */
     putpixel(pix_x, pix_y, pix_color);

     return;
}
```

```
/* -------------------- PIX_LEFT.C -------------------- */
/* ----------- Move pixel left and display it --------- */

#include<graphics.h>

void pix_left()
{
     /* ------ Declare external globals used ------- */
     extern int pix_x, pix_y, pix_color;

     /* ----- Move x left but not off screen ------- */
     pix_x = pix_x - 1;
     if (pix_x < 0 )  pix_x = 0;

     /* ----------- Draw the point ----------------- */
     putpixel(pix_x, pix_y, pix_color);

     return;
}
```

Try running the program. Remember to compile all the different modules below and to link object code in order to create the executable module:

```
\lib\graphics.lib
prog-18.c
pix_ctrl.c
pix_up.c
pix_rght.c
pix_down.c
pix_left.c
```

Not only can you move the pixel around the screen and leave a trail as would a pen or paintbrush, but you can also change the color of the pixels being turned on by entering 0 through 3. Note that changing the color to 0 (the background color) will allow you to erase or move to another part of the screen without leaving a trail.

Here you have the beginning of your own paintbrush program and can draw images on the screen at will; however, the objective is to understand graphics. Note that it takes a while to draw a line across the screen, using your paintbrush. Perhaps it would be worthwhile to examine other ways to draw a line on the screen.

UNDERSTANDING CURRENT POSITION AND COLOR

Before you look at drawing lines, you must understand the concepts of **current position** and **current color**. In the paintbrush program, there was a point that the program kept track of with the variables *pix_x* and *pix_y*. These were the coordinates of the last point drawn. In a way, the program created a situation that is similar to the normal character or text mode screen. When you are typing on a text screen, the blinking cursor tells you exactly where you are on the screen. There is software in the system that keeps track of the current position of the text cursor and causes it to blink on the screen. The paintbrush program simulated this concept on the graphics screen, but it did not have a cursor that showed you the current position. The software engineers who designed the Turbo C graphic functions decided that some of the graphic functions would benefit from the idea of a **current position** (CP) for a graphics screen, and they created one. This is an imaginary point that can be used as a starting point for some of the graphic functions.

Some of the Turbo C graphic functions affect this CP while others do not. No cursor is built into the graphics system that shows where the CP is located, but the C run-time graphic routine does keep track of this imaginary point on the screen. For those C functions that affect it, the CP is updated appropriately. Following are some functions used to control the CP (the variables *x* and *y* are integers):

`x = getx();`	Return the *x* value of the CP.
`y = gety();`	Return the *y* value of the CP.
`moveto(x,y);`	Relocate the CP to the coordinates *x,y*. Nothing is drawn on the screen.

`moverel(5,-9);`	Relocate the CP by using the x value of the first argument as a relative displacement for *x* and the second argument as a relative displacement for *y*. If the CP was (40,40), the new CP would be (45,31). Nothing is drawn on the screen.

In addition to the CP, the graphics screen also has something called the **current color** (CC) and **current background color** (CBC). The CC is one of the three color codes (1, 2, or 3) from the initialized palette, or the background color code (0). The CBC is any of the 16 background color codes (0 through 15). There are some graphics instructions that use whatever color the CC or CBC is presently set to. For this reason, you may want to also control these current colors. The following instructions allow you to do just that (the variable *c* is an integer):

`c = getcolor();`	Return the code for the CC.
`c = getbkcolor();`	Return the code for the CBC.
`setcolor(c);`	Set CC to *c* (*c* = 0 to 3).
`setbkcolor(c);`	Set CBC to *c* (*c* = 0 to 15).

Setting the CC to 0 is not necessarily the same as setting the CBC to 0. Setting the CC to 0 means that the current color will be the same as the current background color (whatever that color is), so the pixels set with the current color will contain a 0. All pixels set to the color code 0 will change whenever the background color is set to a new color code. On the other hand, setting the CBC to 0 means setting the background color to the color black and changing all the pixels with a color code of 0 to the color black.

Now that you have been introduced to the current position and current colors formally, the topic of drawing lines in C can be considered. This introduction was necessary because some of the line-drawing functions affect and use these current settings. (Some other graphic functions, including the putpixel() function, do not use the current colors or the imaginary current position on the screen.)

DRAWING STRAIGHT LINES

If you wanted to draw a line more rapidly than the paintbrush could produce it, you could modify the code in PROG-17.C to plot each point instead of every third point. However, C provides you with a few alternatives for drawing lines. These functions are similar to PROG-17.C in the way they draw, but they allow you to choose the end points of the line, and some of them use the current colors or position settings.

line()

The **line**() function does not use or affect the CP. It simply requires that you designate as arguments the beginning and ending coordinates of the line you want displayed on the screen. The function will produce a line between these two sets of points, using the current color. The general form of the line() function is as follows:

```
line(x1, y1, x2, y2);
```

The arguments *x1* and *y1* are the coordinates of the first point, and *x2* and *y2* are the coordinates of the second point. The CP is not used or changed.

lineto()

In this function, a line will be drawn with the current color between the current position and the coordinates given as arguments. The general form of the lineto() function is as follows:

```
lineto(x2, y2);
```

The arguments *x2* and *y2* are the coordinates of the second point, and the first point is the CP. After the line is drawn, using the CC, the CP is changed to the position (*x2*,*y2*).

linerel()

In this function, both the CP and the CC are used. A line will be drawn from the CP to a point that is computed from the relative differences given as arguments in the function call. The general form of the **linerel()** function is as follows:

```
linerel(dx, dy);
```

The arguments *dx* and *dy* are the differences between the current position and the new point. Assume that the current position was (100, 50) and the following function call was made:

```
linerel(-20, 17);
```

A line would be drawn in the current color between the points (100,50) and (80,67). After drawing the line, the CP would be changed to (80,67).

rectangle()

Lines can be combined to enclose areas and make shapes. Turbo C has library functions to speed up that process. An example is the function **rectangle()**, shown in its general form here:

```
rectangle(x1,y1,x2,y2);
```

The arguments *x1* and *y1* are the coordinates for the upper left corner of the rectangle, and *x2* and *y2* are the coordinates for the lower right corner. In BASIC, the same instruction that will draw lines (LINE) is used to produce rectangles.

Following is a sample program that demonstrates the use of some of the previous line-drawing graphics:

```
/* ---------------------- PROG-19.C ------------------- */
/* --------- Demonstrate line drawing graphics -------- */

#include<graphics.h>
#include<stdlib.h>

void main()
{
     int graph_driver=1, graph_mode=0;
     int x, y, c, i;

     /* ----------- Initialize graphics ------------ */
     initgraph(&graph_driver, &graph_mode, "");

     /* --------- Draw a random star burst --------- */
     for (i=1; i<100; i++) {

          /* ---- Put CP in center of screen ---- */
          moveto(160, 100);

          /* --- x is a number from -90 to 90 --- */
          x = (rand() % 181) - 90;

          /* --- y is a number from -90 to 90 --- */
          y = (rand() % 181) - 90;

          /* ---- c is a number from 1 to 3 ----- */
          c = (rand() % 3) + 1;

          /* ----- Set CC and draw the line ----- */
          setcolor(c);
          linerel(x, y);
     }
     getch();

     /* ------------ Turn graphics off ------------ */
     closegraph();
}
```

The program produces a starburst pattern. If you examine the loop, you will see that each iteration first sets the CP back to the center of the screen. The random number generator is used to produce a range of numbers from -90 to +90 for displacements from the center of the screen for both the X and Y coordinates. A random number from 0 to 2 is produced with the rand() % 3 expression. Adding one to that number gives a number from 1 to 3. This number is then used to set the CC for the next line. The getch() function is used to hold the image on the screen until you are ready to exit by pressing a key.

If you are interested in the difference in speed between C and BASIC, you might want to run the following BASIC program and compare the times:

```
1 '* --------------- PROG-20.BAS ----------------- *
9 '* ---------- Initialize graphics -------------- *
10 KEY OFF
20 SCREEN 1,0
30 COLOR 0,0
99 '* --------- Draw random star burst ----------- *
100 FOR I = 1 TO 100
110      X = (INT(RND * 181)) - 90
120      Y = (INT(RND * 181)) - 90
130      LINE(160,100)-(160+X,100+Y)
190 NEXT I
200 IF INKEY$ = "" THEN 200
299 '* ----------- Turn graphics off ------------- *
300 SCREEN 0
310 WIDTH 80
```

Note that the BASIC version is actually performing fewer tasks than the C version. The color of the line is not being changed; and even so, the actual execution takes longer than the C version.

DRAWING CURVED LINES

The straight lines discussed so far are only one of many types of lines that might be drawn. The ability to draw curved lines is equally important in graphics. Turbo C gives you a variety of functions that will draw curved lines.

circle()

The circle is one of the more common curved lines you might want to draw. The **circle()** function has the following general form:

```
circle(x, y, r);
```

The arguments *x* and *y* are the coordinates of the center of the circle, and *r* is the radius of the circle. Modify PROG-19.C slightly, and try this new function. You can remove the following lines because the CP is not used by circle():

```
/* ---- Put CP in center of screen ---- */
moveto(160,100);
```

Now change the following line

```
linerel(x, y);
```

to read

```
circle(160,100,abs(x));
```

Again, the center of the screen is to be used. It will become the center of the circles that are drawn. The random values that were generated for *x* will be turned into positive numbers and then used as the radius for the circles. (Although the *y* is not necessary here, leave it in; you will use it later.) Run this new code.

arc()

A special function for a circle allows you to draw just part (an arc) of the circle. This function has the following general form:

```
arc(x, y, sa, ea, r);
```

The arguments *x* and *y* are the coordinates of the center of the arc; *sa* is the starting angle; and *ea* is the ending angle. Of course, *r* is the radius of the arc. Think of the center and radius as being from a circle that is only partially drawn. The angles *sa* and *ea* can range from 0 to 360 degrees; they run counterclockwise as shown in Figure 8.2:

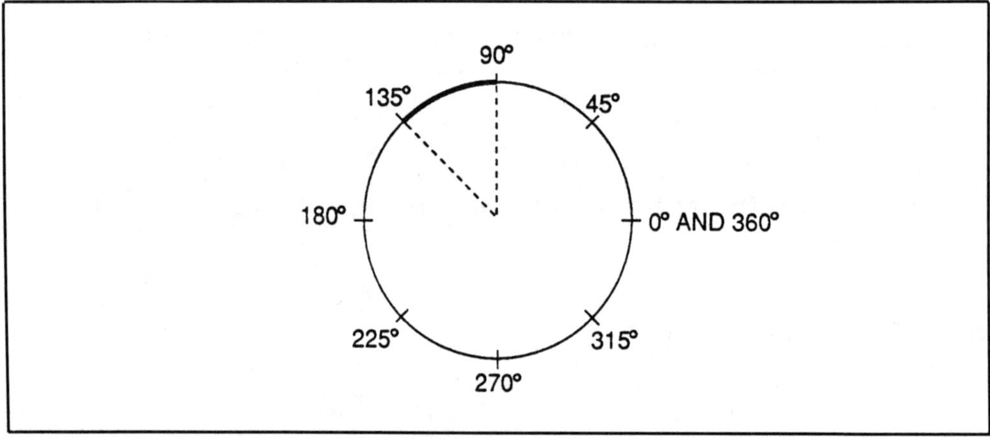

Figure 8.2 *Relative degree positions for arcs*

An arc starting at 90 degrees and going to 135 degrees is indicated in bold in the figure.

ellipse()

The arc() function produces a limited portion of a circle, but actually the circle is simply a special case of the ellipse. **Ellipse** is a geometric term representing all ovals, including the circle. Take an ordinary drinking glass or coffee cup. Hold it up straight in front of you so the top edge is slightly below the level of your eye. The apparent oval-shaped image that the top edge makes is an ellipse (see Figure 8.3).

Figure 8.3 *Ellipse*

Figure 8.4 *Circle*

As you lower the cup, the oval widens and becomes more symmetrical. Finally, when you look directly down into the cup, the top edge appears as a circle (see Figure 8.4). The general form of the function that produces ellipses is as follows:

```
ellipse(x, y, sa, ea, xr, yr);
```

The coordinates *x* and *y* represent the pseudo-center of the ellipse. The argument *xr* is the radius when the ellipse crosses a horizontal line passing through the pseudo-center, and *yr* is the radius when the ellipse crosses the vertical line passing through the pseudo-center (see Figure 8.5). All other points on the ellipse are mathematically derived from these points.

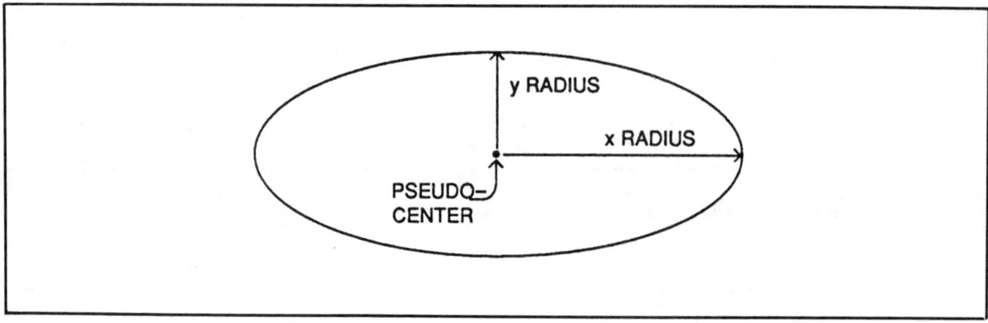

Figure 8.5 *Pseudo-center of an ellipse*

The function for an ellipse will also produce an arc of the ellipse. The *sa* and *ea* are the starting and ending angles for the arc. Again, modify program PROG-19.C. This time, remove the call to the function circle() that you just put in a few lines back. Add the following line:

```
ellipse(160,100,0,270,abs(x),abs(y));
```

This time, the program will produce the major portion of a group of random ellipses in the center of the screen. The overlay might remind you of a colorful Pacman game screen.

DRAWING AREAS

Drawing with points and lines has been discussed. The next step is to consider areas. Simply outlining the desired shape will give the impression of a two-dimensional figure. A stronger impression can be created by filling that area with color. It is possible to take an area bordered by either straight or curved lines and fill in the area with a color and a pattern. Turbo C has various ways of doing this, but to understand these functions, you must first understand two concepts: **fill color** and **fill pattern**.

Understanding Fill Color and Fill Pattern

An area can be filled with a color and a pattern of your choice. In the same way that there is a current color, there is also a current fill color (FC), which may be different from the CC. In addition, there is a current fill pattern (FP). The FC and FP are used when you call those library functions that fill a designated area. You can set the FC and FP with the **setfillstyle()** function, which has the following general form:

```
setfillstyle(fp, fc);
```

The argument *fc* is the fill color code. This is a color code from 0 to 3, indicating either the background color (0) or one of the three palette colors (1 through 3). The argument *fp* is the code for the fill pattern and can be any of the following:

Fill Patterns:

Code	Description of Fill
0	solid using background color
1	solid color
2	horizontal lines
3	thin / lines
4	thick / lines
5	thick \ lines
6	patterned \ lines
7	thin hatch lines
8	thick crosshatch lines
9	interleaving pattern
10	dots widely spaced
11	dots closely spaced

After the fill pattern and fill color have been set, you can use a function that will fill an enclosed area.

floodfill()

An area bordered by a single color may be filled with the FC and the FP when you call the following function:

```
floodfill(x, y, c);
```

This is the general form of the **floodfill()** function, where *x* and *y* are the coordinates of any point inside the enclosed area, and *c* is the border color code. If the point (*x*,*y*) falls outside the enclosed area, the area outside the boundary lines will be filled with the FP. The FP will start spreading from the coordinates given and spread until stopped by the border color.

Other graphic library functions automatically fill the area as it is drawn. The next few functions are examples.

bar() and bar3d()

Both the **bar()** and **bar3d()** functions will fill the designated area without regard for any boundary. They both use the FP and FC. The bar() function will not outline the bar, but will simply fill the area; however, bar3d() will not only outline the area with the current color, it will create a three-dimensional (3D) box around the area if you want. The general form for these functions is as follows:

```
bar(x1, y1, x2, y2);

bar3d(x1, y1, x2, y2, d, t,);
```

The *x1* and *y1* are the upper left coordinates of the bar, and *x2* and *y2* are the lower right coordinates of the bar. The *d* is the pixel depth of the three-dimensional box, and a nonzero *t* indicates the desire for a top to the three-dimensional box. The following sample program will show the use of the three-dimensional bar when the depth is set to one pixel and no top is requested. The result is simply an outline. No three-dimensional box is drawn.

```
/* ------------------- PROG-21.C ---------------------- */
/* -------- Demonstrate bars and fill patterns -------- */

#include<graphics.h>
#include<stdlib.h>

void main()
{
     int graph_driver=1, graph_mode=0;
     int x, y, c, fc, fp;

     /* ---------- Initialize graphics ------------- */
     initgraph(&graph_driver, &graph_mode, "");
```

continued...

...from previous page

```
     /* ----- Using FP from 0 to 11, draw bars ----- */
     for (fp=0; fp<12; fp++){
          x = fp*20;
          y = fp*10;
          c = (rand() % 4)+1;
          fc =(rand() % 3)+1;
          setcolor(c);
          setfillstyle(fp,fc);
          bar3d(x,y,x+30,y+60,1,0);
     }
     getch();

     /* ---------- Turn graphics off ------------- */
     closegraph();
}
```

This sample program also shows all the predefined fill patterns, using random colors for both fill color and current color. The current color is used to outline the bars. When the CC is randomly set to 0, you will not see an outline on the bar. All bars drawn with the bar() function will have this appearance.

pieslice()

Another function that automatically fills an area is **pieslice()**. There are functions for drawing bars and parts of a circle such as a pieslice because of the large amount of statistical graphing performed with computers. The term 23% is easier to comprehend if you can show a visual aid in the form of a pie chart. A 23-cent slice of a silver dollar pie is easy to understand. Professional graphics programming is frequently concerned with graphs or charts of this nature. You can build your own pie chart with individual pixels; however, this function makes it easier. The general form of the pieslice() function is as follows:

```
pieslice(x, y, sa, ea, r);
```

The arguments here are the same as for the arc() function: *x* and *y* represent the center of a circle of radius *r*, and *sa* and *ea* are the starting and ending angles of the arc. Lines are drawn from the ends of the arc to the center of the circle, and the enclosed area is filled with the FP and FC.

cleardevice()

By far the easiest area to fill with a color is the whole screen. You can achieve this effect by clearing the screen of all but the background color. You can call the following function when in graphics mode:

```
cleardevice();
```

You see the general form of the **cleardevice**() function here. Calling the function not only clears the screen but puts the CP at position (0,0).

WORKING WITH IMAGES

So far, you have learned how to create drawings on the screen. These drawings are made up of dots, lines, and areas; however, if you wanted to move your drawing to another part of the screen, you would need to recreate a similar drawing. You had no way to pick the drawing up and move it. The concept of an **image** was created to give you a way to move your drawing and at the same time let you perform such tasks as storing an image for later use or even creating animation. This concept allows you to make a copy of some rectangular portion of the screen and recall it at a later time. Before you can create and recall that copy, you must set aside a special area of memory to hold this image.

Getting Ready for Images

To work with images, you must have activated the graphics screen. In addition, you must reserve an area of memory large enough to hold the image you want to work with. Following are the steps necessary to reserve that space in memory. First, declare the following two variables:

```
unsigned int pic_size;

void *pic_buf;
```

The names are up to you, but one variable is a type unsigned int and the other a type void pointer. The integer must be large enough to hold the pixel count for any size image on the screen, including a full screen — thus, the reason for an unsigned int. The pointer is needed to point to the actual picture buffer in memory. The next step is to find out the size of the image by calling a function and indicating the upper left and lower right points of the rectangle you want to save. This function does not need to point to the actual rectangle, but it should be one of the same size:

```
pic_size = imagesize(0,0,50,60);
```

The function **imagesize()** produces the correct number of bytes needed to store the image. In this example, it is an image of 51 by 61 pixels. Next, you must reserve sufficient memory for that amount of space by calling another function:

```
pic_buf = malloc(pic_size);
```

The function **malloc()** will reserve a special block of memory that is outside of the data segment and the program stack. The pointer will contain the starting address of this block of memory when control returns from the function. Once these steps are completed, you are ready to get an image from the screen.

getimage()

The library function that will retrieve an image from the screen takes the following general form:

```
getimage(x1, y1, x2, y2, pointer);
```

The arguments *x1* and *y1* are the coordinates for the upper left corner of a rectangle you want to save. The lower right corner of the image is represented by *x2* and *y2*. The argument *pointer* is an address pointer to the reserved memory buffer you set aside for this image. This rectangle will be copied from the screen and placed in the buffer. The color codes for each pixel within the rectangle will be stored in the buffer. This image may be retrieved at will and placed back on the screen at the same or another spot.

putimage()

The method for placing the image back on the screen requires the **putimage()** function, which has the following general form:

```
putimage(x1, y1, pointer, cd);
```

The arguments *x1* and *y1* are the coordinates of the position on the screen in which you want to place the upper left corner of the image. Because the image is fixed in size, there's no need to give the lower boundary. The argument *pointer* points to the buffer that contains the image you want placed on the screen, and *cd* is a code from 0 to 4 that specifies how you want each colored pixel to be combined with the existing pixel color that is already on the screen. You can, of course, just replace the old color with the new one, but other options produce some interesting results. Following is a list of putimage() operators:

putimage() Operators:

Code	Description
0	Replace old image with new one.
1	Exclusive OR screen pixel with new one.
2	Inclusive OR screen pixel with new one.
3	AND screen pixel with new one.
4	Replace old pixel with the inverse of the new one.

The codes 0 and 4 both replace the existing screen image. Codes 1, 2, and 3 will combine the existing screen image with the new one to form still another image. These combined images create some interesting results. At times, it will appear that the original image is transparent and the first image can be seen through the second.

If you want to place your image on the screen temporarily, you could always save an image of the existing screen area as it is. Then, replace the existing area of the screen with your temporary image. Finally, you replace the temporary image with the original image that was first saved. This method is slow and requires twice as much memory as the following method. Code 1 (XOR) gives you a better alternative. Just XOR your new image right over the existing screen. Then, when you are ready, XOR the new image again at the same spot. The second XOR will erase the temporary image completely and will leave the original screen as it was. Examine what happens to the bits:

```
1  1  0  0          original screen bits

1  0  1  0          new image bits
----------------
0  1  1  0          first XOR combined image

1  0  1  0          new image bits again
----------------
1  1  0  0          result of final XOR—
                    same as original bits
```

Consider the following example program:

```
/* ------------------- PROG-22.C ---------------------- */
/* ----- Demonstrate getimage and putimage options ---- */

#include<graphics.h>
#include<stdlib.h>

void main()
{
     int graph_driver=1, graph_mode=0;
     int i;
     void *pic_buf;
     unsigned int pic_size;

     /* ---------- Initialize graphics ------------- */
     initgraph(&graph_driver, &graph_mode, "");
     pic_size =imagesize(0,0,30,30);
     pic_buf = malloc(pic_size);

     /* ---------------- Draw face ---------------- */
     setcolor(3);
     circle(15,15,15);        /*    head     */

     circle(8,10,3);          /*    eyes     */
     circle(22,10,3);
     putpixel(8,10,1);
     putpixel(22,10,1);

     circle(4,4,3);           /*    ears     */
     circle(26,4,3);

     circle(15,15,4);         /*    nose     */

     setfillstyle(1,2);       /*   color     */
     floodfill(15,4,3);

     setcolor(0);             /*   mouth     */
     arc(15,17,220,320,8);

     /* ---------- Pick up the image -------------- */
     getimage(0,0,30,30,pic_buf);
```

continued...

...from previous page

```
    /* -- Put rows of images using each operator -- */
    bar(161,10,310,189);
    for(i=0; i<5; i++){
         putimage(85,15+i*34,pic_buf,i);
         putimage(145,15+i*34,pic_buf,i);
         putimage(205,15+i*34,pic_buf,i);
    }

    getch();

    /* ---- Erase original and middle XOR face ---- */
    putimage(0,0,pic_buf,1);
    putimage(145,49,pic_buf,1);

    getch();

    /* ---------- Turn graphics off ------------- */
    closegraph();
}
```

This program will demonstrate a few of the graphic drawing functions along with the image capability. A face is drawn. The image is then picked up and placed back on the screen, using each of the five putimage() operators. Run the program. (Please overlook the choice of colors.) The face in the upper left corner of the screen is where the original was drawn. It was then picked up and saved in memory. The top row is just a straight replacement (code 0). The bottom is also a replacement, but with the inverse image (code 4).

Note that, in both situations, the background is gone and has no effect on the new image. The second row is the XOR (code 1). Here, the image looks normal on a plain background, but you can see that although the image is recognizable, it is affected by a different background. The third row is the OR (code 2). This row has similar characteristics to the XOR; it has no effect on the plain background, but it is affected by a new background. The fourth row is the AND (code 3). Here, against the original background, the image is invisible. Only when it appears against a different background do you get a recognizable image; however, even that image has been changed.

By examining the code, you will note two getch() function calls. When you are finished looking at this example, press any key once. The program will respond by placing an XOR image over both the original drawing and the center image in row two. Note that the image is completely removed in both cases, leaving the background intact. When you are ready to exit, press another key.

These C operations are quite similar to the BASIC ones you would use to accomplish the same tasks. You reserve the space by dimensioning an array and then using the GET and PUT instructions to remove and replace the image on the screen.

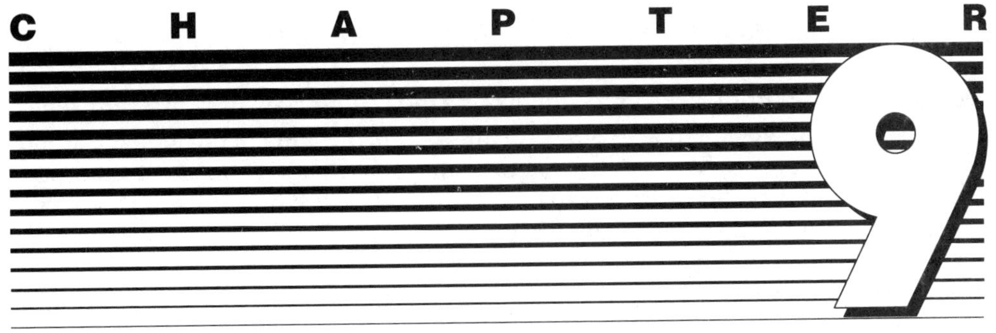

MASTERING THE SCREEN

The screen is an output device. Information is sent from the CPU to the outside world via the screen. The term **screen** as it is used here means all types of electronic video output devices. Numerous kinds of devices use different technologies to produce a video display on a screen, ranging from conventional television monitors to flat liquid crystal displays (LCDs). The most common device in use today is the cathode ray tube (CRT). For the purposes of this book, they will all be referred to as screens.

The screen is almost an ideal terminal output device because it is fast. Information on the screen is easily modified, partially or totally. The one big disadvantage of a screen is that it does not produce a permanent record; however, with a printer and the print screen (PrtSc key) capability of personal computers, the inconvenience has been reduced considerably—at least for text screens.

The screen is also a versatile device. It allows varying sizes of character output; it can produce colored results, as well as both text and graphic output. In addition to all of these features, the screen can be used as a programming tool. The screen has some features (which will be discussed later) that will aid programmers and allow them to produce results that would be quite difficult otherwise. Right now, the task is to understand how the screen functions.

UNDERSTANDING THE SCREEN

You already have some information about the screen. It can be switched between two different types of screens—text and graphics. You know quite a lot about the graphics screen. You are familiar with the different graphic modes, high and low resolution. You know about the different possible graphic colors. You also know that there is a screen buffer that keeps track of the color of each pixel on the screen. It may or may not surprise you to learn that the text screen is also quite versatile and has similar features. It is capable of a variety of modes and of using colors. The text screen also has a screen buffer that keeps track of each character on the screen along with some other factors that relate to the character.

Instead of being divided into pixels, the text screen is divided into columns and rows of characters. There are 25 rows or lines on a text screen, and the text screen can be switched between 40 and 80 columns (or characters) per line. Each character position can be addressed with an X and a Y coordinate. The X represents the horizontal or column position, and the Y represents the row or the line of text. Unlike the graphics screen, the upper left corner of the text screen is designated as (1,1). The lower right corner of the text screen will be either (80,25) or (40,25), depending on which text mode is active. Using coordinates, you can address any character position on the text screen in a way similar to that used to address any pixel on a graphics screen.

Each character is made up of high-resolution pixels. When the screen has 80 characters per line, a character is built from an 8-by-8 array of pixels. When the screen has 40 characters per line, a 16-by-8 array of pixels is used. The characters are larger in that they are twice as wide, but they are the same height as the 80-column characters.

Screen Modes

Both types of screens, text and graphics, have different modes. In the graphics screen, the two modes are high resolution and low resolution. In the text screen, you have different modes for color and for black and white. You also have a mode change for the number of character columns on the screen.

There is a library function that will allow you to change the mode of a text screen. The general form of this function is as follows:

```
textmode(m);
```

where *m* is the mode code. Following is a list of possible text modes:

Text Mode Codes:

Codes	Description
-1	reuse the last used text mode
0	40 columns wide—black and white
1	40 columns wide—color
2	80 columns wide—black and white
3	80 columns wide—color
7	80 columns wide—monochrome

When you change the mode of a text screen, the contents of the screen are removed. The screen is cleared in the same way that it is cleared when you switch from a text screen to a graphics screen. If you set the screen mode to code 3, the total screen is governed by those conditions—80 characters per line and in color. There are other conditions that relate to each character position, but the mode applies to the total screen.

Text Screen Attributes

Each character coordinate position on a text screen can have the following conditions set uniquely for that spot on the screen:

- the ASCII code for the character in that position
- foreground color (color of the character)
- background color
- character blinking or not blinking

This information is stored in memory in the text screen buffer. In addition to the ASCII code for the character being stored, the other information is packed together and is also placed in the screen buffer. This additional information that applies to each character is called the **position attribute**. There is a function that will let you set this attribute, and its general form is as follows:

```
textattr( a );
```

where *a* is the full attribute. Executing this function will not affect any characters or positions already on the screen. Nor will it affect characters subsequently placed on the screen with the conventional printf() function. The printf() function does not change the attribute. It is a general-purpose function that can be used for other types of output devices that do not have this attribute. Only those characters placed on screen by a direct console output function will have this attribute. (The **console** is the master terminal of the computer. For the PC, the console is the keyboard and screen.) The direct console output function that is comparable to the printf() function is the cprintf() function; therefore, after setting the attribute, you must place the text on the screen, using cprintf() to set the attribute for those screen positions.

Incidentally, once the attribute has been especially set for a given position on the screen, printing over that position again with the printf() function will only change the characters; the attribute will remain as it is. For example, if you have a blinking field on the screen, printing over it with printf() will not affect the blinking; the field will continue to blink with the new text. To remove the blinking field, you must change the attribute with the textattr() function and print with the cprintf() function on each position in the field.

The full attribute you use in the textattr() function must be an integer, either decimal or hex. It must be an integer that will set the bits that will give you the desired color codes and indicate whether the character is blinking or not. The ASCII code for the character is an eight-bit code that can be stored in one byte. The attribute can also be stored in eight bits. It is packed into those eight bits as follows:

Attribute Bit Positions

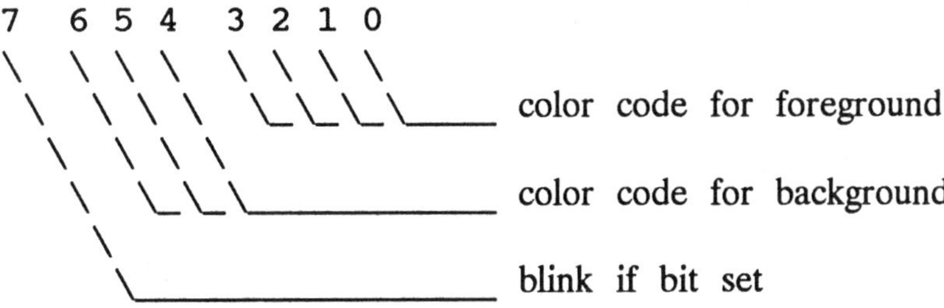

You can see from this diagram that the foreground has four binary bits in which to store a color code (the right-most four bits), which means there are 16 different colors. Remember that there were 16 different background colors in a graphics screen. Here, in a text screen, there are the same 16 possible colors. In this case, though, they are for the foreground. However, unlike the graphics screen, these 16 different colors can be on the text screen at the same time. They are the same color codes as before. The background in the text screen can have only eight different colors—bits 4, 5, and 6. These bits will hold the color codes 0 through 7. Finally, the left-most bit in the attribute indicates whether the character is to blink or not.

The following table indicates what colors are possible for both the foreground and background. It also shows the color code as a hex positional value so that you can just add or combine them to create the desired attribute.

Text Screen Attributes
(codes in relative positional hex value):

Color	Background Color Code Blinking Off	Background Color Code Blinking On	Foreground Color Code
black	00	80	0
blue	10	90	1
green	20	A0	2
cyan	30	B0	3
red	40	C0	4
magenta	50	D0	5
brown	60	E0	6
lightgray	70	F0	7
darkgray			8
lightblue			9
lightgreen			A
lightcyan			B
lightred			C
lightmagenta			D
yellow			E
white			F

Just add the foreground color code you want to the appropriate background code to compute the number of the attribute in hex. If you wanted to have a green background with a yellow foreground, you would take the 20 from the background column and the E from the foreground column and add them for a result of 2E. This would be the hex number of your attribute and would be used in the textattr() function as follows:

```
textattr( 0x2E );
```

The **0x** prefix tells the C compiler that this is a hex value. If you want a character to stand out by making it blink while keeping the same background and foreground colors, you would go back to the table and get the codes A0 and E. Combining these codes and using the result in the function would produce the following:

```
textattr( 0xAE );
```

This would make a yellow character blink on a green background. Note that it is the foreground that blinks, but it is the background code that changes when setting the blink bit in the attribute.

Once the attribute has been set, it applies to all characters that are placed on the screen by using the cprintf() function from that point on. Each character placed on the screen in this way will have that attribute saved with it in the screen buffer; however, the attribute can be reset at any time. This means you could set it once and forget it, or you could reset it for each character placed on the screen.

The following sample program shows a text screen with all the different attributes:

```
/* --------------------- PROG-23.C -------------------- */
/* ----------- Show text screen attributes ------------ */

#include <conio.h>
#include <stdlib.h>

void main()
{
     int s, t;

     /* -- Show sequence of all screen attributes -- */
     for (t=0; t<256; t++){
          textattr(t);
          cprintf("O");
     }
     cprintf("\n");

     /* -- Randomly display all screen attributes -- */
     for (t=1; t<20;t++){
          for (s=1; s<80;s++){
               textattr(random(256)+1);
               cprintf("*");
          }
          cprintf("\n");
          }
}
```

The first loop in the program displays the letter **O** to show all the 256 different attributes in sequence. The second loop displays the * character with a random attribute for the remainder of the screen to demonstrate the uniqueness of the attribute for each character position on the screen.

Note the use of the cprintf() function. (You might also note the use of the random() function. It performs the modulo operation on the rand() function for you, saving you that one step.)

With statements such as WIDTH, COLOR, and SCREEN, BASIC has screen capabilities similar to those of C. This is understandable because both Turbo C and BASIC work with the INTEL-8086 family of chips. They take advantage of fundamental hardware design. The position attributes look the same in BASIC and C, so many of the topics covered in this chapter and the other chapters dealing with the peripherals are independent of the programming language and will be similar in most languages using this same hardware.

Text Windows

Perhaps one of the most popular techniques in producing marketable software today is the use of **windows**. When a user wants to jump momentarily from one task to another, a small window will pop up on the existing screen. Then, when the task has been completed, this little window disappears and the original screen is left intact. It is as if you were working at a desk with paper and pencil. You momentarily place a note pad on top of the page you are working on. When finished, you remove the pad, and the original page remains intact. A utility such as Turbo C's TC Integrated Environment is a prime example of how windows are used.

Many of the new programming instructions that have been added to languages are there to help implement window software. Both BASIC and C now have a window instruction or function. Although BASIC's WINDOW instruction is for a graphics screen and the C window() function is for a text screen, they are similar in nature. Consider the C **window()** function. Its general form is as follows:

```
window( x1, y1, x2, y2 );
```

In this function, *x1* and *y1* are the position coordinates on the total physical screen. They represent the upper left corner of the chosen window. The second set of coordinates, *x2* and *y2*, represents the lower right corner of the window. This new active window, regardless of where it is on the actual physical screen, will have a new set of relative coordinates. The upper left corner of the active window will now be indicated by the coordinates (1,1). The lower right corner will have coordinates that are limited by the size of the active window.

After this function has been called, and until it is changed again with another call to the window() function, this area becomes the total active screen or window. All the rest of the full screen is inactive. There is no apparent change in the screen to indicate this has happened. The user may notice the cursor move, but that is no real indication as to the magnitude of this change in the usable part of the screen. For this reason, you need to plan how you will let the user know where the active part of the screen actually is. This is often done by setting the background color attribute to something other than the existing background color and then clearing the active window, as in the following example:

```
textattr(0x30);
clrscr();
```

This is the general form of the **clrscr()** function, which will clear the active window. It will set all attributes to the current background color and all character codes to spaces. This gives the appearance of putting a blank notepad on top of the existing text.

The problem that must now be resolved is getting the original text screen back when you remove the notepad. Somehow, the original text must be put back onto the area that was cleared for the window when the active window is reset to the total screen. Again, the library of functions has a solution. The first step is to make a copy of the original area of the screen. This copy must be more than just the text that appears there. It must also include the colors and the blinking status of each character and its relative position on this portion of the total screen. That means the function must copy and save both the characters and their attributes for the total area that is to hold the window, and it must save this information in such a way that it can restore it to the original position in that area of the screen. The general form of the function that will perform these tasks is as follows:

```
gettext( x1, y1, x2, y2, *b);
```

The arguments *x1* and *y1* represent the physical screen coordinates of the upper left corner of the area involved. Arguments *x2* and *y2* are the coordinates for the lower right corner. The currently active window has no effect on these coordinates because they relate to the physical screen. The last argument (**b*) is the starting address of a string array in which both the text and attributes are to be stored. (Remember that the name of a string array is a pointer to the array, so when using an array name, no * is necessary in the argument for the gettext() function.) You must declare this array or text buffer of sufficient size to hold both the characters and the attributes. Following is an example for a 20-by-10 window:

```
char textbuf[ 20 * 10 * 2 ];
```

Because the character takes one byte and the attribute takes a second byte, the array is multiplied by two to get a buffer of sufficient size.

After the text and attributes have been saved, you can clear the window and eventually use it. When finished with the window, you need a way to get the text and attributes back in that portion of the screen. This is accomplished with the **puttext()** function, which has the following general form:

```
puttext( x1, y1, x2, y2, *b);
```

The arguments here are the same as for the gettext() function. The coordinates relate to the full physical screen, not to any currently active window.

To effectively use an active window and some of the other functions this book will cover, you need a way to move the cursor around under program control without printing anything. This is accomplished with yet another C library function, which has the following general form:

```
gotoxy( x, y);
```

The argument *x* is the character column position, and *y* is the row position you want to go to in the active text window. If your code has not changed the active window, the active window is the total screen by default. When control is returned from this function, the cursor will be located at position (*x*,*y*). If you choose to print at that time, the first character printed will be at location (*x*,*y*). Remember that the upper left corner of any active window, or the full screen if it is active, is position (1,1).

The following sample program demonstrates all of the new functions that have been discussed:

```
/* ------------------ PROG-24.C --------------------- */
/* ---- Demonstrate placing and removing windows ------ */

#include <stdio.h>
#include <conio.h>

void main()
{
     /* -- Declare buffers for text under windows -- */
     char textbuf1[41*5*2], textbuf2[31*16*2];
     int i, c;

     /* ------- Fill main screen with text ------- */
     clrscr();
     for(i=1; i<60; i++){
          printf("This is the main screen text.  ");
     }
     getch();

     /* -------- Overlay first window ------------ */
     gettext(20,10,60,14,textbuf1);      /* save text */
     window(20,10,60,14);            /* window active */
     textattr(0xB0);                /* set attribute */
     clrscr();                       /* clear window */
     gotoxy(10,3);                    /* move cursor */
     cprintf("This is the first window.");
     getch();                       /* wait for user */
```

continued...

...from previous page

```
    /* --------- Overlay second window ------------ */
    gettext(10,5,40,20,textbuf2);       /* save text */
    window(10,5,40,20);         /* (make a shadow for */
    textattr(0x07);             /*     second window) */
    clrscr();
    window(10,5,39,19);     /* second window active */
    textattr(0x27);           /* set new attribute */
    clrscr();                         /* clear window */
    gotoxy(1,1);                       /* move cursor */
    for(i=1; i<17; i++){
         cprintf("THIS IS THE SECOND WINDOW.  ");
    }                       /* fill window with text */
    getch();                                  /* wait */

    /* ---------- Remove second window ------------ */
    puttext(10,5,40,20,textbuf2);  /* put text back */
    window(20,10,60,14);      /* first window active */
    textattr(0xB0);  /* set attribute, first window */
    getch();                                  /* wait */

    /* ---------- Remove first window ------------- */
    puttext(20,10,60,14,textbuf1); /* put text back */
    window(1,1,319,199);       /* full screen active */
    textattr(0x07);     /* set to default attribute */
}
```

Examine this program carefully. Note that the text buffers are doubled in size to hold the attributes as well as the characters. You will see the steps necessary to create a window. First, save the existing text. Then, create the active window. Set a new attribute and clear the active window. Move the cursor to the position you want in the window, using the relative text positions of the active window. Finally, use the window. When setting the second window, you will see the attribute and window set twice. This is another trick that will cause the window to stand out from the background. A shadow is created at the bottom and side of the intended window. This shadow can be set to any color you choose by setting the attribute and clearing a window that is slightly larger than the intended one. To restore the screen properly, you need to save the text of the total area (both the window and the shadow). This shadowing technique is much easier to use and more realistic if you are using a graphics screen but can be simulated on a text screen as well.

When you are finished with a window, you must perform three tasks to return to the original screen. First, you must restore the original text to the spot on the screen where it first existed. Second, you must reset to the proper attributes. Third, you must set the active window back to the appropriate area of the screen. Now, run this program, and you will see all of the effects discussed here. A getch() after each step causes the program to wait so you can examine the screen. Pressing any key causes the program to continue.

This program demonstrates the use of a window over the top of an existing screen; however, there may be times when you want to take the whole screen off momentarily and then put it back intact. An example would be if you wanted to switch to a graphics screen for a while and then return to the text screen. The gettext() and puttext() functions can save the total screen as well.

Scrolling

The screen has some special features you may take for granted, so perhaps a review is worthwhile. If you print a character in the 80th column of an 80-column mode screen, after printing, the cursor is repositioned to the first position of the next line. You will be given a carriage return and a line feed automatically. You are probably aware that if you print a carriage return (also called a new line character) on the 25th line, the total screen will scroll up one line. The top line is lost and a blank line appears on the bottom of the screen. The cursor is positioned on the first column of the new blank 25th line.

In fact, if you print a character in the 80th column of the 25th row, the screen will scroll up one line and the cursor will again be repositioned in column 1 of the new blank 25th line. When the screen scrolls up, all the position attributes will scroll up with the text. A blinking field will scroll up and off the top of the screen. The new lines that are generated at the bottom of the screen all have new default attributes. Incidentally, this scrolling will also work when you print on a graphics screen. The graphics screen can be made to scroll up by these same operations. It is this built-in feature that allows some interesting screen control techniques.

With the scrolling technique, a large block of text is transformed from today's concept of individual pages in a book to the ancient concept of a continuous scroll. Text can be unrolled and read from the bottom of the screen in a continuous process. On a graphics screen, this scrolling can appear to be the result of a video pan from the top of an object to the bottom. If, as the screen scrolls up, you add a new "line" of graphics to the bottom of the screen, you see a continuous top-to-bottom panning. You have probably seen this concept used in video games in different ways.

Consider the text screen for a moment. Features mentioned here in relation to a text screen also work in a text window. When you reach the right edge of an active text window, there is an automatic carriage return and line feed generated. When you print in the lower right corner of the window, the window will scroll up, leaving a new bottom blank line. You can create this miniature scrolling in a window without affecting the surrounding screen at all. You must keep in mind, however, that if you don't want the screen or window to scroll, you cannot print a character in the lower right corner.

Using the **insline()** function on a text screen will enable you to scroll down or return to text that has scrolled off the top of the screen. This function has the following general form:

```
insline();
```

This function will insert a blank line of text at the current cursor position. All lines from the current cursor position down will scroll down, including the current line. The bottom line will scroll off the screen and be lost. All lines of text above the cursor will remain unchanged. The blank line created will be filled with a line of spaces. The attributes for all positions in this empty line of text will be set using the current active background color.

Scrolling only half the screen is actually quite valuable. This action generates the feature called a **split screen**. Suppose you want to compare two documents visually. There is no problem if you have a hard copy of at least one of the documents, but on a screen it is difficult to remember what is in one document while you display the contents of the other. By splitting the screen and, in a sense, making two screens, you can display parts of both documents simultaneously. Then, you can scroll each document separately on the same physical screen by scrolling either the top half or the bottom half.

If you place the cursor at the top of the screen and insert a new line there, you will cause the whole screen to scroll down. Immediately printing the text you want in that new blank line at the top of the page will complete the illusion of scrolling backward through that text. You must, of course, keep in memory the total text that is being read and be able to tell which line of text must be placed on the screen to complete the scroll. This is necessary when scrolling either up or down.

The insline() function will also work inside the active window. It will cause only the text in the window to scroll down, leaving the rest of the screen unchanged.

On a split text screen, it is also possible to scroll up only part of the screen in the same way that you were able to scroll down part of the screen by using the insline() function. The library function **delline()** will assist you in this task. It has the following general form:

```
delline();
```

When called, this function deletes the line of text that the cursor is on. All lines below the deleted one will scroll up to fill the gap. The line of text deleted is of course lost, and a blank line is left at the bottom of the screen. By deleting the top line, you create the same effect as you did by printing a carriage return at the bottom of the screen. The total screen will scroll up. This function, like its counterpart, works on the active window; the remainder of the screen remains unchanged. Examine the following program:

```
/* ------------------- PROG-25.C ---------------------- */
/* --------- Demonstrate scrolling up and down -------- */

#include <stdio.h>
#include <conio.h>

void main()
{
     char c;
     int i, j;

     /* -------------- Give instructions ----------- */
     clrscr();
     printf("Press 'U' to scroll up, ");
     printf("'D' to scroll down, and ");
     printf("anything else to quit.  \n");
     printf("FIRST, ANY KEY FOR SAMPLE SCROLLING.");
     getch();

     /* --------- Scroll screen up and down -------- */
     for(j=1; j<3; j++){
         clrscr();
         for(i=1; i<36; i++){
             gotoxy(1,25);
             printf("%d SCREEN IS SCROLLING UP.\n",i);
         }
         clrscr();
         for(i=1; i<36; i++){
             gotoxy(1,1);
             insline();
             printf("%d SCREEN IS SCROLLING DOWN.",i);
      }
  }
```

continued...

...from previous page

```
    /* ----------- Scroll on request ------------ */
    i = 25;
    while (i != 0) {
        i = i - 1;
        c = getch() | 0x20;
        gotoxy(1,1);
        switch(c) {
            case 'd':
                insline();
                printf("%d SCROLL SCREEN DOWN.",i);
                break;
            case 'u':
                delline();
                gotoxy(1,25);
                printf("%d SCROLL SCREEN UP.",i);
                break;
            default:
                i = 0;
        }
    }
    clrscr();
}
```

This program demonstrates scrolling. The two different approaches to scrolling—rapid and one line at a time—are used. First, a carriage return is printed on the 25th line. Second, the top line is first deleted, and then text without a carriage return is printed on the bottom line.

Graphic Viewports

Turbo C has similar window capabilities when you are using a graphics screen. The use of the getimage() and putimage() functions allows you to pick up any part or all of a graphics screen and put it back at will. They perform the same task as the gettext() and puttext() functions on a text screen except that they get and save the color for each pixel.

There is another function that will allow you to set a graphics window as active; however, when you work with Turbo C graphics, this active window is called a **viewport** instead of a window. The viewport is set to active by calling the **setviewport()** function, which has the following general form:

```
setviewport( x1, y1, x2, y2, i);
```

The arguments *x1*, *y1* and *x2*, *y2* are the absolute full screen graphic coordinates. They designate the upper left and lower right corners of the viewport. Once set to active, the viewport will have relative coordinates. The upper left corner of the viewport is addressed as (0,0). The lower right coordinates are set by the size of the viewport. Unlike the text window, the rest of a graphics screen is still active when you set a viewport to active. Points outside the port are addressable. Functions such as **setbkcolor()** affect the whole screen.

In the general form of the **setviewport()** function, *i* is a flag that will terminate all graphic lines at the boundaries of the viewport if *i* is nonzero. On the other hand, when *i* is a zero, any graphics will be allowed to complete even if they go outside the viewport boundaries. Actually, this function allows a viewport to be used for two different concepts. When the flag *i* is nonzero, the option is as a window. It is almost as if the viewport is a miniature graphics screen. When *i* is zero, the option is an entirely different concept. It allows you to shift the origin, or the point that has the coordinates (0,0), to different parts of the screen. In the second case, the full screen still remains active in that you can draw on it. By shifting the origin, you introduce negative coordinates. See Figure 9.1:

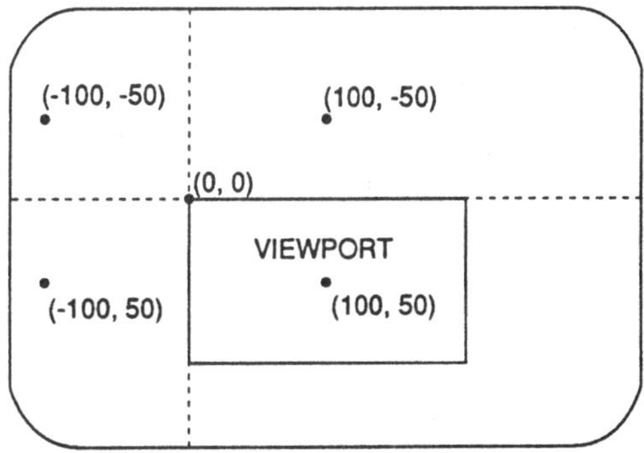

Figure 9.1 *Shifting the origin*

In Figure 9.1, the origin is the upper left corner of the viewport. Because this pixel has coordinates (0,0), any pixel to the left of it or above it must have at least one negative coordinate. Also, the negative coordinates are addressable and accessible on the screen, which means that you can draw curves from algebraic equations that produce both positive and negative results. (With the flag set to zero, you can still address the negative pixels, but only the parts of the figure that have positive coordinates will appear.) Another use of this second type of viewport is to redraw an image in another part of the screen without changing the pixel coordinates in your code. You just shift the relative positions of the screen so the same pixel coordinates will produce the image elsewhere on the screen.

Consider the following example of a program using viewports:

```
/* ------------------- PROG-26.C ---------------------- */
/* --------- Demonstrate graphic viewports ------------ */

#include<graphics.h>
#include<stdlib.h>

void main()
{
        int i, graph_driver=1, graph_mode=0;
        void *port1_buf, *port2_buf;
        unsigned int port1_size, port2_size;

        /* ---------- Initialize graphics ------------- */
        initgraph(&graph_driver, &graph_mode, "");
        port1_size = imagesize(100,50,200,120);
        port1_buf = malloc(port1_size);
        port2_size = imagesize(150,30,250,90);
        port2_buf = malloc(port2_size);
```

continued...

...from previous page

```
/* ------------- Fill main screen ------------- */
setcolor(3);
line(0,170,319,50);
line(200,0,150,199);
line(0,40,319,180);
for (i=1; i<15; i++){
     line(random(319)+1,0,random(319)+1,199);
     setfillstyle(random(12),random(3));
     floodfill(random(318)+1,random(198)+1,3);
     floodfill(random(318)+1,random(198)+1,3);
}
getch();

/* ------- Make and fill first view ----------- */
getimage(100,50,200,120,port1_buf);
setviewport(100,50,200,120,1);
clearviewport();
for (i=2; i<80; i=i+5){
     circle(15,15,i);
}
getch();

/* ------- Make and fill second viewport ------ */
setviewport(0,0,319,199,1);
getimage(150,30,250,90,port2_buf);
rectangle(150,30,250,90);
setviewport(151,31,249,89,1);
clearviewport();
for (i=3; i<50; i=i+6){
     circle(80,20,i);
}
getch();
```

continued...

...from previous page

```
    /* --- Return to first viewport - color ring -- */
    putimage(-1,-1,port2_buf,0);
    setviewport(100,50,200,120,1);
    floodfill(17,52,3);
    getch();

    /* --------- Return to full screen ----------- */
    setviewport(0,0,319,199,1);
    putimage(100,50,port1_buf,0);
    getch();

    /* ---------- Turn graphics off ------------- */
    closegraph();
}
```

Examine the code step by step. Note how the buffers that will hold the original screen images are sized and declared differently from those on a text screen. You can remember how this is done from the chapter on graphics. Next, the full screen is filled with a random design, again using functions that were also covered before. Now, construct a viewport. First get and save the background image in the array you had declared earlier. Second, set the viewport active. Third, clear the viewport. If you want to cause the port to stand out by making it a different color, you can't do so by resetting the background color. Because the whole graphics screen is semiactive, resetting the background color will change the background for the total screen. You could call for floodfill(), which would flood the cleared viewport with any desired color and would stop at the boundaries of the viewport—that is, assuming you are using the appropriate flag setting (nonzero).

The next step in the sample program is drawing in the viewport area. Note how the circles stop at the boundaries of the viewport and don't continue into the remainder of the screen. You can see that the code creates a second viewport on top of the first. To do this, the program must set the whole screen active for a moment. First, the desired area is saved. Then, a border is drawn around the area. Finally, the viewport is cleared, and circles are drawn again. Note how the border helps the viewport stand out from the background. Again, the circles are terminated at the border.

The next-to-last block of code visually removes the second viewport from the screen by putting the background back into that area of the screen. Take a look at the coordinates in the putimage() call. The image is larger than the viewport because of the border, and negative coordinates are used to align it properly. Something else is revealed here. Although the putimage() function recognized the viewport coordinates, it did not limit the image to the border. It extended the image to the area outside the viewport. Now that the viewport is visually removed, the next step is to deactivate it by making the first viewport active again. This time, one of the rings is flood filled. This function does recognize the boundary of the viewport and stops as intended.

The last block of code returns to the full screen, removing the last traces of the viewports.

Menus and Screens

This book has been using the term **screen** to refer to the physical equipment. The term is also used in the computer industry to mean a **menu**. A menu gives the user numerous options to choose from or to fill in. In some cases, the user will enter a response, but there are times when the menu software will allow the user to move around the screen with a mouse, a joystick, or the cursor keys and make a selection by placing the cursor on the desired choice and then pressing some key or button. When this method is used, the program must be able to determine where the cursor happens to be at that moment in order to determine which option was chosen. As you might expect, there are functions that will give you this information. If you were in a text screen, you would use the following functions:

```
x = wherex();

y = wherey();
```

You can get the same information from a graphics screen by calling similar functions that return the coordinates of the current position:

```
x = getx();

y = gety();
```

BASIC can also perform these operations, using functions called CSRLIN and POS().

USING THE SCREEN AS A TOOL

The screen has some features and characteristics that allow it to be used for more than just displaying information or graphics. You can use the screen and/or its screen buffer as a temporary work space to create new images from ones that are on the screen. Before you do that, however, you must put the first image on the screen.

Producing Graphic Images

One technique for producing an original graphic image on the screen is to start with a piece of graph paper. The grid should contain four or five squares per inch. This graph paper will represent a magnified portion of the graphics screen. Each square on the paper will represent one pixel on the screen. Even though a pixel is not quite a square in shape, the distortion is generally not a problem because of the reduction in size that takes place. Number each square across the top. These squares represent the X coordinates. Down the left side, label the Y coordinates. For convenience, make the upper left corner (0,0).

Now, draw or trace the outline of the image you want on the graph paper. You may use a single color or multiple colors to make the outline. If you use colors, the colors should correspond to those you can produce on the screen. After you have finished the sketch, take the same colors you were using and fill in or shade each square on the graph paper that has a line going through it. The image may look rather crude, but remember that each square you shaded in will appear as a point on the screen. If there are areas you want to be one color, shade those squares in as well.

The next step is to write the program code that will transform the image you have on graph paper to the screen. You do this by getting the coordinates of each point and putting them in the appropriate function calls that will cause the desired pixels to display on the screen. You could get the coordinates and color of each pixel and then use the putpixel() function to put them all on the screen, but you would save time by recognizing that some of the pixels form a straight line. For these pixels, you could just get the beginning and end points and use the line drawing functions. Also, once you have an area completely surrounded with the same colored pixels, you could flood fill the area with a desired color. The code could be a series of calls to the line() function, or it could be a single call within a for loop, using coordinates that are stored in an array. Whatever way you write the code, get the image on the screen, and then let the screen help you modify the image.

Turning the Image

After you have an image you like, it may not be necessary to draw a completely new image just because you need a different view of it. The getimage() function will let you pick this image up and save or move it to some other place on the screen. It will look the same in this new position as it did originally. You also have a getpixel() function that will let you pick up each individual pixel and save or move it to some other place on the screen. Depending on how you put it on the screen in relation to the other pixels, it may or may not have the same appearance it started with. The getpixel() function has the following general form:

```
c = getpixel( x, y)
```

The variable *c* will contain the color code of the pixel located at the coordinates (*x,y*). Examine the following code:

```
for (x=0; x<4; x++) {
      for (y=0; y<3; y++) {
            c = getpixel(x,y);
            putpixel(100+x,100+y,c);
      }
}
```

This code will pick up pixels in a three-by-four array at the origin and move them toward the center of the screen. The new image will look exactly like the original. Each pixel in the array is picked up and placed back on the screen in the same position relative to the others. Although it may appear that only the foreground colors are involved, both foreground and background are picked up and moved.

Suppose you want to turn an image that is located in the upper left corner of the screen, and the image is facing left. You can use the screen as a tool or temporary buffer to make the image face to the right. Assume the following four points represent your image:

```
(p1)(p2)(p3)
        (p4)
```

If you could pick up the points one at a time and place them down on the screen in the following order, you would have turned the image to face the right:

```
(p1)        (p2)(p1)        (p3)(p2)(p1)    (p3)(p2)(p1)
                                            (p4)
```

All points are represented; only their relative placement with one another is changed. Examine the following code to see if it will accomplish the result you want.

```
for (x=0; x<4; x++) {
     for(y=0; y<3; y++) {
          c = getpixel(x,y);
          putpixel(100-x,100+y,c);
     }
}
```

Note that the only difference between this code and the one that exactly reproduces the image is in the last line. The putpixel() function has a minus sign instead of a plus sign. Each pixel is picked up one place to the right of the previous one. It is then placed back on the screen one place to the left of the previous point. This reverses the right-left direction of the image. Try reversing the up-down direction of the image. Did your method resemble the following?

```
putpixel(100+x,100-y,c);
```

You can turn the original image any direction you want by placing the points in proper relation to each other. After you have used the screen as a tool to create this new image, you can use getimage() to save it for later use.

Recoloring the Image

In the previous example, *c* is the color code of the pixel being moved. When *c* is a 0, you know it is the background color. If it is a 1, 2, or 3, you know it is a foreground color. Suppose you want to change the color of the image but not alter the shape. What would the following line of code do?

```
if (c==3) putpixel(100+x, 100+y, 2);
```

As long as the background code 0 and the color code 3 were the only ones involved, this one line would reproduce the image in a new color. If you had all four colors involved and wanted to change them all, four such lines would allow you to test for each color picked up and then change a pixel to the color you want.

There is still another way you could change the colors of an image. If you give a color code that is greater than 3, the C compiler will do a modulo operation on the color code to reduce it to an acceptable color code. As an example, the following line of code will change all colors, including the background:

```
putpixel(100+x, 100+y, c+1);
```

If a 4 is generated as a color code, it will be converted to a 0 when the pixel is drawn on the screen.

Changing the Image Size

You can also modify the size of an image. Obviously, some detail is lost when you reduce an image, and when you directly enlarge an image from a smaller image, you will not have any more detail than was originally there; it will just appear larger and coarser.

The following line of code will reduce the width of an image by half:

```
putpixel(100+x/2, 100+y, c);
```

Only integer values can be plotted on the screen, and the previous line of code will generate half as many horizontal points as were in the original image. Try doubling the horizontal width of an image. If your attempt resembles the following line of code,

```
putpixel(100+x*2, 100+y, c);
```

you are partially correct. This code will produce an image that is twice as wide as the original, but every other point will be left out. This result may not be bad. In fact, the resulting image may appear smoother than if you had filled in each point, but to get an image that is filled in, you would need to use lines similar to the following:

```
putpixel(100+x*2, 100+y, c);
putpixel(100+x*2+1, 100+y, c);
```

No doubt you understand how to make the image both wider and taller, so try the following code:

```
/* ------------------- PROG-27.C --------------------- */
/* ---- Using the screen as a tool to modify image ---- */

#include<graphics.h>

void hand();

void main()
{
     int graph_driver=1, graph_mode=0;
     int c, x, y;

     /* ---------- Initialize graphics ------------- */
     initgraph(&graph_driver, &graph_mode, "");

     /* ---- Display image in upper left corner ---- */
     clearviewport();
     hand();
     getch();

     /* --- Pick up each pixel in a 38 X 26 array -- */
     for(x=2; x<41; x++){
        for(y=4; y<31; y++){
               c = getpixel(x,y);

               /* ------ Reproduce image as is ------- */
               putpixel(140+x,56+y,c);
               /* ---------- Point it left ----------- */
               putpixel(136-x,56+y,c);
               /* --- Make reflection point right ---- */
               putpixel(140+x,122-y,c);
               /* --- Make reflection point left ----- */
               putpixel(136-x,122-y,c);


               /* ------- Point reflection down ------ */
               putpixel(139+y,120+x,c);
               /* ------------- Point down ---------- */
               putpixel(137-y,120+x,c);
               /* -------------- Point up ----------- */
               putpixel(139+y,58-x,c);
               /* ------- Point reflection up -------- */
               putpixel(137-y,58-x,c);
```

continued...

...from previous page

```
                /* ---- Point diagonally down right --- */
                putpixel(180+x,100+x+y,c);
                /* ---- Point diagonally down left ---- */
                putpixel(96-x,100+x+y,c);
                /* ----- Point diagonally up left ----- */
                putpixel(96-x,30-x/3+y,c);
                /* ----- Point diagonally up right ---- */
                putpixel(180+x,30-x/2+y,c);
        }
    }
    getch();

    /* --- Pick up each pixel in a 38 X 26 array -- */
    for(x=2; x<41; x++){
         for(y=4; y<31; y++){
              c = getpixel(x,y);

              /* ------ Change colors of image ------ */
              if(c==1) putpixel(250+x,y,3);
              if(c==1) putpixel(250+x,32+y,2);
              /* --- Change background colors also -- */
              putpixel(250+x,64+y,c+1);
              putpixel(250+x,96+y,c+2);
              putpixel(250+x,128+y,c+3);
         }
    }
    getch();

    /* --- Pick up each pixel in a 40 X 26 array -- */
    for(x=2; x<43; x++){
        for(y=4; y<31; y++){
              c = getpixel(x,y);
```

continued...

...from previous page

```
                /* ------ Change size of images ------- */
                if(c==1) putpixel(10+x/4,32+y/4,1);
                /* ------ Make image 1/3 its size ----- */
                if(c==1) putpixel(10+x/3,42+y/3,c);
                /* ------ Make image half its size ---- */
                if(c==1) putpixel(10+x/2,56+y/2,c);
                /* ----------- Regular size ----------- */
                if(c==1) putpixel(10+x,76+y,c);
                /* ----- Make image twice as big ------ */
                putpixel(10+x*2,110+y*2,c);
                putpixel(10+x*2,110+y*2+1,c);
                putpixel(10+x*2+1,110+y*2,c);
                putpixel(10+x*2+1,110+y*2+1,c);
            }
        }
        getch();

        /* ----------- Turn graphics off ------------- */
        closegraph();
}
void hand()
{
        /* ------------ Draw pointing hand ----------- */
        setcolor(1);            setfillstyle(1,1);
        line(26,21,27,20);      line(24,22,25,21);
        line(22,21,23,22);      line(26,17,27,17);
        line(24,18,25,18);      line(23,19,23,19);
        line(21,20,22,20);      line(19,22,19,27);
        line(20,24,28,24);      line(29,23,30,22);
        putpixel(19,24,0);
        line(30,19,30,21);      line(27,26,28,25);
        line(20,27,26,27);      line(19,29,21,29);
        line(12,30,18,30);      line(6,28,10,28);
        line(2,29,5,29);        line(2,19,2,28);
        line(7,16,9,14);        line(17,7,18,6);
        line(2,18,4,18);        line(5,17,6,17);
        line(9,13,12,10);       line(13,10,16,7);
        line(18,4,18,5);        line(18,4,19,4);
        line(21,6,21,7);        line(21,8,19,10);
```

continued...

...from previous page

```
        line(18,11,18,12);  line(17,13,20,13);
        line(17,14,17,15);  line(21,12,23,12);
        line(24,11,39,11);  line(40,12,40,14);
        line(29,15,39,15);  line(31,18,31,17);
        line(28,20,29,20);  putpixel(20,5,1);
        putpixel(30,16,1);  putpixel(20,21,1);
        putpixel(22,28,1);  putpixel(11,29,1);
        putpixel(13,21,1);  putpixel(15,20,1);
        putpixel(17,17,1);
        return;
}
```

This program will place a graphic image in the upper left corner of the screen. When you are ready to continue, press any key. The image will be lifted from the screen pixel by pixel, and each pixel will be used to simultaneously draw 12 different images. You will be able to see each of the new images take form. If you examine the hand() function, you can see how much code it took to produce the first image. Once that image is on the screen, it just takes the double for loop to pick up the pixel, and each of the new images is produced with one additional line of code.

Note that the image can be turned in almost any position you want without your having to redraw the image on graph paper. Compare each image with the line of code that produced it. When you are ready, press any key again. The original image will be reproduced in different colors. Make sure you understand the code that produces the color changes, and then press another key. This time, the image is reproduced in different sizes. When you are satisfied with how each is produced, press any key to end the program.

Any or all of these individual lines of code along with the for loops involved could be made into separate library functions that you could call to turn an image in a desired direction, change its color, or change its size.

Using the screen in this way as a tool is also valuable when working with text. Although it may be awkward to work with text on a graphics screen, the results are sometimes well worth the effort. Try the following code:

```
/* ------------------- PROG-28.C --------------------- */
/* ---- Using the screen as a tool to modify text ----- */

#include<graphics.h>

void main()
{
     int graph_driver=1, graph_mode=0;
     int c, x, y;

     /* ---------- Initialize graphics ------------- */
     initgraph(&graph_driver, &graph_mode, "");

     /* ---- Print a word in upper left corner ----- */
     clearviewport();
     printf("Graphics");
     getch();

     /* --- Pick up each pixel in a 64 X 8 array --- */
     for(x=0; x<65; x++){
          for(y=0; y<9; y++){
               c = getpixel(x,y);

               /* ------ Reproduce image as is ------- */
               putpixel(164+x,y,c);
               putpixel(250+x,y,c);
               putpixel(x,38+y,c);

               /* -------- Make mirror image --------- */
               putpixel(160-x,y,c);
               /* ------- Make reflected image ------- */
               putpixel(164+x,16-y,c);
               /* --- Make reflected mirror image ---- */
               putpixel(160-x,16-y,c);

               /* --- Make reflected vertical image -- */
               putpixel(152+y,20+x,c);
               /* -------- Make vertical image ------- */
               putpixel(172-y,20+x,c);
```

continued...

...from previous page

```
/* -------- Make diagonal image ------- */
putpixel(180+x,20+x+y,c);
/* ---- Make diagonal mirror image ---- */
putpixel(144-x,20+x+y,c);

/* ------ Change colors of image ------ */
if(c==3) putpixel(250+x,10+y,1);
if(c==3) putpixel(250+x,20+y,2);
/* --- Change background colors also -- */
putpixel(250+x,30+y,c+1);
putpixel(250+x,40+y,c+2);
putpixel(250+x,50+y,c+3);

/* -------- Make smaller image -------- */
if(x%2==1&&y%2==0)putpixel(x/2,11+y/2,c);
/* -------- Make half as wide --------- */
if(x % 2 == 1) putpixel(x/2,18+y,c);
/* -------- Make half as tall --------- */
if(y % 2 == 0) putpixel(x,30+y/2,c);

/* --------- Make tall image ---------- */
putpixel(x,50+y*2,c);
putpixel(x,50+y*2+1,c);

/* -------- Make taller image --------- */
putpixel(x,70+3*y,c);
putpixel(x,70+3*y+1,c);
putpixel(x,70+3*y+2,c);

/* --------- Make wide image ---------- */
putpixel(x*2,102+y,c);
putpixel(x*2+1,102+y,c);

/* ----- Make tall and wide image ----- */
putpixel(x*2,120+y*2,c);
putpixel(x*2,120+y*2+1,c);
putpixel(x*2+1,120+y*2,c);
putpixel(x*2+1,120+y*2+1,c);
```

continued...

...from previous page

```
                /* --- Make taller and wider image ---- */
                /* --- But, don't fill in all points -- */
                putpixel(x*3,140+y*3,c);

                /* ----- Make it big and colorful ----- */
                if(c==3) putpixel(x*5,167+y*4,2);
                if(c==3) putpixel(x*5+2,167+y*4+2,1);
            }
        }
        getch();

        /* ---------- Turn graphics off ------------- */
        closegraph();
}
```

Instead of an image of a hand, the word **Graphics** is placed in the upper left corner. Pressing a key will cause the word to be produced with a variety of changes. You will see that the direction, color, and size of the word can be changed in the same way that the image of the hand was changed earlier. You will find in two of the enlargements that all of the points are not printed, which creates a dotted image, but there is no doubt about what the word is.

Using this type of code, you could create functions for your personal library that would allow you to produce headings or special titles for a screen. Turbo C already has two functions to help you with this task: **settextstyle()** and **gettextsettings()**. You may not find it necessary to produce any of your own text functions when working with C; however, BASIC does not provide you with such functions. If you choose to work in BASIC, you can also accomplish the same tasks in a similar way:

```
1 '* --------------- PROG-29.BAS ----------------- *
2 '* -- Using screen as a tool to modify text ---- *
9 '* ---------- Initialize graphics -------------- *
10 KEY OFF
20 SCREEN 1,0
30 COLOR 0,0
99 '* --------- Print word in upper left --------- *
100 PRINT "Graphics";
199 '* -------- Pick up each pixel of word ------- *
200 FOR X = 0 TO 64
210    FOR Y = 0 TO 8
220       C = POINT(X,Y)
299       '* ------- Reproduce word as is -------- *
300       PSET(164+X,Y),C
310       PSET(250+X,Y),C
320       PSET(X,38+Y),C
329       '* ------- Make mirror image ----------- *
330       PSET(160-X,Y),C
339       '* ------- Make reflection ------------- *
340       PSET(164+X,16-Y),C
349       '* ------- Make mirror reflection ------ *
350       PSET(160-X,16-Y),C
359       '* ------- Make vertical image --------- *
360       PSET(172-Y,20+X),C
369       '* ----- Make vertical reflection ------ *
370       PSET(152+Y,20+X),C
379       '* -------- Make diagonal image -------- *
380       PSET(180+X,20+X+Y),C
389       '* ----- Make diagonal mirror image ---- *
390       PSET(144-X,20+X+Y),C
399       '* --------- Change colors ------------- *
400       IF C=3 THEN PSET(250+X,10+Y),1
410       IF C=3 THEN PSET(250+X,20+Y),2
419       '* --- Change background colors also --- *
420       PSET(250+X,30+Y),C+1
430       PSET(250+X,40+Y),C+3
439       '* ------ Make smaller image ----------- *
440       IF X MOD 2=1 AND Y MOD 2=0 THEN 442 ELSE 450
442       PSET(X/2,11+Y/2),C
449       '* ------ Make half as wide ------------ *
```

continued...

...from previous page

```
450         IF X MOD 2=1 THEN PSET(X/2,18+Y),C
459         '* ------ Make half as tall ------------ *
460         IF Y MOD 2=0 THEN PSET(X,30+Y/2),C
469         '* -------- Make tall image ------------ *
470         PSET(X,50+Y*2),C
472         PSET(X,50+Y*2+1),C
479         '* -------- Make taller image ---------- *
480         PSET(X,70+Y*3),C
482         PSET(X,70+Y*3+1),C
484         PSET(X,70+Y*3+2),C
489         '* ---------- Make wide image ---------- *
490         PSET(X*2,102+Y),C
492         PSET(X*2+1,102+Y),C
499         '* ----- Make tall and wide image ------ *
500         PSET(X*2,120+Y*2),C
502         PSET(X*2,120+Y*2+1),C
504         PSET(X*2+1,120+Y*2),C
506         PSET(X*2+1,120+Y*2+1),C
508         '* ---- Make taller and wider image ---- *
509         '* ---- But don't fill in all points --- *
510         PSET(X*3,140+Y*3),C
519         '* ------ Make it big and colorful ----- *
520         IF C=3 THEN PSET(X*5,167+Y*4),2
522         IF C=3 THEN PSET(X*5,167+Y*4+2),1
880     NEXT Y
890 NEXT X
900 IF INKEY$ ="" THEN 900
920 SCREEN 0
930 WIDTH 80
```

For a good example of the difference in speed between BASIC and C, run the compiled PROG-28.C and the BASIC version PROG-29.BAS. Observe the difference. You won't need a stop watch, but a calendar might help.

Kerning and Leading on the Screen

The terms **kerning** and **leading** come to us from the printing profession. When setting the type for printing on an old-style printing press, the printer would adjust the spacing between letters in a word (kerning) and the spacing between lines (leading) so that the text would look good on the page.

Most documents are left-aligned, meaning that each new line starts at the same column on the page. However, by kerning (adjusting the space between the characters in each word), you can make the document justified as well. Justified text is blocked without a ragged right edge. With computer screens and printers, justifying text is not easy to do. You will find that some programs make a halfhearted attempt at justifying text on a screen or printer by adding more spaces between words, as in the following example:

```
To   fill    the  line    it    starts   looking  like   this.
```

In these programs, nothing can be done to compact or expand the space between individual letters. Only the spaces between words can be expanded. With this approach, you determine the length of a line by counting the number of characters on the line.

A new concept has become popular with the advent of desktop publishing: **wysiwyg** (what you see is what you get). If you want to write a program that shows on the screen just what will appear on a printed page, you must change the way text is currently displayed on the screen. You will need three things: a special font, a new way of keeping track of the position on the screen, and a program to simulate the kerning done by typesetters.

First, the font must match that used on the printer. This type font will have to match not only the style but the width of each character. Unlike the letters you use when displaying a character on a screen, the width of a letter used by a typesetter varies. On the screen, all letters are the same; they are either 8 or 16 pixels wide, depending on the mode of the screen. The letter **w** is the same width as an **i**. Not so in typesetting. The **w** takes more space than the **i**.

Next, you need an algorithm to keep track of the spacing on a line of text. In typesetting, the letters used as well as the number of letters on the line determine the length of the line. You need to know the pixel width of each character, not just the number of characters, to know where you are on the line.

Finally, this algorithm would need to be incorporated in a program to simulate the kerning and leading techniques used in typesetting.

The following program demonstrates that simulation of both kerning and leading is possible on screens. When you run this program, you will see the word **information** displayed in the upper left corner of the screen. Repeated pressing of a key will cause that word to show the effects of both kerning and leading.

```
/* ------------------- PROG-30.C ---------------------- */
/* --------- Demonstrate kerning and leading ---------- */

#include<graphics.h>
#include<stdlib.h>

void main()
{
     int graph_driver=1, graph_mode=0;
     int c, x, y, j;
        void * i, *n, *f, *o, *r, *m, *a, *t;
     unsigned int sz;

     /* ---------- Initialize graphics ------------- */
     initgraph(&graph_driver, &graph_mode, "");
     sz = imagesize(0,0,7,7);
     i = malloc(sz);      n = malloc(sz);
     f = malloc(sz);      o = malloc(sz);
     r = malloc(sz);      m = malloc(sz);
     a = malloc(sz);      t = malloc(sz);

     /* ----------- Print normal text -------------- */
     clearviewport();
        printf("information  (Press any key.)");
```

continued...

...from previous page

```
    /* ----------- Build new type font ------------ */
    y=0;
    getimage(1,0,4,6,i);
    getimage(8,0,13,6,n);
    getimage(16,0,21,6,f);
    getimage(24,0,29,6,o);
    getimage(32,0,38,6,r);
    getimage(40,0,46,6,m);
    getimage(48,0,54,6,a);
    getimage(57,0,61,6,t);
    getch();

    /* ------ Show both kerning and leading ------- */
    for (j=0; j<6; j++){
         y = 8+j*(8+j);
         putimage(1,y,i,0);
         putimage(5+j,y,n,0);
         putimage(11+2*j,y,f,0);
         putimage(16+3*j,y,o,0);
         putimage(22+4*j,y,r,0);
         putimage(29+5*j,y,m,0);
         putimage(36+6*j,y,a,0);
         putimage(42+7*j,y,t,0);
         putimage(47+8*j,y,i,0);
         putimage(51+9*j,y,o,0);
         putimage(57+10*j,y,n,0);
         getch();
    }

    /* ----------- Turn graphics off -------------- */
    closegraph();
}
```

Creating Animation

The screen can also be used as a tool to create the illusion of movement. Once again, it is the screen, accompanied by the human eye and brain, that allows the illusion of movement to take place—just as the eye will take a group of dots and put them together to form a complete image and will mix colored dots to create a new color. The eye will also take a series of slightly different still images and send them to the brain in such a way that you see one image moving.

A child's pastime can demonstrate this. Take a pad of paper or the pages of a book. Draw a dot on the first page in the upper right corner about 1/2" down from the top and in from the edge. Go to the next page and draw a very small circle in the same position. Make it slightly larger than the dot. Go on to the next page and draw a slightly larger circle. Continue to do this for about fifty pages. Using your thumb, fan through the pages so that you can see your drawings. The dot will inflate like a balloon. You have created animation.

The same thing can be done on your computer screen. Many of the films you see today are created, at least in part, with the aid of a computer. Timing is the key to creating this illusion of movement. Today's modern films at normal speed will run at 16 to 24 frames per second (FPS). Silent films run at 16 FPS, and film with a sound track runs at 24 FPS. If pictures are taken of a moving object at 24 FPS (normal speed), your eyes see and transmit to the brain normal movement rather than still pictures.

When you vary the speed, you create different illusions. Slow motion is created by taking pictures at 48 FPS or faster and then displaying those pictures at 24 FPS. Movement that took 10 seconds to actually perform would take 20 seconds or more to view, making the action appear to slow down. You can also speed up actions by taking pictures at 6 FPS and then projecting them back at 24 FPS. If a car took 20 seconds to actually drive across a bridge, it would then appear to race across the bridge in only 5 seconds. The extreme of this speeding up action is time lapse. Time-lapse films are created by taking one picture of the same flower about every 6 hours for weeks. This must be done without moving the camera. You would then display those still pictures at a rate of 24 FPS. What the eyes see is a flower that magically blooms and dies in a matter of seconds.

The screen on your computer is fast enough for you to use it as a tool to create animation. You can display a series of individual still images in such a way that the eye will see a single image moving. You can create the film techniques mentioned in this chapter on your screen by using the concepts of timing just discussed. The first step is to draw or create a series of still images of your subject. Each image should be slightly different—as if you had stopped the subject a number of times during some action or movement. If you display these still images sequentially at the same place on the screen, you have created moving animation. You could use the expanding circle as an experiment. First, place a single dot on the screen, and erase it. Then, place a small circle on the screen, and erase it. Keep repeating with larger and larger circles. When you run your program, the dot will appear to grow to a large circle.

The next example program to be discussed produces slightly more involved animation. First, there are some functions for drawing the still images. These are functions that will be called by the main program to create the initial still images. There are six different stop-action views of a running horse and then one view of a small pine tree.

Each separate function that actually draws an image does so by using a series of pixel coordinates that are defined in an array (*p[ ]*) when the array is declared. These coordinates are used in the for loops to draw lines and individual pixels. You will notice that when horse() is called, it first puts a solid rectangle on the screen. The body of the horse is carved or sculptured from this block by drawing with the background color. This block becomes the body of the horse. Just this part of the whole horse is captured as *body* and is used in creating each new view of the horse. The remainder of the horse (legs, tail, and head) is created by drawing with the foreground color 1. After the image is drawn, it is captured with a getimage() function for later use. Note that all of the arrays that hold these images are declared extern and will be used in the main program. These functions will not run alone, but will require the globals declared in the main program:

```
/* -------------------- HORSE.C --------------------- */
/* ---------- Draw all views of horse and tree -------- */

#include<graphics.h>
#include<stdlib.h>

void horse6();    void horse5();    void horse4();
void horse3();    void horse2();    void horse1();
void tree();

void horse()
{
     extern void *h6,*h5,*h4,*h3,*h2,*h1,*t,*body;

     /* -------------- Set conditions -------------- */
     setcolor(1);        setfillstyle(1,1);

     /* -------- Call all drawing functions -------- */
     horse6();                       /* Go draw horse  */
     getimage(11,12,32,20,body);     /* Save body only */
     getimage(0,0,40,30,h6);         /* Save the horse */
     cleardevice();                  /* Clear screen   */

     putimage(11,12,body,0);     /* Put body on screen */
     horse5();                   /* Draw next horse    */
     getimage(0,0,40,30,h5);     /* ...                */
     cleardevice();

     putimage(11,12,body,0);
     horse4();
     getimage(0,0,40,30,h4);     cleardevice();

     putimage(11,12,body,0);
     horse3();
     getimage(0,0,40,30,h3);     cleardevice();

     putimage(11,12,body,0);
     horse2();
     getimage(0,0,40,30,h2);     cleardevice();
```

continued...

...from previous page

```
     putimage(11,12,body,0);
     horse1();
     getimage(0,0,40,30,h1);    cleardevice();

     tree();
     getimage(0,0,20,22,t);     cleardevice();

     return;
}

/* --------------- Draw horse number 6 ---------------- */
void horse6()
{
     int i;

     /* ---- Define points for lines and pixels ---- */
     int p[100]={19,12,27,12, 32,14,32,19, 31,16,31,17,
                 16,19,20,19, 15,20,22,20,
                 30,11,36,11, 31,10,35,10, 33,9,34,9,
                 33,12,37,12, 35,13,38,13, 33,21,37,25,
                 27,21,27,24, 28,21,28,22, 26,25,26,26,
                 8,21,13,21,  8,22,10,22,  7,23,9,23,
                 5,24,7,24,   3,14,7,14,   4,15,8,15,
                 37,14,       32,21,       38,25,
                 29,21,       25,27,       26,28,
                 25,28,       5,25,        9,14,
                 10,13  };


       /* ----- Start with solid block for body ------ */
       rectangle(11,12,32,20);
       floodfill(15,15,1);

       /* ------- Erase areas from body block -------- */
       setcolor(0);
       for (i=0; i<20; i=i+4){
               line(p[i],p[i+1],p[i+2],p[i+3]);
       }
       putpixel(11,12,0);
```

continued...

...from previous page

```
        /* -------------- Draw solid lines ------------ */
        setcolor(1);
        for (i=20; i<80; i=i+4){
                line(p[i],p[i+1],p[i+2],p[i+3]);
        }

        /* -------------- Draw pixels ----------------- */
        for (i=80; i<100; i=i+2){
                putpixel(p[i],p[i+1],1);
        }

        return;
}

/* --------------- Draw horse number 5 ---------------- */
void horse5()
{
        int i;
        int p[82]={27,21,27,22, 28,21,28,25, 29,25,29,28,
                   33,21,36,21, 33,20,34,20, 37,22,38,22,
                   39,23,40,23, 8,21,13,21,  12,22,8,27,
                   10,23,11,22, 4,23,6,23,   4,13,7,13,
                   5,14,9,14,   31,10,36,10, 29,11,39,11,
                   33,9,34,9,   39,12,30,12, 30,28,
                   32,19,       7,22,        10,13,
                   38,13,       33,13,       10,20   };

          for (i=0; i<68; i=i+4){
                line(p[i], p[i+1], p[i+2], p[i+3]);
          }

          for (i=68; i<82; i=i+2){
                putpixel(p[i],p[i+1],1);
          }

          return;
 }
```

continued...

...from previous page

```
/* --------------- Draw horse number 4 ---------------- */
void horse4()
{
        int i;
        int p[90]={30,10,36,10, 30,11,39,11, 30,12,39,12,
                   33,9,34,9,   32,19,33,19, 33,20,35,20,
                   36,21,38,23, 32,26,34,28, 32,25,29,22,
                   29,21,31,23, 9,27,9,24,   10,24,13,21,
                   10,23,12,21, 10,18,10,21, 5,23,7,21,
                   7,22,9,20,   2,24,4,24,   9,13,10,13,
                   4,14,9,14,   2,15,7,15,   38,13,
                   33,13,       30,21,       10,28,
                   9,21    };

        for (i=0; i<80; i=i+4){
              line(p[i],p[i+1],p[i+2],p[i+3]);
        }

        for (i=80; i<90; i=i+2){
              putpixel(p[i],p[i+1],1);
        }

        return;
}

/* --------------- Draw horse number 3 ---------------- */
void horse3()
{
        int i;
        int p[94]={28,11,37,11, 29,10,36,10, 30,9,35,9,
                   31,8,33,8,   19,12,20,12, 7,16,9,16,
                   4,17,8,17,   6,18,8,18,   13,21,11,23,
                   12,24,14,26, 13,22,16,19, 16,19,16,24,
                   17,19,17,24, 18,25,19,25, 20,26,21,26,
                   26,21,34,21, 34,22,32,24, 29,22,29,24,
                   25,24,27,26, 27,12,       36,12,
                   9,15,        3,16,        31,24,
                   22,27,       28,25,       15,26,
                   28,22    };
```

continued...

...from previous page

```
        for (i=0; i<76; i=i+4){
              line(p[i],p[i+1],p[i+2],p[i+3]);
        }

        for (i=76; i<94; i=i+2){
              putpixel(p[i],p[i+1],1);
        }

        setcolor(0);
        line(13,12,11,14);      line(12,12,11,13);
        line(11,19,12,20);      putpixel(11,20,0);
        putpixel(30,21,0);
        setcolor(1);

        return;
}

/* --------------- Draw horse number 2 ---------------- */
void horse2()
{
        int i;
        int p[100]={9,21,12,24,  10,21,13,24, 14,21,15,22,
                    16,19,16,20, 14,23,16,25, 14,24,16,21,
                    9,14,10,14,  6,15,9,15,   4,16,8,16,
                    21,26,23,26, 26,21,26,23, 25,23,25,24,
                    28,21,30,23, 29,21,31,24, 30,25,29,25,
                    27,24,28,25, 29,11,38,11, 30,10,36,10,
                    30,9,35,9,   31,8,33,8,   36,12,37,12,
                    11,21,       15,20,       17,25,
                    3,15,        20,25,       24,25,
                    27,21,       15,21    };

        for (i=0; i<84; i=i+4){
              line(p[i],p[i+1],p[i+2],p[i+3]);
        }

        for (i=84; i<100; i=i+2){
              putpixel(p[i],p[i+1],1);
        }
```

continued...

...from previous page

```
        setcolor(0);
        line(11,16,11,19);  line(30,20,32,20);
        line(31,18,31,19);  putpixel(12,24,0);
        putpixel(11,13,0);  putpixel(12,12,0);
        putpixel(12,18,0);  putpixel(32,14,0);
        setcolor(1);

        return;
}

/* -------------- Draw horse number 1 --------------- */
void horse1()
{
        int i;
        int p[102]={29,20,33,20, 30,19,33,19, 30,18,33,18,
                    11,17,11,18,
                    28,11,38,11, 29,10,38,10, 30,9,35,9,
                    31,8,33,8,   27,21,27,22, 26,21,26,25,
                    23,25,26,25, 25,26,24,27, 9,19,15,19,
                    9,20,15,20,  9,21,14,21,  11,22,15,26,
                    7,24,8,24,   9,20,9,24,   3,13,4,13,
                    9,13,10,13,  4,14,9,14,   5,15,7,15,
                    27,12,       22,24,       25,28,
                    12,22,       14,26,       6,25,
                    16,19  };

        setcolor(0);
        for (i=0; i<16; i=i+4){
             line(p[i],p[i+1],p[i+2],p[i+3]);
        }
        putpixel(32,14,0);  putpixel(17,18,0);

        setcolor(1);
        for (i=16; i<88; i=i+4){
             line(p[i],p[i+1],p[i+2],p[i+3]);
        }

        for (i=88; i<102; i=i+2){
             putpixel(p[i],p[i+1],1);
        }
```

continued...

...from previous page

```
        return;
}

/* ------------------ Draw the tree ------------------- */
void tree()
{
        int i;
        int p[112]={9,3,10,3,     7,4,11,4,     9,5,12,5,
                    9,6,11,6,     8,7,11,7,     6,8,10,8,
                    8,9,11,9,     9,10,12,10,   8,11,14,11,
                    7,12,12,12,   6,13,13,13,   8,14,14,14,
                    8,15,15,15,   6,13,13,13,   8,14,14,14,
                    7,15,15,15,   6,16,13,16,   5,17,15,17,
                    4,18,17,18,   3,19,4,19,    8,19,14,19,
                    9,20,10,20,   9,21,10,21,   2,20,
                    7,20,         15,20,        18,19,
                    5,14,         5,9,          6,5,
                    13,6,         10,2,         9,1  };

        for (i=0; i<92; i=i+4){
              line(p[i],p[i+1],p[i+2],p[i+3]);
        }

        for (i=92; i<112; i=i+2){
              putpixel(p[i],p[i+1],1);
        }

        putpixel(7,17,0);  putpixel(12,18,0);
        putpixel(9,12,0);  putpixel(10,15,0);

        return;
}
```

The following program calls the horse() function. It will use the images created by horse() to create the illusion of movement or animation.

```
/* ------------------ PROG-31.C --------------------- */
/* --------- Demonstrate graphic animation ------------ */

#include<graphics.h>
#include<stdlib.h>
#include<bios.h>

void horse();
void put_horse();
void erase_horse();
void animate_horse();
void move_trees();
void move_horse();
void move_horses();

void *t, *h1, *h2, *h3, *h4, *h5, *h6, *body;
int image_num, x, y, horse_flag;
int treex1, treey1, treex2, treey2;
int newx, newy, newx1, newy1, newx2, newy2;
int slow, stride, key;

void main()
{
     int graph_driver=1, graph_mode=0;
     unsigned int sz;

     /* ---------------- Initialize ---------------- */
     initgraph(&graph_driver, &graph_mode, "");
     sz = imagesize(0,0,40,30);
     h1 = malloc(sz);      h2 = malloc(sz);
     h3 = malloc(sz);      h4 = malloc(sz);
     h5 = malloc(sz);      h6 = malloc(sz);
     body = malloc(sz);    t = malloc(sz);
     image_num = 1;

     /* ------- Clear screen and draw images ------- */
     clearviewport();
     horse();
```

continued...

...from previous page

```
    /* --------- Show all images used ------------- */
    putimage(0,165,h1,1);    putimage(40,165,h6,1);
    putimage(80,165,h5,1);   putimage(120,165,h4,1);
    putimage(160,165,h3,1); putimage(200,165,h2,1);
    putimage(250,165,t,1);

    /* --------- Set and outline viewport --------- */
    rectangle(39,19,231,151);
    setviewport(40,20,230,150,0);
    printf("         Press any key.");

    /* --------------- Show animation ------------- */
    animate_horse();
    move_trees();
    move_horse();
    move_horses();

    /* ----------- Turn graphics off -------------- */
    closegraph();
}


/* ---- Animate horse with two images then with six --- */

void animate_horse()
{
    /* ---------------- Initialize ---------------- */
    stride=5;  key=0;  horse_flag=3;
    x=60;  y=60;
    clearviewport();

    /* --------------- Animate horse -------------- */
    while (key == 0){

         /* ----------- Display horse ---------- */
         put_horse();

         /* ----- Check for a pressed key ------ */
         if (bioskey(1) != 0) {
             key=bioskey(0);
```

continued...

...from previous page

```
                /* - Show all horses if first key - */
                if (horse_flag == 3) {
                        horse_flag=1;
                        key=0;
                }
            }

            /* -- Slow down - let user see image -- */
            for(slow = 1; slow<14000; slow++) { }

            /* ----------- Remove horse ----------- */
            erase_horse();
        }
}


/* ------ Move the background keep horse in place ----- */

void move_trees()
{
        /* ---------------- Initialize ---------------- */
        stride=5;  key=0;
        treex1=170;  treey1=random(100)+5;
        treex2=50;  treey2=random(100)+5;
        x=60;  y=60;
        clearviewport();

        /* ------- Animate horse and move trees ------- */
        while (key == 0){

            /* -------------- Put trees ----------- */
            putimage(treex1,treey1,t,1);
            putimage(treex2,treey2,t,1);

            /* ----------- Display horse ---------- */
            put_horse();
```

continued...

...from previous page

```
        /* ----- Check for a pressed key ------ */
        if (bioskey(1) != 0) {
            key=bioskey(0);
        }

        /* ---- Generate next tree position --- */
        newx1=treex1-stride; newy1=treey1;
        newx2=treex2-stride; newy2=treey2;

        /* -- If at end of screen start over -- */
        if (newx1 < 0){
            newx1=170;
            newy1=random(100)+5;
        }
        if (newx2 < 0){
            newx2=170;
            newy2=random(100)+5;
        }

        /* -- Slow down - let user see image -- */
        for(slow = 1; slow<5000; slow++) { }

        /* ------ Remove horse and trees ------ */
        erase_horse();
        putimage(treex1,treey1,t,1);
        putimage(treex2,treey2,t,1);

        /* ---- Set up new tree positions ----- */
        treex1=newx1;       treey1=newy1;
        treex2=newx2;       treey2=newy2;
    }
}
```

continued...

...from previous page

```
/* ------- Move the horse keep background still ------- */

void move_horse()
{
     stride=5;  key=0;
     x=0;  y=60;

     /* ------- Place permanent background --------- */
     putimage(170,24,t,1);
     putimage(20,106,t,1);
     putimage(140,90,t,1);
     putimage(70,5,t,1);
     putimage(45,10,t,1);

     /* ------- Move the horse across screen ------- */
     while (key == 0){
          put_horse();

          /* ------ Check for pressed key ------- */
          if (bioskey(1) != 0)  key=bioskey(0);

          /* ---------- Advance horse ----------- */
          newx=x+stride;
          if (newx > 150) { newx=0; }

          /* ----- Slow down so user can see ---- */
          for(slow=1; slow<6500; slow++) { }

          /* - Erase horse - get ready to move -- */
          erase_horse();
          x=newx;
     }
}
```

continued...

...from previous page

```
/* ---------- Move many horses across screen ---------- */

void move_horses()
{
     int i, ima[3]={1,2,4};
     int hx[3]={50,0,120};
     int hy[3]={60,70,20};
     int nx[3], ny[3];

     stride=5;  key=0;

     /* --------- Put horses on the screen --------- */
     for (i=0; i<3; i++) {
         x=hx[i];  y=hy[i];  image_num=ima[i];
         put_horse();
         ima[i]=image_num;
     }

     /* ------- Move the horses across screen ------ */
     while (key == 0){

            /* ------------ One at a time ------------- */
            for (i=0; i<3; i++) {

               /* ---------- Advance horse ----------- */
               nx[i]=hx[i]+stride;  ny[i]=hy[i];
               if (nx[i] > 150) {
                   nx[i]=0;
                   ny[i]=random(90)+10;
               }

               /* ----- Slow down so user can see ---- */
               for(slow=1; slow<1000; slow++) { }

               /* ------ Check for pressed key ------- */
               if (bioskey(1) != 0)  key=bioskey(0);

               /* ------------ Erase horse ----------- */
               x=hx[i];  y=hy[i];  image_num=ima[i];
               erase_horse();
```

continued...

...from previous page

```
                /* ----- Set up new x and y values ---- */
                hx[i]=nx[i];  hy[i]=ny[i];

                /* --------- Put horse back ----------- */
                x=hx[i];  y=hy[i];  image_num=ima[i];
                put_horse();
                ima[i]=image_num;
          }
      }
}


/* --- Advance image_number and put horse on screen --- */

void put_horse()
{
        image_num = image_num + horse_flag;
        if (image_num > 6) image_num = 1;

        switch (image_num) {
          case 1:
               putimage(x,y-3,h1,1);
               putpixel(-20,150,1);
               break;
          case 2:
               putimage(x,y-2,h2,1);
               putpixel(180,150,1);
               break;
          case 3:
               putimage(x,y-1,h3,1);
               putpixel(140,150,1);
               break;
          case 4:
               putimage(x,y,h4,1);
               putpixel(100,150,1);
               break;
          case 5:
               putimage(x,y-1,h5,1);
               putpixel(60,150,1);
               break;
```

continued...

...from previous page

```
            case 6:
                 putimage(x,y-2,h6,1);
                 putpixel(20,150,1);
                 break;
        }
}


/* ------------- Remove horse from screen ------------- */

void erase_horse()
{
        switch (image_num) {
          case 1:
               putimage(x,y-3,h1,1);
               putpixel(-20,150,0);
               break;
          case 2:
               putimage(x,y-2,h2,1);
               putpixel(180,150,0);
               break;
          case 3:
               putimage(x,y-1,h3,1);
               putpixel(140,150,0);
               break;
          case 4:
               putimage(x,y,h4,1);
               putpixel(100,150,0);
               break;
          case 5:
               putimage(x,y-1,h5,1);
               putpixel(60,150,0);
               break;
          case 6:
               putimage(x,y-2,h6,1);
               putpixel(20,150,0);
               break;
        }
}
```

When you run this program, you will first notice a flickering image in the upper left corner of the screen. This is where HORSE.C is creating the images. You can, of course, create these images where they will first be used and eliminate the flickering in the corner. Each of these images is then displayed at the bottom of your screen, so you can see in detail what they look like. Then, a viewport is created and outlined on the screen.

In the viewport, you can make the horse appear to run by placing one image of the horse on the screen and then erasing it. Putting a different image of the horse at the same place makes it appear as if the first image moved. If you look at the still images at the bottom of the screen, you will see two blinking pixels above two of the images. The animation of the horse in the viewport is created by using only the two still images that have the blinking pixels. The illusion of a running horse is there, but it could be better.

The more stop action images you use in the simulated movement, the more fluid and lifelike the action will appear. Press any key and you will cause the program to begin using all six of the still images. Note that the blinking pixel is momentarily above each still image as that image is used. Also, the movement in the viewport is less jerky and more closely imitates the movement of a horse. Because the six images represent a complete cycle of the stride of a running horse, they can be repeated or looped again and again. If you were to go to the trouble of creating even more stop action images, you could create animated motion that is as smooth and lifelike as you want.

Looking at the code, you will see that the image is first put on the screen with the function put_horse(). It is later removed in erase_horse() by XORing the same image directly over the first. Then, a new image is put down. The galloping motion of the horse is further simulated by having the image rise and fall slightly through the cycle of the stride. Notice that the *y* coordinate varies slightly from image to image in put_horse(). These elements give the illusion that the horse is in full gallop. You see a moving pliable image rather than six separate rigid figures.

While you are looking at these two functions, you might notice the putpixel() calls. These calls blink the pixels above the still image that is currently in the viewport. Look at the coordinates of the pixel in case 1. The *y* value is a negative 20 because a viewport is active, and the coordinates of the origin have shifted.

The illusion of movement can be further enhanced by considering the background. You might have the impression that this horse is running on a treadmill. The horse gets nowhere. This image can be eliminated by putting in some background for the horse to run through. Because the horse is not actually moving on the screen, it will be necessary to move the background to simulate the illusion of a horse moving through the environment. If you press a key, background will be inserted into this animation. The effect would then be similar to a camera panning or moving to follow the galloping horse. Look at the move_trees() function. If you go down to below the comment "Generate next tree position," you will see that the next position of each tree is generated by subtracting the variable *stride* from the current *y* coordinate. These positions are temporarily stored in the variables *newy1* and *newy2* because the old coordinates are still necessary to erase the last trees, and you want to leave these trees on the screen for just as long as possible. Changing the variable *stride* will speed up or slow down the movement of the trees and thus give the impression of the horse traveling faster or slower.

You can also simulate movement through an environment by reversing the process—leaving the background stationary and placing one image of the horse slightly to the right of the previous one. This way, the horse would literally move across the viewport. Press a key again to see this approach to movement. Now it is as if the camera were stationary and the horse were running across the field of view. Although this may be the most natural approach, the time the horse is actually on the screen is short. If this time is sufficient to create the desired impression, fine. If it is not, then perhaps the previous approach would be better for your needs. The current process of starting the horse over gives the impression of multiple horses following each other across the screen.

If you want multiple horses, the same six images can be used to create multiple horses on the screen at the same time. Press another key to observe this effect. By making sure the same image is not used for different horses at the same time, and randomly placing them on the screen, you can make it appear that there are many horses.

If the movement of the horses does not appear realistic on your computer, go to the following functions:

```
animate_horse(), move_trees(), move_horse(), move_horses()
```

Locate the following line of code in each function:

```
for (slow=1; slow<5000; slow++) { }
```

Modify the limit of the loop up or down to adjust to the speed of your computer. You can also add a do-nothing instruction in between the braces to slow the action down even more. Note that this slow operation takes place while the image is on the screen. You want to do as little as possible while the screen is blank or between images, because prolonged operations at this point will cause the image to blink.

Take some time to observe how each of the different approaches is created in the code. Try to modify the code to do other things. Do you remember how to reverse an image? How would you make the horse run from right to left across the screen? How would you make the horse run from right to left when you also have a horse running from left to right? How would you do it when the other horse is actually stationary on the screen and the background is moving from right to left?

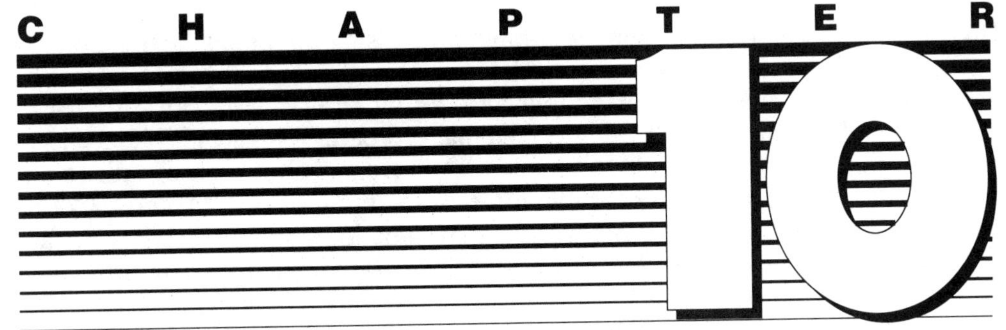

UNDERSTANDING STREAMS AND FILES

This chapter discusses something you have been using all along: **text streams**. You may not have realized it because C has been opening them automatically. A stream is the way that C handles input and output (I/O). You can think of a stream as an I/O buffer or device interface that C creates to make all I/O devices look the same to you (well, almost the same). Streams allow you to talk to all devices in the same way. They are an attempt to standardize I/O, and make it **device independent**. To your program, all streams look alike even though the devices they may be sending data to and receiving data from are different.

These different devices are referred to as **files**. C makes all I/O appear as if it were to and from a disk file. In a language such as BASIC, all I/O devices are handled differently because of their different characteristics. By using a C stream, you can generally handle all I/O devices or files in the same way. Most C I/O functions are designed to be used with streams. The functions cprintf() and cscanf() are examples of exceptions. They send data directly to and from the console without going through a stream. (The operator console is the primary I/O device for controlling the CPU. In the case of a PC, the console is your keyboard and screen.)

Each time one of your programs executes, C opens three text streams automatically. You pass data to a stream every time you use a printf() function. You also take data from a stream each time you use the scanf() function. The three streams that are automatically opened are as follows:

stdin	standard input
stdout	standard output
stderr	standard error

These streams direct data to and from the console. Do not try to open, close, or otherwise modify these streams yourself. If you want to use them to send data to a different device, you can, because MS-DOS allows redirection. You can use DOS to redirect your input and output from these streams to other devices without changing the streams, or you can create your own streams.

CREATING A STREAM

There are certain steps you must take to create an I/O data stream in C:

- Include stdio.h in your code.
- Declare a stream file pointer.
- Open the stream.

The first step in creating a stream is to include the stdio.h header file in your program. Part of the purpose of this header file is to define some of the constants and macros you will be using. Following is a partial list of them:

PRN	system line printer
LPT1	alternate line printer
LPT2	second alternate line printer
FILE	data type used to declare the pointer to the file
NULL	binary zero
EOF	end-of-file mark
SEEK_SET	beginning-of-file position (code 0)
SEEK_CUR	current position in file (code 1)
SEEK_END	end-of-file position (code 2)

The next step is to declare a stream file pointer, which is a FILE address pointer (defined in stdio.h). It is used to point to information about the stream and file. Following is a sample declaration for a stream file pointer:

```
FILE *stream_file_pointer_name;
```

The name assigned to the pointer is up to you. This pointer points to information about the stream and stream file. The information pointed to is as follows:

- **The device name or filename**. The device name is the name of the physical device. Where the device is the disk, the device name is the actual disk filename.

- **The device or file status**. This status is the mode the stream file was opened with. For example, the mode might have been "r"—open for reading from a text file (see next page).

- **The stream position pointer**. The position pointer points to some character or byte within the stream of data. This is perhaps most meaningful when you think of an actual disk file. Think of a position pointer as pointing to some byte in the disk file.

In addition to a pointer name pointing to the above information, the stream file pointer name is used to identify the particular stream you want to use.

The last step in creating a stream is to open it, using the **fopen()** function.

fopen()

When you have declared the stream file pointer, you use its name to open the stream. That step is accomplished with the **fopen()** function, which has the following general form:

```
stream_file_pointer_name = fopen("device","mode");
```

In this function, "device" is a string that is a device name or a disk filename, and "mode" is a string that is a code designating the desired status in which you want the device or disk file. Following are the mode options:

Stream Modes:

Mode	File Status
"r"	open existing text file for reading
"w"	create new text file for writing *
"a"	open or create text file for appending to end
"rt"	open existing text file for reading
"wt"	create new text file for writing *
"at"	open or create text file for appending to end
"r+t"	open existing text file for update **
"w+t"	create new text file for update * **
"a+t"	open or create text file for update at end **
"rb"	open existing binary file for reading
"wb"	create new binary file for writing *
"ab"	open or create binary file for appending to end
"r+b"	open existing binary file for update **
"w+b"	create new binary file for update * **
"a+b"	open or create binary file for update at end **

*	Erases any existing file with the same name.
**	Both read and write are possible if separated by an fseek() or a rewind() (explained later).

As you can see, there are two types of streams: text and binary. A **text stream** is a sequence of characters terminated by a new line character or a carriage return/line feed. It may or may not contain the same number of characters that were sent by the peripheral device, depending on possible substitution of ending characters made by the computer. The **binary stream** is a sequence of bytes that has the same number of bytes as the peripheral device. No substitutions are made by the computer.

Following is an example of how you would open a stream to the line printer:

```
#include<stdio.h>

void main()
{
     FILE *sfp;
     sfp = fopen("PRN", "w");
     ...
```

The mode "w" designates the stream as a text stream for writing. The "PRN" designates the file to be the line printer (defined in stdio.h). The stream file pointer name is *sfp* in this case.

After you have opened this stream, you are free to use it as an output interface to the printer. You can send it the data you want printed on the printer. The stream does function as a buffer. It will not necessarily print each character as you send it, but it will send the data to the printer in blocks. When you are finished sending data, the stream may still contain the last of the data. It is sometimes necessary to force the stream to send this remaining data to the printer, which is referred to as **flushing the stream**. One way of flushing the stream is to send a new line character to the stream.

DATA TRANSFER FUNCTIONS FOR STREAMS

You send data to a stream with a function. One that you are already familiar with is the printf() function; however, this function will only send data to the stdout stream. There is a similar function that can be used to send data to any stream.

fprintf()

This function works just like printf() except that it will accept an argument that designates which stream the data is to be sent to. The general form of the function is as follows:

```
fprintf( sfp, "format", arguments );
```

The only difference between fprintf() and the printf() function is the stream file pointer name (*sfp*), which designates the desired stream.

fscanf()

Another function you are familiar with is the scanf() function, which always takes data from the stdin stream. The scanf() function also has a counterpart that can be directed to accept data from any stream. The general form is as follows:

```
fscanf( sfp, "format", arguments);
```

Again, the *sfp* is the stream file pointer that designates which open stream the function is to accept data from. In all other aspects, this function acts the same as scanf().

fputc()

The **fputc()** function can be used to send a single character to a stream. The general form is

```
fputc( ch, sfp);
```

where *ch* is the character you want to send, and *sfp* is again the stream file pointer name you want to send the character to.

fgetc()

This function will take a character from a selected stream. Its general form is as follows:

```
ch = fgetc( sfp );
```

The next character in the stream *sfp* is converted to an integer and returned to *ch*. If the end of file has been reached or an error has occurred, EOF (defined in stdio.h) is returned.

CHANGING THE CURRENT POSITION POINTER

When you open a stream, you also establish the **current position pointer** for that stream. This is a software pointer that is set to point to the beginning character of the file when the stream is opened. It points to the next character or byte that will be read, or it points to the location the next character or byte will be written into. Each time you read from or write to the stream file, the position pointer is advanced. It will continue to advance until the end-of-file mark is reached. Allowing the pointer to advance in a normal fashion is the way you would use a sequential device such as a tape drive. You start at one end of the tape and read until you reach the EOF; however, it is possible to redirect the current position pointer. In the case of a tape drive, you can rewind the tape and start over. In the case of the disk, you can start over or randomly access different bytes in the file. These actions are accomplished with two functions.

rewind()

The **rewind**() function will simply reset the current position pointer back to the first character or byte in the stream file. Depending on the physical device involved, it may actually perform a rewind or some comparable action, but all you care about is that the pointer is now pointing to the first character in the file. Because of the standardized nature of a C I/O stream, you needn't be concerned about what must be done to any particular device to get the pointer there. The general form of the function is

```
rewind( sfp );
```

where *sfp* identifies the stream involved.

fseek()

Another way to reposition the current position pointer is with the **fseek()** function. It is used to randomly reposition the position pointer to any desired byte in a stream file. C allows any file on the disk to be randomly accessed for either reading or writing. The general form of the function is as follows:

```
fseek( sfp, offset, start );
```

In this function, *sfp* identifies the stream file, and *offset* is a type long int that designates how far you want to move the pointer. This number is the offset that will be added to the *start* position. The *start* position is not necessarily the current position; it may be one of the following three choices:

- Use 0 or SEEK_SET to start at the beginning of the file.
- Use 1 or SEEK_CUR to start at the current position.
- Use 2 or SEEK_END to start at the end of the file.

Following is a sample use of the function:

```
fseek( apple, -5L, SEEK_END ;
```

In this example, *apple* is the stream file pointer, and **-5** is the offset. The **L** forces C to handle the -5 as a long integer, which is what C expects. A long integer is necessary to have large enough numbers to access files over 64K bytes in size. The **SEEK_END** was defined in the header file stdio.h as a 2, and in this case the position pointer will be positioned five bytes in from the end-of-file mark.

HANDLING STREAM EOF AND ERRORS

When working with external or peripheral I/O devices, you have situations that are difficult to predict. The device may be turned off. An end of file may be unexpectedly reached. A printer may run out of paper. A diskette may be full. An anticipated disk file may not exist, or the diskette may be write protected. All of these situations will create error conditions. If your program has not been set up to handle these error conditions, control will be taken away from your program, and its run will be aborted. This result will irritate the user of the program, and should be avoided if possible. Most functions will return an error status if an error condition has been encountered. Setting up code to recognize and handle this error return is the programmer's job.

When opening a stream file, you can test to make sure it was successful before you attempt to go on and use an unopened file. Assume that you have opened a file for writing with this line of code:

```
sfp = fopen( "junk.fil", "wb" );
```

You could then immediately test the stream file pointer as in the following example:

```
if ( sfp == NULL ){
     printf("\nCould not open file!");
     ...
}
```

If an error occurs, the stream file pointer will be given a NULL value (defined in stdio.h). When this if condition tests true, you should have the code available to resolve the problem.

Streams, like some physical devices, have the data terminated with an end-of-file mark (EOF). It can save you time and code when programming to check for the EOF instead of trying to keep an exact count on the number of bytes in the file. Consider the following code:

```
ch = fgetc(sfp);
if ( ch == EOF ) exit(0);
...
```

When the fgetc() function reaches the end of the file, it will return EOF. Simply testing for this condition allows you to know when all the data has been read.

feof()

When working with a binary file, it is possible for the combination of bits that are being transferred to look like an end-of-file mark when you are not actually at the physical end of the data. C has a function to solve this problem, and its general form is as follows:

```
i = feof( sfp );
```

The *sfp* indicates the stream. The *i* will be nonzero when the end of file has been reached. You should call this function with each read of data from the stream.

ferror()

Another function that is provided in the library of functions allows you to test for an error with each action relating to a stream. The general form of the **ferror()** function is as follows:

```
i = ferror( sfp );
```

Again, *sfp* indicates the stream. The function returns nonzero when an error is detected in the stream.

TERMINATING THE STREAM

After you have finished using a stream, there are still some tasks to perform. The stream should be closed, and any unnecessary disk files should be removed.

fclose()

When you have finished with a stream, you must close it. Failure to properly close a stream file could cause serious problems, including loss of data. Closing is accomplished with the following function,

```
fclose( sfp );
```

where *sfp* is the name of the stream file to be closed.

unlink()

When working with streams that involve disk files, you often create temporary or scratch files. Good sense dictates that these files should be promptly removed to ensure that the disk has the maximum available space free to use. Under program control, it is possible to remove a disk file from the disk. This task is accomplished with the following function,

```
unlink( "file_name" );
```

where *file_name* is a string that designates the path and name of the file you want removed from the disk.

USING STREAMS WITH THE PRINTER

It was stated earlier that streams allow you to access and work with all I/O devices in the same way. Examine the following example of writing to a line printer:

```
/* ------------------- PROG-32.C ---------------------- */
/* -------- Demonstrate writing to printer ------------ */

#include <stdio.h>

main()
{
     /* ------------- Initialization --------------- */
     int i;
     char ch[28] = "abcdefghijklmnopqrstuvwxyz ";

     /* --------------- Open stream ---------------- */
     FILE *stream_dev;
     stream_dev = fopen("PRN" ,"wb");

     /* ----------- Put data in stream ------------- */
     for (i=0; i<27; i++) {
         putc(ch[i], stream_dev);
     }

     /* ------------ Flush the stream -------------- */
     putc('\n',stream_dev);

     /* -------------- Close stream ---------------- */
     fclose(stream_dev);
}
```

This is a straightforward program to have the line printer print out the alphabet. No error checking was included, so make sure the printer is turned on.

USING STREAMS WITH THE DISK

Now examine the same program modified to output to the disk:

```
/* ------------------- PROG-33.C ---------------------- */
/* ------- Demonstrate writing to disk file ----------- */

#include <stdio.h>

main()
{
     /* ------------- Initialization --------------- */
     int i;
     char ch[28] = "abcdefghijklmnopqrstuvwxyz ";

     /* --------------- Open stream ---------------- */
     FILE *stream_dev;
     stream_dev = fopen("junk.fil" ,"wb");

     /* ----------- Put data in stream ------------- */
     for (i=0; i<27; i++) {
         putc(ch[i], stream_dev);
     }

     /* -------------- Close stream ---------------- */
     fclose(stream_dev);
}
```

Except for the line of code that flushes the stream when sending data to the line printer, the only difference in the two is when the stream is opened. Examine the following two lines of code:

```
stream_dev = fopen("PRN", "wb");

stream_dev = fopen("junk.fil", "wb");
```

In one case, the printer is designated with "PRN," and in the other, a disk file is specified with "junk.fil." For the most part, both devices are written to in the same way. You will not be aware of anything happening after running the second program, but you should find on your disk a new file called "junk.fil." (Make sure it is there before going on with the other examples.)

Sequential Access

You work with most devices in a sequential manner. The two previous examples were sequential writes to the respective devices. This is also the way you usually access the data on the device—starting at the beginning and reading sequentially through the data. In the next example, PROG-33.C was modified to make two sequential reads of data from the file that was created by that program:

```
/* ------------------ PROG-34.C ----------------------- */
/* --- Demonstrate sequential reading of disk file ---- */

#include <stdio.h>

main()
{
     /* -------------- Initialize ------------------ */
     int i, ch;

     /* -------------- Open stream ----------------- */
     FILE *stream_dev;
     stream_dev = fopen("junk.fil" ,"rb");

     /* ---------- Read data from stream ----------- */
     for (i=0; i<15; i++) {
         ch = getc(stream_dev);
         printf("%c ",ch);
     }
     printf("\n");

     /* ------ Start over and read all data  ------- */
     rewind(stream_dev);       /* Start pointer over  */
     while (ch != EOF) {       /* Read to end of file */
         ch = getc(stream_dev);
         printf("%c ",ch);
     }

     /* ------------- Close stream ----------------- */
     fclose(stream_dev);
}
```

The first change that was made in the program was to eliminate the defined array *ch[ ]*. You will not need all those letters because they are in the file that is going to be read. The stream file was opened to read from instead of write to, and fgetc() was used instead of fputc(). The size of the loop was also reduced so only part of the file would be read the first time. The first loop relies on knowing what data is in the file. Finally, an output statement was added to show on the screen just what was read.

A second loop was included to read the total file while demonstrating how you would look for an EOF. Using the rewind() function, you will also observe the resetting of the current position pointer.

Random Access

The data from any disk file may be accessed randomly when you are using streams. Accessing the data is a matter of repositioning the position pointer to the desired byte in the file before each read. In some cases, this will save considerable time. If you are repeatedly looking for individual elements, records, or structures in a file and are forced to read sequentially from the beginning of the file each time, a random capability is extremely useful. The following sample program demonstrates the process of accessing a file randomly:

```
/* -------------------- PROG-35.C --------------------- */
/* ------ Demonstrate random access of disk file ------ */
/* --( To be run after file is created by PROG-33.C )-- */

#include <stdio.h>

main()
{
     /* --------- Initialize variables ------------- */
     long d[13] = {17,0,13,3,14,12,26,0,2,2,4,18,18};
     int i, ch;

     /* --------------- Open stream ---------------- */
     FILE *stream_dev;
     stream_dev = fopen("junk.fil" ,"rb");

     /* ---------- Access stream randomly ---------- */
     for(i=0; i<13; i++) {
         fseek(stream_dev, d[i], SEEK_SET);
         ch = getc(stream_dev);
         printf("%c", ch);
     }
     printf("\n");

     /* ------------- Close stream ----------------- */
     fclose(stream_dev);
}
```

Note the offset data that is defined in *d[ ]*. These offsets, of course, represent the positions of each of the desired characters in the file. They are offsets from the beginning of the file (SEEK_SET). You will see that they are declared long because they are intended to be used in the fseek() function.

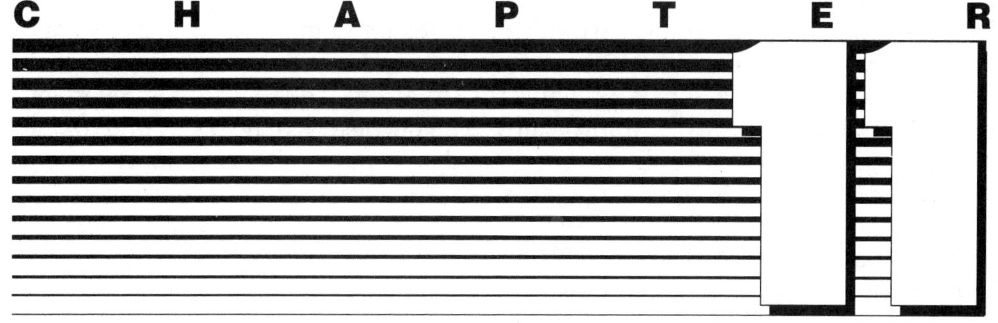

DATA-HANDLING TECHNIQUES

In professional programming, certain techniques for handling data are used over and over again; however, different ways can be found to accomplish the same task. You choose the approach that best suits the situation. The techniques covered in this chapter represent typical approaches. The purpose is to help you understand what techniques are available for handling data and to provide at least one approach that will work for you. In some cases, the language you are using will include a statement or function that will accomplish the task. A good example is a sort routine. However, you may well run into a language that does not have the function you need. If that is the case, this chapter will hopefully give you a technique to use.

Data-handling techniques tend to fall into four general categories: checking the validity of input data, storing data for later retrieval, manipulating data, and ensuring the security of data.

CHECKING THE VALIDITY OF DATA

A constant concern when data is being entered into a computer is that it be entered and captured correctly. It is usually the system analyst's responsibility to devise a plan for catching errors before they get into the computer database. The plan will often include both the procedure that is to be followed for entering the data and the design of the programs accepting the input.

It is common for data entry or keypunch operators to enter everything twice. The second pass is called **verification**. This second time through, the input data is compared to the data that was entered earlier. If the entries are not the same, the computer will notify the data entry operator that there is a discrepancy so that the item can be corrected. Also, there is usually a rule that prohibits the same person from entering the data both times. There is a good chance that the same person will take the same action the second time (for example, misinterpret poor handwriting the same way a second time).

Often, the staff entering the data is not the staff using the data. Someone unfamiliar with the data would not recognize when a number was an illogical entry for a given situation. Some systems are designed so that users enter their own data because they are familiar with it. This has a drawback in that it may be less expensive to hire someone who is very fast (although unfamiliar with the data) than to require a nontypist or a highly paid supervisor to enter the data.

Visual verification is sometimes used to catch errors in input data. An example is a process referred to as **full-duplex**. This process is often used when keyboard input is sent over phone lines or from remote terminals to a computer located elsewhere. In this type of environment, errors are sometimes introduced by noise on the phone lines. When the user presses a key on the keyboard, the terminal does not echo what has been typed. The code is sent to the remote computer. The computer then sends back to the terminal the character that it received, and the terminal displays it on the screen. This happens very fast and you most likely could not tell that it was not a direct result of your typing. What you might see is that you typed an **A** and the screen shows a **B**. When this happens, you can correct the error on the spot. **Half-duplex** is the situation in which the character is displayed as you press the key and before it is sent to the computer. Most terminals can be used in either way. It is a matter of setting a switch. If you want the full-duplex capability, make sure that the terminal and the computer system are both set for the full-duplex mode.

Some systems use software input screens that offer visual verification to confirm the appropriateness of data. Suppose you were entering invoice data about a customer. Your first entry is the customer number. The computer looks up the customer name from that number and places the name on the input screen. You can then check the name on the screen against the name on the invoice to make sure that the right customer is going to be billed, which also saves having to enter the name so the computer can verify that it is the right customer.

Usually, the program that controls an input screen will run limit or bounds checks on the incoming data where appropriate. For example, the processor knows the current date. It can then put reasonable limits on which dates it will accept. In some situations, dates in the future or dates that go back past the last accounting period may not be appropriate. When the processor works with dollar amounts, there are usually some reasonable limits that an amount will fall between. This amount can often be determined as a plus or minus percentage of the average amounts a given account has in its past history. If an unusually large or small amount appears, the computer can stop and request a verification on the amount. Assuming the amount was correct, a similar amount would not be questioned the next time. With a table lookup, the user can verify that part numbers are valid active numbers. Most analog data (such as time, temperature, weight, and flow volume) has an acceptable range. These can all be programmed into the input routine in an attempt to catch errors before they get into the system.

The check digit is a technique used with identification numbers that are permanently assigned to some entity. An ID such as an insurance policy number will often have a built-in check digit.

Check Digit

A **check digit** is commonly the first or last digit of some identification number such as an insurance policy number. This digit is a built-in code to verify that the number is correct. If the person entering the number enters it incorrectly, the computer will immediately determine that there is an error and will ask for a correction. It can tell without having to look anything up. You first add all the digits of the number together. The unit value of your sum is the check digit. This is the result of a modulo 10 operation on the sum. See the following example:

```
policy number        253104
sum of digits        15 = 2+5+3+1+0+4
check digit          5 = 15 % 10

policy number
with check digit     5-253104
```

Someone mistakenly typing a 7 in place of the 4 in the previous example would produce the number 5-253107. The computer would generate a resulting check digit of 8 and this would not match the check digit of 5 that it was supposed to generate. As a result, the computer would know that there was an error and would refuse to accept the entry as a valid policy number.

You can no doubt see that the technique is not foolproof. For example, it will not catch a two-digit transposition of digits, and transpositions are common typing errors. Suppose someone typed 5-523104 instead of 5-253104. With the algorithm above, both of these numbers would produce the same check digit. To catch transposition errors, the check digit algorithm would have to be improved. It might be modified in the following way (before adding the digits, multiply every other digit by 2):

```
policy number          2    5    3    1    0    4
multiply by 2              *2        *2        *2
                      ---------------------------
new values             2   10    3    2    0    8

add new values         25 = 2+10+3+2+0+8
check digit            5 = 25 % 10

policy number
with check digit       5-253104
```

Again, the check digit happens to be 5, but the check digit that would be generated for the transposition (5-523104) is 2 and would be found to be an error. So you now have an improved algorithm, and it will trap more errors; however, this algorithm will not catch a three-digit transposition. A number such as 5-352104 instead of 5-253104 will slip through. One method you can use to trap this error is to multiply each digit by a consecutively larger value before you add up the digits.

You must keep in mind that no single check digit can catch all possible errors because every tenth number would generate the same check digit, which means that 10% of all policy numbers will have the same check digit. All you have done is reduce the probability of an error getting through. You have not stopped errors entirely. With a good algorithm, you might catch the most common errors, but you will not get them all.

There is a way of further reducing the error rate. You could reduce the number of policies with the same check digit. This could be done by using a two-digit check number in front of the policy number. Here, with a good algorithm, you produce a sum. Instead of modulo 10, you use modulo 100 division to get the check number. Only one in every 100 policy numbers would generate the same check number. This method, however, has a disadvantage in that it increases the size of the policy number.

Yet another method is a compromise that keeps the policy number small and, at the same time, reduces somewhat the repetition of identical check digits. This method is to use modulo 26, take the result, and convert it to an alphabetic character. You can do this by adding the result to a decimal 65. The resulting number will be the decimal ASCII code for an uppercase letter, which becomes the check digit. The policy number would resemble the following: Z-253104.

You could expand on this idea by using both uppercase and lowercase letters. You might even throw in numbers as well, which would allow you up to 62 policies with unique check digits before you need to use the same check digit again.

A word of caution about check digits. If you are thinking of implementing one in a system, make sure the algorithm is one that you can live with. It is virtually impossible to change the algorithm once the check digit numbers have been issued and are in use. Changing the algorithm means that all check numbers issued with the old algorithm will be rejected by the new approach, and allowing either check digit increases the possibility of error.

Another technique called a **hash total** is commonly used when working with long lists of identification numbers such as customer numbers, policy numbers, and phone numbers.

Hash Total

A hash total is a way of verifying that a long list of identification numbers is correct. Suppose you want to design a system that will allow a person to enter payroll information into a computer system. You would have to input the identity of the person and the hours that person worked for the current period, and the computer would figure out the deductions and print the check. The problem is how to get the information into the system correctly.

Suppose you use social security numbers to identify individuals. A hash total is generated by adding up all the social security numbers for everyone entered into the payroll system for a pay period. A sum made up of social security numbers may seem meaningless, but can be useful. You design a system that requires the data entry person to add up, on an adding machine, all the social security numbers that were entered into the computer that day. Then, have that person enter this hash total into the computer as well. The payroll program will create its own hash total by adding up all social security numbers it received and compare that total with the hash total it was given. The computer will accept the data as correct or require a correction to be made, depending on whether the hash totals match. This method does not tell you where the error is—only that there is one.

Check Sum

The hash total is obviously an outgrowth of the long-term accounting practice of adding up columns of numbers in different directions or by different people to verify the accuracy of the result. When you produce a total such as this for a computer, it is referred to as a **check sum**. If you were entering the bank receipts for the day into a computer, you would use the same technique as the hash total to verify that the amounts were entered properly. An adding machine tape would be produced with the total of all the amounts. This check sum would also be entered into the computer. The computer would verify that it generated the same total as you did on the adding machine.

Like the check digit, neither the check sum nor the hash total will catch all possible errors. Two errors that are complementary will cancel each other out. You could reduce the potential for this problem by preparing check sums or hash totals for fewer entries (for example, each 20 entries). This approach serves two purposes. First, the chance of the two errors canceling each other out is reduced because they may now be in different groups. Second, you will have isolated the error to a smaller group and made it easier to find.

STORING DATA FOR RETRIEVAL

After data is in the computer, it is usually necessary to arrange and hold it in some way. The **array** is perhaps the most used programming tool for holding data while it is in the CPU. If you were going to create a list of names for all 50 of the United States, you would do so in an array. In BASIC, you might dimension the array with DIM STATES$(50), where each element would be addressed as STATES$(1), STATES$(2), ... STATES$(50). However, you will find that most data has other information that is related to it. Perhaps with the name of the state you would like to save the name of its capital city. This could be done by using a two-dimensional array in the form DIM STATES$(50,2), where STATES$(23,1) would be the name of a state and STATES$(23,2) would be the name of its capital city.

A better example of the need for related data is the phone book. Phone numbers alone would be of no value. You need the names and addresses attached to the phone number. It is reasonable to hold this related information together. This way, it would be easy to extract all the information on a particular person at one time. You could use a two-dimensional array that might resemble the following: PHBOOK$(34,1) is the person's name, PHBOOK$(34,2) is the person's phone number, and PHBOOK$(34,3) is the person's address.

This technique works fine as long as all the elements of the array are the same type of data. In this case, they are all alphanumeric strings. What would happen if for some reason you wanted to keep the phone number as a true number? You might have a series of arrays such as NAME$(), PHONE(), and ADDRESS$(), where the name and address are kept as strings and the phone number is held as a number. The array index would tie common data together. For example, the 25th entry in each array would relate to the same person. This method would work and is often used in BASIC. In C, you are given another option. C has a special way to keep all these related pieces of data together, using what is called a **structure**.

Structures

A structure is the way C allows the programmer to hold related but different types of data together. Pieces of information can be different data types, but they can be collectively referred to with a single identifier or structure variable name. You could compare a structure with what other programming languages call a record. Each element or variable in the structure is the same as an item in a record.

To establish a data structure, you first define a structure **type**. You are familiar with data types such as int and char. With a structure, you construct and name your own structure types. They are not predefined. The structure type can be made up of as many data types and variables as you want. You use the keyword **struct** to define the structure template and associate it with a name that will be the structure type. Following is an example:

```
struct date {
     int day;
     char month[4];
     int year;
};
```

(Take particular note of the final semicolon, which is required to terminate the definition of a structure type.)

The structure type is **date**. The template is made up of the three elements: day, month, and year. After the structure type is defined, you can declare as many structure variables of that structure type as you want:

```
struct date today, birthday, anniversary;
```

At this point, you have three date structure variables: *today*, *birthday*, and *anniversary*. Each structure variable can be defined as follows:

```
anniversary.day = 8;
strcpy( anniversary.month, "Aug" );
anniversary.year = 1988;
```

The elements of a structure are referred to by giving the structure variable name followed by a period. That, in turn, is followed by the desired element of the structure. Also, don't forget the use of the strcpy() function when assigning a value to a string variable.

Arrays of Structures

After a structure type has been declared, it is also possible to define an array of structures instead of just a structure variable as was shown previously. Using the same example, suppose you want to keep a list of 32 special holidays. You could declare an array as follows:

```
struct date holidays[32];
```

Each of the 32 holidays in the array would have the three elements of the **date** structure: *day*, *month*, and *year*.

Consider a second example. If you were working in a factory that manufactured widgets, you might define a structure template in the following manner:

```
struct parts {
     char dept;
     int part_num;
     char description[30];
     int on_hand;
     float cost;
};
```

The structure type is *parts*. Assume that the factory has three different inventories, one for each of the three kinds of widgets that are manufactured. You could define three different arrays of structures, one for each widget inventory of parts:

```
struct parts a_widget[20], b_widget[30], c_widget[10];
```

The first inventory is called **a_widget** and is made up of the 20 different parts that are used in the construction of the a_widget. Five elements of information are known for each part. For example, if you wanted to look at quantity on hand and cost of the seventh part for the a_widget, you could do so with the following function call:

```
printf("%d  %f", a_widget[7].on_hand, a_widget[7].cost);
```

Again, the period (.) is used to separate the structure variable name from the element name. The array index is designated in brackets as usual.

Arrays and structures are tools for holding and working with lists of data while the data is in the CPU. If you want to store this information for a long time, you must transfer it to a disk or some other mass storage device. How you transfer it varies depending on what language you are working with. With C and streams, you write it on the desired stream byte by byte. For retrieval purposes, it is important to know the number of bytes each entry in a structure uses. This way, you can easily go directly to the entry you want and reconstruct the elements of that entry and any entries in a structure. To get the byte count, add up the bytes required for each element of the structure template.

TYPES OF LISTS

Although you have read about the tools that exist for holding data in a list, nothing as yet has been said about how you might use those tools to make a different order or arrangement of a list for a particular purpose. Even though you may use the same tools (arrays and structures), you could easily make different lists and types of lists out of the same data, or you could construct a new tool of your own to hold the data in a particular way. The type of list you choose depends on the nature of the information in the list and how you intend to work with it.

One type of list is referred to as a **stack**. Think of a stack of dinner plates. If you add a plate to the stack, it goes on the top. When you take a plate from the stack, it comes off the top. Perhaps you have heard of LIFO—last in first out. This description applies to a stack. In the discussion of interrupt traps, it was said that you had to save all the registers when an interrupt occurred. Then, when you had completed servicing the interrupt, you had to restore all the registers to their initial state. A stack is used to store the registers during an interrupt. Stacks are such an important concept and are used so often that your PC hardware has stacks and stack registers built into it for system software to use.

Another type of list is called a **queue**. The FIFO (first in first out) principle is used in a queue. When you must process transactions chronologically, you would use a queue. Place data temporarily in a queue until you have time to process it. I/O buffers are examples of queues. The first key pressed on the keyboard is the one you must process first.

Another important form of list is the **circular list**. Although the entries may actually be in a physical line, think of them as being placed in a circle. The program will keep track of the index. When the index reaches the end of the array, the code will start the index over at the beginning, forming a circle. Circular lists are sometimes referred to as **rings** or **ring buffers**. See the following illustration of an array:

```
              c[0]
        c[11]      c[1]
     c[10]            c[2]
   c[9]                 c[3]
     c[8]             c[4]
        c[7]       c[5]
              c[6]
```

This type of list is particularly suited for use as a queue and for FIFO. You are simply storing data here temporarily until you can process it. If you wanted a buffer to temporarily hold input from the keyboard until you could get to it, you could use a circular list. The circle would be large enough to absorb a burst of typing speed from the user until the program could catch up. You put data into the array sequentially, but after you reach the end of the array, you start over at the beginning, thus creating a circle. This type of list requires that characters be removed from as well as placed into the circle; otherwise, you would just catch up with the beginning of the data and overwrite it. Building this buffer requires two index pointers for the array: one to keep track of the next place to put data and one to keep track of the next place to remove data. Call the input index **inpt**, and the index to remove data **outpt**. The code to put data into the buffer would look something like the following, where *chi* is the incoming character:

```
if (inpt == outpt) {                /* Head bite the tail? */
    printf("Overflow");             /* Yes - data lost     */
    ...
}
c[inpt] = chi;                      /* Put chi in list     */
inpt = inpt + 1;                    /* Increment pointer   */
if (inpt > 11 ) inpt = 0;           /* Start circle over?  */
```

The first line of code checks the two index pointers to see if the program is about to write on top of the output end of the circle. If it is, the user is alerted, and the program then processes the overflow as you see fit. Ring bells. Cuss out the user. Dynamically expand the circular list. Do what you think would be the best solution to the problem. If the input end has not reached the output end, the third line from the end of the code places the new character in the array. The index is then incremented, and, if the program has reached the end of the array, it circles around and starts over at the beginning.

The code for removing data from the circular list might resemble the following:

```
if (outpt != inpt) {                    /* Circle empty?         */
    process_input( c(outpt) );          /* No - send char. out */
    outpt = outpt + 1;                  /* Increment pointer     */
    if (outpt > 11) outpt = 0;          /* Start circle over?    */
}
```

The first line of code checks to see if there is anything in the array. If the program is about to take a character from the first empty space in the circle, the list is empty, and there is nothing to do. On the other hand, if the buffer has a character to be processed, the program sends it off to a function for whatever processing is required. When control is returned, it increments the index pointer. The last line checks to see if the end of the array has been reached. If it has, the index is started over at the beginning of the array.

Stacks and queues are types of lists used in a dynamic or rapidly changing environment; however, some situations require lists that are more permanent in nature. An example might be a list of cities with some associated statistical data (such as crime rate or population density). The statistical data might change now and then, but the city part of the list would stay the same. You just need to access the data on a particular city to look at or change the data associated with it. FIFO and LIFO are not appropriate. You want to access a particular entry in the list, so it is important to have a fast and easy way to find any particular entry.

This means that the order of the list becomes important. Put the cities in an order (such as alphabetical) that lets you find an entry faster than just starting at the top of the list and looking for the one you want. You can put the list in the desired order by sorting it, but sorting usually means moving items around to get them in the right order. That technique works fine if it is just a city name and population you want to move around, but suppose you wanted to keep much more information on all cities over a given size. If you wanted exact geographical boundaries, social and economic profiles, biographies on current and past city officers, and a detailed history of the city, sorting entries of this size would mean physically moving thousands of characters. You might not feel that strategy to be the best way to handle the situation. Instead, you could leave all data in its current physical order and just have a pointer to the first entry. Then, have that entry point to the next ordered entry in the list. This means you must keep track of additional information (the pointer), but you do not need to rearrange anything.

Lists that are ordered using pointers to indicate the next entry rather than physical proximity to the next entry are referred to as **linked lists**. They might resemble the following:

```
1          2          3          4          5          6 ...
city-C     city-M     city-H     city-G     city-K
point->4   point->6   point->5   point->3   point->2
```

Here, the first entry points to the fourth entry. The fourth entry points back to the third, and so on. This way, you can make your way alphabetically from the beginning of the list to the end. You will want to keep track of where the first entry can be found, and the last entry could point to the first empty space for the addition of new entries. All entries will be in the desired order, but it is not necessary to physically move them when they are sorted. More time and work is saved each time a new city gains enough population to be added to the list. There is no need to move all entries down to make space for the new one. Just add it onto the end and change two pointers to include the new entry in its proper position. If you added **city-I**, you would have the following:

1	2	3	4	5	6
city-C	city-M	city-H	city-G	city-K	**city-I**
point->4	**point->7**	**point->6**	point->3	point->2	**point->5**

It would only be necessary to modify the list to the extent that the entry is appended to the end and the two bolded pointers are changed. Time would also be saved when an entry is removed. Taking out **city-K** is accomplished as follows:

1	2	3	4	5	6
city-C	city-M	city-H	city-G		city-I
point->4	point->7	point->6	point->3		**point->2**

You don't have to remove the entry and then move everything up to fill the gap. Only the pointer directly following the one removed must be changed to contain the pointer of the item removed. The empty space can be left as is and used later when a new entry is added.

If you use linked lists in this way, it is possible to order the same list in more than one way. For each new way you want the list to be ordered, you just add an additional pointer. One pointer could link all entries alphabetically while another links and orders them by population size. This is another timesaver. If you used a physical sort and had the list in actual alphabetical order, you would need to resort each time you needed the list in order of population size, or you would need to keep two lists, one in alphabetical order and the other in population order. This is not a good idea because it requires twice as much storage, and you must update two lists when changes occur.

In a list that is physically sorted, it is possible to proceed in either direction from a given entry. This is not possible with the linked lists just discussed. It is only possible to proceed in one direction. Even though you may have multiple pointers for different orderings, these lists are referred to as **single-linked lists**. They are linked in a single direction only. There are times when it may be necessary to be able to proceed in either direction from a given entry in a list. **Double-linked lists** are used to accomplish this task. A double-linked list has two pointers, one pointing down the list and one pointing up the list. If you were to double-link the previous example, you would get something similar to the following:

1	2	3	4	5	6 ...
city-C	city-M	city-H	city-G	city-K	
point->4	point->6	point->5	point->3	point->2	
point<-	point<-5	point<-4	point<-1	point<-3	

Now, it is possible to proceed in either direction from any entry in the list.

Another way to allow you to get to any entry in a list from any other entry in the list is to turn the list into a **circular list**. Point the last entry back to the first entry as shown below:

1	2	3	4	5	6 ...
city-C	city-M	city-H	city-G	city-K	
point->4	point->1	point->5	point->3	point->2	

You can reach all the entries regardless of where you start in the list.

Another form of list that is often used is called a **tree**. Although it is normally drawn as if one were looking at the root structure of a tree rather than the trunk and branches, it is called a tree because of the branching nature of its diagram. The point at which branching occurs is referred to as a **node**. The beginning node is called the **root**. You have probably seen the diagram of a family tree at one time or another. This is a type of tree list. The analogy of a family tree is used so often for tree lists that it is common to describe relationships between nodes in a tree list by the terms **parent**, **descendants**, **offspring**, and **siblings**. If you use directories on your PC disk files (especially directories within directories), you are using a type of tree structure. Arrays lend themselves to tree lists as well. See the following diagram:

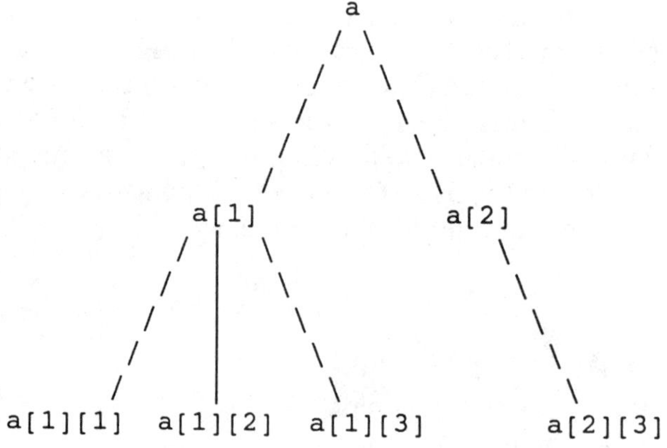

MANIPULATING DATA

Now that you understand something about the types of lists you can create for the orderly storage of data on a computer, a word or two should be said about how to manipulate the data in those lists. Following are some of the data manipulations you might want to perform on a list:

- Insert an entry into the appropriate place in a list.
- Purge an entry from the list.
- Find an entry, using its numeric position in the list.
- Search a list by key for the occurrence of an entry.
- Examine an entry in a list.
- Change the contents of an entry in a list.
- Count the entries in a list.
- Duplicate a list.
- Split a list into two lists.
- Merge two lists into one list.
- Sort a list into a desired order.

Some of these actions are pretty straightforward. For example, changing and counting entries should present little problem, and finding an entry by its numeric position in a list is automatic when you are using a structured array. Other types of data manipulation, such as the sort, require more thought.

Sort

A phone book would be of very little value if the names were in random order. Think of the ordeal of trying to find someone's phone number in such a phone book. To be of value to humans, the data in a computer often requires ordering. This process of arranging data into a given order is referred to as **sorting**. Some computer programming languages have a built-in sort operation. Others, such as BASIC, do not.

Sort algorithms abound. Each one has some special feature that makes it more valuable in one situation than another. The equipment used in sorting the data is a factor. Are you sorting in memory, on a disk, or on a tape—or are you using a combination of devices? When the amount of data you are going to be sorting increases in volume, speed becomes more of a concern. As a result, many different types of sorts were developed to improve speed in some special situations. A sort developed by C. A. R. Hoare in 1962 that he dubbed "quicksort" is considered one of the best general-purpose sorts being used today. This quicksort is built into a Turbo C function called **qsort**(). The following program demonstrates it:

```
/* -------------------- PROG-36.C --------------------- */
/* ----------- Demonstrate qsort function ------------- */

#include <stdlib.h>

int list[6] = {423, 200, 657, 102, 356, 278 };

/* --------- Test routine for qsort to use ----------- */
int tst(int *entry1, int *entry2)
{
     return(*entry1 - *entry2);
}


/* -------------- Sort and print out list ------------ */
main()
{
    int i;
```

continued...

...from previous page

```
    /* ---------- Print out array before sort --------- */
    printf("\nArray before sort:\n");
    for (i = 0;  i < 6; i++) {
        printf("list[%d] is %d\n",i,list[i]);
    }

    /* ------- Call qsort function to sort list ------- */
    qsort( list, 6, 2, tst);

    /* ---------- Print out results of sort ----------- */
    printf("\nArray after sort:\n");
    for (i = 0;  i < 6; i++) {
        printf("list[%d] is %d\n",i,list[i]);
    }
}
```

This program prints an array of integers before and after they are sorted. The line below is the qsort() function call in the example program:

```
qsort( list, 6, 2, tst );
```

The *list* is the name of the array to be sorted, **6** is the number of entries in the array or list, and **2** is the byte size of each entry. (An integer is 16 bits or 2 bytes.) Finally, *tst* is a user-defined function that qsort() will call repeatedly to test the relationship of the entries in the list. The user is free to define the relationship between entries in any way. This function must, however, return the following when called with pointers to two entries:

- a value less than zero if the first entry is to be considered less than the second
- a value of zero if the two entries are to be considered equal
- a value greater than zero if the first entry is to be considered greater than the second

You will see an example of a test function, tst(), defined in the code of this sample program. The names of this testing function and the array are up to the user. When qsort() returns control, the array will be in the desired order.

In this example, only the entries in the list were sorted. There was no related data. When working with data, you will be concerned about all the related data for a particular entry in a list as well. In other words, you will want to keep track of all the elements in a C structure for each entry in a list. Again, examine the phone book. You need the names and addresses attached for the phone number to be of value. In this case, the name is considered the key, and the book is arranged by the alphabetical order of names. The phone number has no effect on the order in which the entry appears in the book, but without the phone number the book again has little value. You know from reading about rearranging linked lists that it is not always necessary to move everything related to the key when you move the key. When you sort on the key, you need only move the key and a pointer to the rest of the information, or, in some cases, you can just change the pointer.

Recall the health insurance policy numbers discussed at the beginning of this chapter. If the policy number is the key, the related data might include the name, address, phone number, age, sex, and occupation of the policy holder. It would also include the other family members' names, ages, sexes, and occupations. Additional information would include the effective date of the policy, type of policy, payment history, and claims history. A lot of unnecessary work would be required to move all that information each time you re-sorted the list for some reason. One day you might need a list ordered by zip code for the sales department. The next day you might need a list ordered by name for the claims department. Sorts usually involve moving around the key and a pointer to the related data. The bulk of the data does not move.

Suppose you were asked to write a program to produce a company phone book. The book would be in order by the person's name but would include phone number, title, and office location. The name is the key that you would sort on. The remainder of the information would be stored together, and a pointer to that information would be attached to the person's name. You would rearrange the names, keeping the pointers with them. Then, when the sort is complete, you would print the phone book by taking the names in order and using the pointers to look up the related data. Examine how you might go about writing a sort such as this.

One sort often used because it is easy to program is called a **bubble sort**. It gets its name from the way entries float or "bubble" to the top and settle to the bottom. To perform a bubble sort, you would take the list of names and look at the first and second entries. If the second entry comes alphabetically before the first, you switch the two names and the pointers. Then, you look at the second and third entries, and repeat the process. You continue down the list, always putting the two entries you are examining in alphabetical order. When you reach the bottom of the list, you repeat the process again. This process continues until you go through the entire list without having to make a single switch of names. Then you know the list is in alphabetical order.

The following is a sample program of a bubble sort. This example is written in BASIC because BASIC does not have a built-in sort statement. C includes the qsort() library function you looked at earlier. This program simply uses the name as a sort key to arrange the names in alphabetical order and then prints the ordered list.

```
1 '* --------------- PROG-37.BAS ----------------- *
9 '* --------------- Bubble sort ----------------- *
10 KEY OFF : CLS
20 DIM NA$(16),PT(16),PHONE$(16)
30 DATA Jan,224-2731,Mel,226-7535,Ann,224-3334
32 DATA Joe,375-2121,Pam,224-3621,Bud,247-2441
34 DATA Tim,224-1773,Kim,226-8956,Tom,224-6333
36 DATA Rod,736-0021,Jim,226-2397,Peg,375-1992
38 DATA Rob,226-5041,Don,224-7343,Bob,224-2718
40 DATA Ted,225-1722
50 SIZ = 16
99 '* ---- Initialize arrays and print out ------- *
100 FOR I = 1 TO SIZ
110   READ NA$(I), PHONE$(I)
120   PT(I) = I
130 NEXT I
140 PRINT " This is the way the list starts. "
150 GOSUB 500
199 '* ------------------ Sort ------------------- *
200 FLAG = 1
210 PRINT "You will see the order after each pass,"
212 PRINT "and a count of the number of swaps made."
```

continued...

...from previous page

```
214 PRINT
216 GOSUB 700 : PRINT : PRINT
220 WHILE FLAG > 0
230   FLAG = 0
240   FOR I = 1 TO SIZ-1
250     IF NA$(I) > NA$(I+1) THEN 252 ELSE 260
252       SWAP NA$(I), NA$(I+1)
254       SWAP PT(I), PT(I+1)
256       FLAG = FLAG +1
260   NEXT I
270   GOSUB 700
280   PRINT FLAG;" "
290 WEND
299 '* ---------- Print all of sorted list ------- *
300 GOSUB 600
310 PRINT "This is the sorted list."
320 GOSUB 500
390 END                    '* -- Program ends here -- *
499 '* ------------ List all data as is ---------- *
500 PRINT: PRINT "Pt   Name","Phone number"
510 FOR I = 1 TO SIZ
520   PRINT PT(I);"  ";NA$(I),PHONE$(PT(I))
530 NEXT I
550 GOSUB 600
590 RETURN
599 '* ------------- Wait for user --------------- *
600 PRINT : PRINT "Press any key to continue"
610 IF INKEY$="" THEN 610
620 PRINT
690 RETURN
699 '* ----- Print current order names only ------ *
700 FOR J = 1 TO SIZ
710   PRINT NA$(J); " ";
720 NEXT J
790 RETURN
```

A number of steps in this example program are not really necessary. For example, first, the program prints the unordered list so you can examine it. There is a built-in wait that requires a key to be pressed before the sort will take place. Also, note that in line 20, three different arrays are established: NA$ to hold the names, PHONE$ to hold the phone numbers, and PT to hold the pointer. If this program were to be used to produce the company phone book mentioned earlier, it would need additional arrays for the person's title and office location. Admittedly, in this situation the pointer is extra work because there is only one item, the phone number, that is related to the key. This single item could be moved as easily as the pointer; however, the pointer is used to demonstrate the process for a situation in which the additional related data are to be included. They would be accessed in exactly the same way the phone number is in the example, and, like the phone number, they would not be moved during the sort. Down through line 130 there is only initialization of the unordered arrays. You can see that the pointer starts out as the existing order of the list in line 120.

Begin the sort. A variable called FLAG is used to keep track of how many times entries in the array are switched in each pass. FLAG is initially set to 1 so the WHILE statement in line 220 will start. Remember, when no entry is switched during one complete pass, the sort is complete, so the WHILE statement will stop if it sees that FLAG contains a zero. Once started, FLAG is initialized to zero for each pass through the loop. The variable SIZ contains the size of the array to be sorted. Line 250 compares the entry pointed to with the current index to the next entry in line and swaps the entries if they are not ordered alphabetically. Line 254 swaps the pointer when a name is swapped, and line 256 increments FLAG if a swap took place. Lines 216 and 270 are also unnecessary steps; they call a subroutine that prints the current order of the names only. You can then observe just how each pass in the sort affects the order. Line 280 prints the contents of FLAG after each iteration of the loop, which tells you how many swaps were made on the current pass. Lines 216, 270, and 280 allow you to observe the progress of the sort and the number of passes through the list that are required to sort the entries.

The last section of code prints out the sorted list and is another unnecessary part of this sort program. You will see that the same pointer is still associated with each name. You will also see that the correct phone number is printed adjacent to the name, even though the phone number was not touched during the sort. This is accomplished by keeping the original pointer attached to the name and then in line 520 using that pointer as the index in the PHONE$ array.

For any value of I in the range from 1 to 16,

- NA$(I) is the name.
- PT(I) is the pointer to the PHONE$ array.
- PHONE$(PT(I)) is the phone number that goes with NA$(I).

Consider how you could improve or speed up this sort. If you look at the results printed for each pass, you will see that after the first pass, the last entry is in its permanent place. After the second pass, the next-to-last entry is also in its permanent position. Will this result always be the case? Could you modify the program to take advantage of this result and speed up the sort?

Other data rearranging operations that professional programmers are often called on to build into their code include searching for or looking up an entry in an ordered list or merging two different ordered lists together.

Merge

A **merge** combines two ordered lists to make one large list. The end result must also be ordered. Again, the lists you are merging are only comprised of the key and a pointer to the mass of related data. This mass of related data is not moved. The process is straightforward. If you want to merge two lists that are ordered from small to large, establish three pointers and set them all to the beginning of three separate arrays: one pointer to each existing list and one to the new empty array that is as large as both of the existing lists together. This empty array will hold the combined data of both lists. The pointer to the new list is simply pointing to the first available opening in this new list.

The two existing lists must already be sorted. Look at the top entry in each list. Take the one that is smallest and move it into the new list. Advance the pointer in the new list to point to the next empty position. Advance the pointer to the entry you moved so that it points to the next entry in line. Now check to see if you have reached the end of that list. If not, again look at the two top entries and repeat the process. When you reach the end of one of the lists, simply append the remaining entries of the other list to the new list, and you have completed the merge.

The code for such a merge might resemble the following:

```
/* -------------------- PROG-38.C --------------------- */
/* ---------- Demonstrate a merge operation ----------- */

main()
{
    int list1[6] = {123, 200, 257, 302, 356, 678 };
    int list2[5] = {321, 445, 598, 709, 864 };
    int listn[11];
    int pn=0, p1=0, p2=0, i=0 ;

    /* ------- Merge list1 and list2 into listn ------- */
    while (1) {
        if (list1[p1] < list2[p2]) {
            listn[pn] = list1[p1];
            p1 = p1 + 1;  pn = pn + 1;
            if (p1 > 5) {
               for (i = p2; i<5; i++) {
                    listn[pn] =list2[p2];
                    p2 = p2 + 1;  pn = pn + 1;
               }
               break;
            }
        }
        else {
           listn[pn] = list2[p2];
           p2 = p2 + 1;  pn = pn + 1;
           if (p2 > 4) {
               for (i = p1; i<6; i++) {
                   listn[pn] =list1[p1];
                   p1 = p1 + 1;  pn = pn + 1;
               }
               break;
           }
        }
    }
    /* ---------- Print out results of merge ---------- */
    printf("\nNew merged list:\n");
    for (i = 0;  i < 11; i++) {
        printf("listn[%d] is %d\n",i,listn[i]);
    }
}
```

In this sample program, the three pointers are *p1*, *p2*, and *pn*. They are pointers for the three arrays *list1*, *list2*, and *listn*, respectively.

Search

Sometimes you may want to find a single entry in an existing list so you can retrieve the related data, update the existing data, or insert an additional entry at that point. You could start at the beginning of the list and work your way down each entry until you come to the one you want. This process will work every time. Sometimes, you will only need to look at one entry—when the one you want is the first one in the list. Other times, you will need to go through the whole list. In a list of 128 entries, the average number of entries you will have to look at to find the one you want is 64. This is called a **linear** (or **sequential**) **search** and would be necessary if the list were not ordered on the key you were looking for.

If the list has been ordered, there are other search algorithms that try to improve this average by taking advantage of the order the list is stored in. One such search algorithm is called a **binary search**. It will find a particular entry out of 128 entries by looking at no more than six other entries. You may have played a game as a child that uses this approach: "Pick a number from one to a hundred. I will guess your number in seven tries, if you will tell me whether my guess is high or low." The process is as follows. Make the first guess half of the total number of entries in the list. If the guess is high, take the lower half. If the guess is low, take the upper half, and repeat the process. In other words, you will have eliminated half of the total list with the first guess. Now do it again and eliminate half of the remaining group by picking a number that is half of the remaining numbers. Assume the person had picked the number 37 out of the numbers from 1 to 128. Your guesses would go as follows:

first guess (midway between 1 and 128)	64	high
second guess (midway between 1 and 64)	32	low
third guess (midway between 32 and 64)	48	high
fourth guess (midway between 32 and 48)	40	high
fifth guess (midway between 32 and 40)	36	low
sixth guess (midway between 36 and 40)	38	high
seventh guess (midway between 36 and 38)	37	HIT

This example demonstrates a binary search. If you were using BASIC, you would have to use this or some other search algorithm.

In C, on the other hand, there are some library functions that you can call to search a list for some key. The functions **lfind()** and **lsearch()** will perform linear searches for you. Also, if you have an ordered list, there is a function called **bsearch()** that will perform a binary search. The following code demonstrates how to use the bsearch() function:

```
/* -------------------- PROG-39.C --------------------- */
/* ----------- Demonstrate bsearch function ----------- */

#include <stdlib.h>

int list[6] = {123, 200, 357, 402, 456, 678 };

/* ---------- Test routine for bsearch to use --------- */
int tst(int *entry, int *key)
{
     return(*entry - *key);
}


/* --- Search array and print address pointer of key -- */
main()
{
    int skey = 200;
    int *pt;

    /* ---- Call bsearch function to look for key ----- */
    pt = bsearch( &skey, list, 6, 2, tst);

    /* -------- Print out results of search ----------- */
    if (pt != NULL) {
        printf("List starts at %p - Key at %p\n",list,pt);
    }
    else {
        printf("Key not in list.\n");
    }
}
```

The bsearch() function is similar in format to qsort(). The following line is the call to the binary search function in the sample program:

```
pt = bsearch( &skey, list, 6, 2, tst );
```

The *&skey* is an address pointer to the key you want to search for in the array, and *list* is the name of the array that is to be searched. The number **6** represents the number of entries in the array, and **2** is the byte size of each entry. As in the qsort() function, *tst* is a user-defined test function that must return the following:

- a value less than zero if the entry is less than the key
- a value of zero if the key and the entry are equal
- a value greater than zero if the entry is greater than the key

The *pt* is an address pointer that will contain the address where bsearch() found a match in the array. If no match was found, a NULL is returned. The sample program gives you the address that was returned. Remember, you can access an array, using either an array index or an address pointer. To access the array with an index pointer, just convert the address returned to an index, using the byte count and the address of the array.

The function bsearch() is defined as returning a type void. Because of this, in some cases it may be necessary to change the type of the return value, using a cast. (A **cast** temporarily converts the variable type.) You can do this by changing the bsearch() call in the following way:

```
pt = (int *) bsearch( &skey, list, 6, 2, tst );
```

This cast forces the return to be an integer address pointer.

ENSURING SECURITY

So far in this chapter, you have examined ways to check for valid input of data and ways to handle and store the data once it is in the system. One last topic should be mentioned before you move on to the next chapter: ensuring the security of that data.

Ensuring security of machine-readable data generally centers around two tasks:

- protecting against the physical loss of the data
- keeping the information private or secret

In any environment (professional or personal), you must safeguard your computerized data from physical loss or destruction. The method you use and the degree to which you use it depends on the value of the data and the concerns you have for its safety.

Backups

All machine-readable data of any value should be backed up. This simply means that you make a machine-readable copy. Even if you back up your data to some degree and know of the MS-DOS COPY and DISKCOPY commands, any professional development or operational system should have a regular and systematic procedure for taking and storing backups that will satisfy the needs of the situation.

Timing is important. If the data changes, you should make backups often enough that you can live with loss of the data between backups. If the loss of a week's programming work or a week's collection of data would not create an undue hardship, you could back up once a week. On the other hand, perhaps a day's loss of data would be too much, and you should back up twice a day or even hourly. In some cases, the collection of data is so valuable that it is unacceptable to lose any data. When this is so, a duplicate copy of the data should be made simultaneously with the original capture of the data. To ensure that the data is not lost, redundant computers could be used to safeguard against hardware failure, and auxiliary power sources could automatically take over in case of power failure. You need to weigh how much data can you afford to lose against the time and expense of making the backup and storing it in a safe place.

Backups may involve other concerns. If you have a hard disk on your PC, the time it takes to back up the total disk to diskettes may take so long that you are reluctant to back up as often as you feel necessary. You could establish a procedure to back up only the data that has changed, and thus reduce the time required for the backup, or you could add a streaming tape to speed up the process. The hard disk would then be backed up onto magnetic tape.

Nor is simply making a backup sufficient protection for the data you want to safeguard. Where the backups are stored is also critical. If a fire destroyed the original data, would your backup survive? Not if it was stored in a desk drawer next to the computer. If the backup is not stored in a fireproof safe, it should be kept off site—someplace where the same disaster would not destroy both the original and the backup simultaneously. In the San Francisco area, where earthquakes are a concern, come companies have off-site storage nearly 100 miles away in Sacramento.

Another area of concern is the number of copies of old backups to keep. Do you have only one diskette or one set of diskettes that you use for backups? Each time you make a new backup, do you write over the previous one? What happens if the original data is clobbered without your being aware of it? If you make a backup of that bad data, you will destroy the only good backup you had. Or suppose your backup diskette is physically worn out and will no longer reliably store data. In that case, no backup you make would be any good. Keeping more than one past backup is important. You should keep them all—at least for a while. Keep a sufficient backlog of them around to safeguard against the possibility of having something go wrong with one or more of the backups.

If you are an analyst implementing a computer system, you must design a backup procedure that suits the situation and security needs of the project. The procedure should anticipate the types of problems that could occur. It should allow your computerized data to survive with an acceptable level of loss in case of a disaster or tampering. The following backup procedure might be used in a situation where no loss is preferred, but one to five days' loss of machine-readable data could be accommodated:

Daily Back up the data on diskettes.

Use a seven-day cycle of diskettes, reusing the backup diskettes that are seven days old.

Store diskettes on-site in a fireproof safe.

Hold original hard copy of data for seven days to allow for the reconstruction of the machine-readable data.

Weekly Before making the day's backup, verify that yesterday's backup is good by ensuring all or at least random parts are readable.

Pull yesterday's backup from the daily cycle and store off-site for one month.

Put the off-site backup diskettes that are a month old back into the daily cycle.

Quarterly Retire latest weekly backup diskettes and archive them indefinitely. Put a new set of diskettes into the daily cycle to replace the retired set.

Following are a few more points to consider:

- The storage environment in which you keep these long-term backups is important. Your data can be lost as a result of improper temperature, poor handling, nearby electrical currents, humidity, dust, and smoke.
- In some situations there are legal requirements governing how long data must be kept.
- Magnetic storage media do wear out. It is a good practice to keep a history of use on backup media and not use it for critical data beyond the period suggested by the manufacturer.

This approach assumes that the data is cumulative. Each day builds from the previous day's data. It gives you a week's hard copy from which to reconstruct data. It also gives you copies of machine-readable data for the last seven consecutive days stored on-site in a fireproof safe. Also, you have the four most current weekly copies of history stored off-site. The average age of the newest off-site data is 3.5 days old. The maximum age of the newest off-site data would be seven days. Finally, you have quarterly archive backups dating back as long as the system has been used. The greatest value of these last backups will usually be for historical research. It allows the reconstruction of a time in the past for such purposes as tax audits.

If you are concerned about the privacy of the information as well as its safety, you will want to ensure that both on-site and off-site data storage is secure with restricted and controlled access. The backup approach just described would give some protection against the purposeful and malicious destruction of all data simultaneously.

Limited Access

Your primary concern so far has been for acts of nature and accidental loss or destruction of data, but what about when the concern is the privacy and secrecy of your information? Instead of protecting against accidents, you are attempting to stop an unauthorized person who is purposely trying to tamper with your data. Protecting against unauthorized or malicious access to private information is an entirely different problem. Here you might come up against professional computer criminals, hackers trying to get into your system for the thrill of it, an unauthorized but curious employee, or industrial spies looking for your company's secrets. It is extremely difficult to protect data from a knowledgeable, informed, and malicious individual or team determined to break your security system.

A key word here is **informed**. If you are attempting to keep your data private, a good place to start is to keep all information and procedures relating to the data private. The less that is generally known about how, when, and where your data is used, the harder it will be for the wrong person to get at it. When an informed person leaves the company, you should change the procedures, passwords, and dataphone numbers. It is a good idea to change these on a continuing basis anyway. It can be an inconvenience for the people who work with the system, but it is surprising how often this type of information appears on hacker bulletin boards.

Passwords

Using passwords is one approach for restricting access to a computer or a software system. Passwords are common on larger multi-user systems. The initial programs will not allow a person access to the main programs and the data associated with them until the user gives a proper password. This password might allow the user to have access to only a small amount of data or to the total system, depending on how the security system is designed. Larger multi-user computer systems often have built-in hardware and software security features that will help programmers secure a system and the data.

A password is usually tied to an additional identification number or name. That way, each individual can have a separate password. When you try to enter the system you are asked to identify yourself. This could be your name or ID number, something that would never change. You are then asked to give your password, which should be changed periodically. The password is not displayed on the screen as you type so that it cannot be seen by someone looking over your shoulder. If the password is not the one the computer expects, it will usually allow another try, assuming a typing error; however, if you fail to give the correct password after some set number of tries, the system will assume you are trying to break the code and will take some action at that point. It might simply refuse to respond to anyone using that name or ID number for a period of time, or it may let you continue to try but will not accept even the correct password at that point. It will usually keep track of the unsuccessful attempts to enter the system and report it. If the password is given correctly, you are allowed access to the system and the type of data for which you have clearance.

It is important that each person keep his or her password secure. Unfortunately, people often write down their password so they will not forget it, and they keep it near the computer or terminal where they use it. This is like putting the key under the doormat. In addition, people will often choose a password that is easy to remember—such as their nickname or the name of their cat. It might be some number they know, like their birthday, or the value for pi. All these strategies make it easy for a person trying to break into a system. For your own good, you should avoid making it easy to break your password. Commercial computer systems keep records of who has used the system. You could be blamed or billed for another person's action if that person used your access code. In commercial systems, you are billed for any use made of your ID and password.

Another approach used by someone trying to break into a system is to try and find a list of all the passwords. People have been successful in breaking into a computer by going through the computer room trash. All hard copy reports of passwords and any proprietary data should be destroyed before being discarded. Sometimes that list of passwords or proprietary information can be found near the computer.

When you are given access to a computer system, it doesn't mean that you get access to all parts of it. You are not given access to all the other passwords, for example. You are given access to data on a need-to-know basis, but for a determined individual, limited access might be enough. By looking through "unused" areas of memory or the disk, people have found remnants of old data still there and readable after the original user released the resource. Copies of passwords have been found in this way, allowing security to be compromised. Secure systems will zero out all memory and storage devices before releasing them for others to use.

If you allow a user into a secured area in which proprietary data is kept, you must control all the user's actions from then on. You must not allow users to abort out of the code while they are in the secured area. If they break out, they can look at and do whatever they want in that area. This means you must build in interrupt traps for all possible abort attempts, including error conditions. The traps should remove the user from the secured area and take away all special privileges before releasing program control.

As was mentioned earlier, passwords are generally used on larger systems that have both hardware and software features to aid in restricting a user to only limited areas of the computer and to limited parts of data. On a PC, it is much more difficult to protect against someone getting at proprietary data if that person has physical access to the computer and data. So the first security defense is physical: keep your valuable information and programs locked up.

There are other strategies for protecting your proprietary data and programs. As mentioned earlier, the second line of defense is secrecy. The less that is known about how you operate, the harder it will be for someone to find a way to take advantage of you. To protect their programs against piracy, software manufacturers have gone to great lengths to secure their diskettes so those diskettes cannot be copied. They write on areas of the diskettes that are normally not used or place erroneous information on the diskettes to confuse the conventional COPY utilities. These methods all require secrecy. After someone figures out what was done, it is easy to write a program that will copy these protected diskettes.

The third line of defense in protecting your data also requires secrecy. This defense is to encode your data so that it is meaningless to someone else in its existing form.

Encrypting Data

Some situations require data to be transmitted or physically carried from one location to another. Data is particularly vulnerable at such times. At other times you must have the data available on the computer for its intended use, but you need some way to hide the data so others that have access to the system will not be able to find or understand it. In situations that require a maximum effort to safeguard the data, that data is **encrypted**. Obviously, once encrypted, the data requires some method of getting it back into a usable form at a later date. It must somehow be decoded. This is where the secrecy comes in. If someone knows how you created the encrypted data, that person can recreate the original text. You must also realize that the computer is a perfect tool for someone attempting to break a code.

The following are three rudimentary approaches to encoding data.

A **table lookup** is an often-used technique for creating codes. For each alphanumeric character, there is a matching code in a table. To encipher a character, just look it up in the table and take the code that is equivalent to it. Deciphering simply reverses the process. For computers, this approach has a serious drawback. For someone to decipher the code, the table must exist in the computer. All that person must do to break the code is find the table.

A second method that has advantages and disadvantages is to **embed** your text in extraneous data. For example, create a block of random text, and then insert one character of your proprietary text after every third character of the extraneous data. Your message will be well hidden. A better approach might be to vary the position in which your character is inserted. One way of doing this is to use the random number generator. You know that with the same starting seed, C's random number generator will reproduce the same sequence of pseudo-random numbers time and again; therefore, you could let the random number generator generate the positions to insert and withdraw the good data from the extraneous data. (This is also possible with the random number generator in BASIC.) Although your decoding program would need to exist somewhere, it is not necessary to leave the seed for the random number generator in the computer or in the program. This seed number can be kept in your head. The disadvantage to this approach is the increased memory space necessary to store the extraneous data used to hide the text.

A third approach is to use that wonderful logical operator, the **exclusive or** (XOR). It was used previously in this book on a graphics screen; the image on the screen was completely scrambled when an image was XORed over an existing image; recall how the original image would magically reappear when you would XOR the same image to the same spot a second time. This also happens when you XOR an eight-bit mask to the ASCII code for a character. The ASCII code will be converted into some strange series of eight bits, but the original ASCII code will reappear if you XOR the same mask to this strange series of bits. Note the following example:

0100 0111	ASCII code for letter G in binary
1100 1100	Secret mask in binary
--------------	XOR mask to ASCII code
1000 1011	Encoded result to be saved on disk
1100 1100	Same secret mask again
--------------	XOR mask to encoded byte
0100 0111	The original ASCII code reappears

Again, this mask does not need to be stored in the computer or be part of the program. It can be in your head and only given to the computer when encoding or decoding is required. The mask can be changed whenever you want, as long as the same mask is used to encode as was used to decode.

There is a problem with this approach; only 256 different combinations of bits or possible masks are possible. Someone with a computer could easily write a program to try all the possibilities and break the code. You could improve on this approach by increasing the number of bits in the mask. A mask of 16 bits would encode two characters at once and have over 65,000 different possible combinations someone would need to try in order to break the code. Or a mask of 32 bits would encode four characters at once and have well over four billion different possible masks. If someone wrote a program that would try all possible combinations for masks, and if with each different mask it would check the results against a dictionary of English words, it would only take about 135 years to break the code—assuming the program could check the results of each different mask at a rate of one per second.

The important point is to keep the mask, seed, and/or algorithm that is used to create the coded information a secret. Perhaps you can think of an entirely new and different approach that might be better. For example, you could combine the last two approaches discussed or use the random number generator to constantly change the mask used in the third approach.

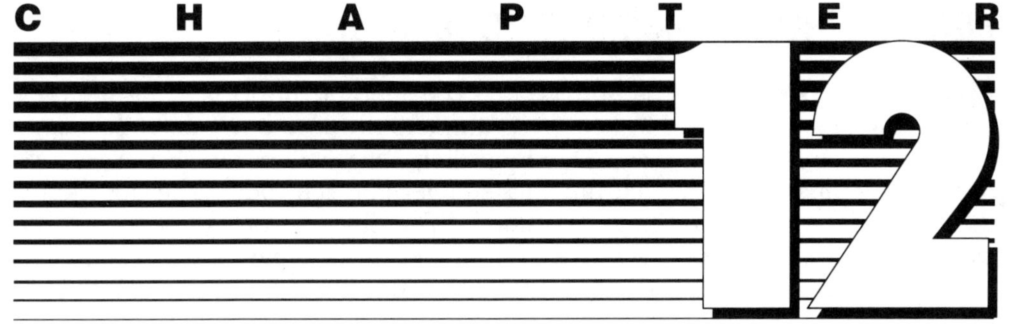

MASTERING PROGRAMMING ERRORS

FINDING PROGRAMMING ERRORS

Earlier in this book, it was mentioned that considerable effort is being spent on developing new techniques to help programmers produce bug-free code—code without errors. Although these techniques help, bugs still occur. From past experience, companies know that the bugs still get into the code. They also know that it is important to find these problems. The obvious errors are recognized early and fixed. It is the bugs that are not immediately apparent that companies spend considerable time and effort trying to find. Statistically they know bugs exist. The problem is finding them. This concern has lead the industry into creating a variety of procedures and techniques just to find problems.

Design Control

Companies are expending a lot of effort to catch problems early—the earlier the better. Finding these programming errors is expensive; the later a bug is found in the development process, the more expensive it is to correct. If a bug is not recognized until after the program gets into the customer's hands, its effect can be quite expensive. The error hurts in two ways: first, it can mean the loss of customer faith in the product, causing reduced sales; second, it means that to correct the problem, you incur the time and expense of fixing the problem at multiple sites rather than just one.

The best place to catch a bug is before it gets into the code. If you catch a problem in the design stage, you have saved over 90% of the potential debugging cost. This process of looking for the problems early is usually called **design control**. Some software development companies have a whole department dedicated to design control. People in this department study designs of any new product. A problem in design logic could mean that the whole concept is wrong and that any and all work in that direction will be wasted. They also examine the problems that occurred in the past. Are there any patterns of where and why problems appear? Does a particular approach or piece of code have a long history of problems? Would it be better to use a different approach or to rewrite a library function from scratch rather than incorporate the old code in a new product and continue to chase bugs?

Most of a design control group's effort goes into design and code reviews. Programmers document the design for the module or function they are developing. The document usually includes the code or at least the pseudo-code. It is distributed to design control and to other programmers and developers on the project for review. Often this review is followed by a **walkthrough**; this is a group session in which the programmer gives a step-by-step explanation of the design (or code). The purpose of the meeting is to find and remove potential problems and errors in an early stage, before the code reaches the computer. The reviewing group is usually made up of peers in order to foster a shared commitment to the success of the project. Managers are often purposely excluded so that programmers needn't be concerned about losing face.

Quality Assurance

No one in a software development company (except the sales staff, of course) really expects code to be bug-free on the first attempt. Some modules simply have fewer bugs than others. The programmer often sees and fixes obvious problems before anyone is aware they existed; however, there are other types of bugs that are not so obvious.

Bugs can be placed into three categories: bugs you have found and fixed; bugs you have found and are looking for a way to solve; and bugs you don't know about yet. It is this last group of problems, the ones the programmer misses, that yet another department dedicates its working life to finding. This is the **quality assurance** (QA) department.

Before you can fix a problem, you must know that the problem exists. Quality assurance groups are made up of people whose job is to find such problems. There are two cardinal rules to follow when it comes to QA. The staff cannot be made up of the same programmers who developed the code, and the staff cannot report to the manager of the development team.

The developer of a piece of code knows what the code will do. He or she will test it to make sure it does what it is supposed to do, but programmers are too close to the code. If they did not think to write code to cover a particular situation, chances are they will not think to test to see what the program will do in that situation. People who don't have any preconceived ideas or limitations in their thinking must test the code to shake out a computer program for bugs. A programmer's primary job is to program. For quality assurance, you need people testing whose primary job is to test.

Development managers are under constant pressure to deliver a product yesterday. When that pressure becomes great enough, the manager will pull resources from testing and put them into development. This solves the problem like magic. With more people working on development, the product is completed sooner. When fewer people are testing the product, fewer problems are found, and the product can be released sooner. Unfortunately, the product is more likely to contain bugs that the customer will find.

Quality assurance is also usually responsible for keeping track of known problems on the system. It will have some type of error-reporting process that describes the problem, usually by means of a report. Common names are "Problem Report" and "Incident Report." The report is submitted by anyone who finds a problem. It records how, when, and who discovered the error. It usually has information about what equipment and what version of the software was being used. If at all possible, all conditions necessary to reproduce the error are listed, along with a description of the erroneous results.

QA gives the report a priority, logs it, and distributes copies to appropriate individuals (usually to someone on the development staff, perhaps also to training and documentation staff). The problem is examined to determine how it is to be fixed. In some cases, when the current result is reasonable and a programming change would be quite difficult, the documentation is simply changed to reflect the current results. When the problem is fixed, a description of how the problem was resolved and what modules or functions were involved is returned to QA. QA logs the solution, tests to ensure it works, and then passes this information on to all concerned, including the person reporting the problem initially.

Types of Tests

How does QA find these unknown bugs? A variety of tests is usually carried out, although QA is not always responsible for all of them. The purpose of each test is the same: to find those hidden bugs. The different types of tests used are as follows:

- **Unit tests.** The first level of test is called the unit test. These tests are on the module or function level. No other development functions or modules are used in the unit test. The purpose is to isolate and test that particular piece of code. The programmer often performs this test because the test usually requires a programmer to write special test interfaces or stubs to call the function with the different arguments in order to test all the options. Also, because it is the programmer's responsibility to produce bug-free code, the programmer should go through this process anyway. Good programmers will try to deliver clean code to QA and not rely on QA to do the programmers' work.

- **Integration tests**. The next level of test is called integration testing. All the individual modules or functions are put together and tested to make sure they fit and work together as a whole. The test is not as concerned about all application features or the end-result as much as it is with making sure all the parts talk to each other. This level of testing often falls to the development staff. Although QA could perform the tests, it is more efficient to have the development staff correct the problems.

- **System tests**. This is where the entire system is tested. There is no question about who should perform these tests — the QA staff should. All modules and options should be tested here in a lifelike environment to ensure the system works properly. A thorough set of tests is made up in advance. (See "General Debugging Concepts and Tools" later in this chapter.) The development staff would not know of or help make up the specific tests. The system is tested until it runs without failing.

- **Acceptance tests**. Sometimes, a customer requires that the product pass a series of tests as a condition of purchase. These are specified in the contract and are similar to but probably not as extensive as the system tests.

- **Regression tests**. This kind of testing is more of a concept than a separate set of tests. Suppose the system test was made up of 200 individual tests and only one of those tests failed. When the problem is corrected and the fix incorporated into the code, it is not sufficient simply to run the one test that failed to ensure the system runs properly. All 200 tests should be run again. Whenever a change is made to the code, it is necessary to go back and retest the entire system to ensure that the change did not inadvertently introduce more bugs. This process of retesting after any change in the product is referred to as regression testing.

Testing Techniques

Finding a bug is only part of QA's task. The other part is to pass sufficient information to the developers so that the bug can be reproduced. One of the most difficult tasks a programmer has is to find what causes a bug. If that bug is known to exist but cannot be reproduced on a predictable basis, the task of finding the problem can be enormous. It is for this reason that testing procedures are controlled. Random testing is not good procedure. Parts of the system are often missed and go untested, and when a problem is found, the tester will often have trouble reproducing all the conditions that led to its appearance.

Knowing the environment that existed at the time of a program failure is very important. You should know what equipment, operating system, and particular software versions were being used at the time, as well as the contents of the disk files or databases before and after the test. In other words, it is important to have a known and controlled test environment.

For this reason, the QA staff will set up what are called **test beds**. These are "snapshots" of files and databases. In the test bed, the contents of all files or databases are known. They are saved in this known state so they can be recalled and used over and over again. In this way, the person performing the tests always knows what the data looked like at the start of the test. All conditions and steps leading to the time when the test bed was created are known and reproducible. Several different test beds can be used during a complete system test. Obviously, one test bed will be empty to ensure that a system can be brought up from scratch. Other test beds will be built to test different parts or options. You should know what the conditions were at the start of a test so you can check the total file system after the test to ensure that the anticipated and correct results occurred and that only the anticipated changes took place.

Another important step in the testing process is to ensure that all portions of the system are actually tested. Some systems are so large and involved that it would be impossible to test all possible branches within a reasonable time frame and with reasonable resources, but certainly all functions or modules of code should be tested, and all options on screens or windows should be tried. You cannot expect to touch on every part of the system by randomly testing different parts. To make sure that all parts of the system are tested at least once, create a test matrix.

A **test matrix** is a two-dimensional array. For example, examine a matrix to test the options on several screens. Across the top of the matrix would be all of the screen options, and down the side would be all of the code modules or functions that make up the total system. It would resemble the following:

Options	Screen 1 A	B	C	Screen 2 D	E	F	Screen 3 ... G	H	...
Function 1									
Function 2				8					
Function 3				8					
Function 4						9			
...									

In this matrix, the different tests are placed so that they indicate what functions or parts of code they use and what screen options are requested. For example, test number 8 exercises option D of screen 2, and in so doing uses function 2 and function 3. Test 9 exercises option F of screen 2 but only uses function 4. The staff building tests must have code listings so that they can see what functions are called with each option. They should also have the documentation to ensure that the programs match what is stated in the documentation. Tests must be made up so that every horizontal line in the array has at least one test on it, and every vertical line in the array has at least one test on it. Important options should have multiple tests so they can hit more of the possible branches within the option.

Because it is important to be able to reproduce a problem, every step must be described and followed precisely, just as you might follow the script of a play. In fact, the write-ups of the tests are called **test scripts**. Following these scripts verbatim will always recreate the problem, if one appears. Anyone should be able to run them. In fact, executing test scripts can be an excellent way for sales staff, installers, or trainers to become familiar with a system while at the same time performing the needed task of testing it. A test script is designed to test one portion of the system. After it is designed, it is incorporated into the test matrix as previously described.

A test script will first describe all the conditions that must exist before the test starts. It tells what equipment must be on-line, which test bed must be in place, how the screen should appear at the beginning of the test, and what, if any, tests must have been previously run. (It is not an efficient practice to have too many tests tied to one another in this way. If the first one fails, none of the others can be run until the first bug is fixed.) After all the prerequisites are specified, the test script will spell out exactly which keys to press and what data to put into the system. The test script then goes on to show what changes are expected as a result of running the test and includes descriptions or samples of changes on the screen, hardcopy printouts, and the expected state of the file data when the test is complete.

In the early stages of testing, it is reasonable to manually test a system because it usually has enough bugs that it will probably not run in an expected or reliable manner for any great length of time; however, once the system starts to perform in a predictable manner, you can think about automating the tests. This means you write a program that will simulate the keystrokes necessary to perform each of the test scripts. This automated program can also look at the results of the test and compare them to what was expected in order to verify that everything is working properly. Automating the system test allows the tedious and time-consuming task of regression testing to take place in a minimum amount of time and with little effort when only a few changes have been made to the code. Because the process is so time-consuming, it is a good idea to automate the checking of changes to data files right from the beginning of testing.

CORRECTING PROGRAMMING ERRORS

Knowing that a bug exists does not mean you know what is causing the problem, and once you find out what is causing the problem, you still may not see a way to solve it. When a bug is known to exist, the programmer's work has just begun. The first and oftentimes most difficult part of this work is to find the cause of the problem. The second part, finding a solution once the reason is known, is conventional programming.

Finding the reason for a bug within a program is a difficult, frustrating, and time-consuming task. Many say that the programmer who is good at finding the cause of a bug has the knowledge of an encyclopedia, the intuition of Sherlock Holmes, the endurance of a marathon runner, and the luck of a riverboat gambler. There are no magic rules to follow that will always give you the reason for a bug. When looking for the cause of a problem, you are like a detective hunting for clues. Sometimes you're lucky—the right clue appears immediately, and you recognize it. Other times, it takes an inordinate amount of effort to uncover the clue that leads you to the reason for the problem.

What you can do with the clues you get depends on your experience and knowledge of the computer and the programming language. You are a detective using all your resources together to help you solve the mystery. At one time, programming was considered an art as much as a science. Today, this is no longer true. Programming is a science. However, debugging code is one aspect of programming that still can be considered an art. The stronger you are with the scientific tools of programming, the better you will be at finding the cause of a problem; however, intuition and creative thought are needed to find and correctly understand the clues that a bug will leave behind.

Once you have discovered the cause of a problem, you must then find a solution. In many cases, solutions are straightforward and obvious. Typing errors are examples that are usually easily corrected; however, some bugs are much more difficult to correct. An example might be one that is the result of an oversight or poor design in program logic. A decision must be made about whether to do a redesign and start over from scratch or to try modifying the existing code to correct the problem. (This is much like the problem programmers have when they are asked to add a feature to an existing system that was not originally designed to handle such a task.) In this situation, the solution may be very complicated and end up affecting many other parts of the system. It is this type of situation that makes regression testing mandatory because even a minor change may have far-reaching ramifications.

The remainder of this chapter is devoted to ways of finding the cause of errors.

GENERAL DEBUGGING CONCEPTS AND TOOLS

You can learn that there is a bug in your program in two ways: You will see an error message, or the program will not do what you expect.

Error messages are generated by the compiler or interpreter when you try to compile or run your program. They might also be generated from software that is active when your program is running. In the latter situation, the messages might be generated by the operating system or run-time modules that were loaded with your program when it started to execute. If you receive an error message, it is often short and cryptic and may not tell much about the actual problem because one message is often used for a variety of situations; however, it is still your best clue for what the problem might be. Look up the message in the appropriate manual. The manual will give more detail about the situations that cause this message to be printed.

If the error message still does not make sense, or if there was no message but just unexpected results, you will have to resort to other measures. Read through the code and consider what caused the error. As you become more familiar with the language, bugs will sometimes jump out at you.

If you still don't have an inkling about what the problem is, you might try to **dry run** the program. With just a listing in front of you, go through each step of the code as if you were the computer. With paper and pencil, keep track of the values for the different variables. Search for that clue. Is there anything that doesn't seem to be right?

A better approach to dry running is to let the computer single-step through the program so you can look at the results of each operation. Unfortunately, this is not always easy to do. Some languages, such as MUMPS, allow you to single-step through high-level code. Some computers have a switch you can set that will cause the system to stop after each machine instruction cycle. Some languages allow you to insert **breakpoints**. When the CPU reaches a breakpoint, it will stop and let you look at the results of the execution up to that point. If these aids are not available, the next best strategy is to simulate single-stepping by creating your own breakpoints in the code. First, make a copy of your source code. With this new copy, feel free to insert as much new debugging code as you need. Add code that will print out the results of questionable variables at appropriate places. Remember, you are looking for some clue to what is happening. Put in extra code that will help by giving you more clues about what the program is doing.

Suppose you put in an instruction to print the value of a variable after a certain piece of code is executed, and the variable is never printed out. This means you did not get to that spot in the code. The program is branching in some way that you did not expect. In this case, you need a **trace routine**—a routine that will show you exactly what path the program takes when it executes. BASIC has a built-in trace routine. If you are writing in a language without one, put in additional debugging print instructions at critical branch points to see which way the program is going.

After you find what path the program is taking, add more code to find out why it goes that way. Perhaps a variable contains a value that it should not have in a branch instruction. Think about where the variable got such a value. In a large block of code, it is difficult to find all the places in which a given variable is used or modified. This is particularly true of a language such as BASIC, in which all variables are global in the sense that they have a scope equal to the total program in memory. In this situation, you need another tool or utility program called a **cross-reference listing** (XREF). This utility will print a source listing of your program in which each line of code is given a line number. (The line numbers are for languages that do not have a built-in line number.) It will print out a list of all variables and labels. Each variable and label will be followed by a series of line numbers. These are all the program lines in which the variable or label was referenced. This XREF utility is very useful for debugging, and most professional programming shops have them available for their staff.

One type of problem immediately stands out when you use a cross-reference listing. Any variable or label that is referenced only once is an error of some kind. It may be a remnant from some old code, and all but this one reference was removed. It may be a variable that was intended to be used in some way, but all the code is not yet implemented. In languages that do not require a variable to be declared, it could be a typing error that was really intended to be a different variable.

Now that you have an idea where the variable was changed, ask yourself why the value was changed. You could add some code that will act as a trap. Whenever the variable is changed, this trap will spring and you will know when it was changed and what it was changed to, which should also give you a clue about why it was changed.

There may be times when you can't seem to isolate where a problem is happening. The best approach for this problem might be to again make a copy of the source program, but this time, instead of adding extra debugging code, start removing code. Try to isolate the offending code. When the problem disappears, you know you have removed too much. You have found the problem. Put it back and try to isolate the bug to just the one offending line of code. Suppose you find the exact line of code that is causing the problem, but you still don't see what is wrong. Then, start isolating the problem in that line of code. Remove or change parts of that one instruction until you can see exactly what is happening.

Another type of problem you might encounter is that the program worked last week, but it is not working now. You made a few changes and can't seem to remember just where they all were. You need a different tool for this—a **source compare**. This type of utility will compare two program source files and print out only the differences between them. Run the source compare against your current program and an old backup copy, and you will be able to isolate the changes that have been made.

The file or **memory dump** is another tool used by professional programmers. The contents of a file or an area of memory are dumped to a printer. You can look for differences between what you expect and what is actually there. This will help you verify that arrays and data files are getting the right data. You could compare a memory dump of your program before it starts to run with a dump of the code after it has run or when it has crashed. You might discover something such as a string variable in C that is longer than the declared size of the variable; as a result, some of your machine language code would have been written over by data. With a dump, you are looking at the machine language. This is usually printed in octal or hex, and, to be of much value, you would need to be able to read and make sense out of the machine language.

The debugging concepts discussed here are general and can be applied to any language; however, each language is different and might need slightly different variations in these methods. For this reason, BASIC and Turbo C will be examined separately.

Debugging with BASIC

BASIC has some very powerful aids for debugging code. The first is a built-in trace routine. If you want to follow the path a program takes, you simply enter the command TRON before entering RUN. The trace routine will display on the screen the BASIC line number of each line of code it is going to execute before it executes that line. The line numbers will appear between brackets. With this feature, you can follow program execution line by line.

The TRON command can also be used as an instruction. If you want to trace only one section of code, then add a temporary line of code to your BASIC program where you want the trace to start. That line of code might resemble the following:

```
840 ...
841 TRON
850 ...
```

Turning the trace routine off requires a different command: TROFF. It can also be incorporated in the BASIC code and made part of the program.

Another feature of BASIC is the ability to put breakpoints in your code. This is done with the STOP instruction. When BASIC encounters a STOP instruction, it will stop execution and display a message. The important point is that STOP leaves everything in the computer ready to continue if you want to continue. A sample instruction might resemble the following:

```
1251 STOP
```

The message printed by BASIC before it stops would be

```
Break in 1251
```

At this point, you may want to examine or change the contents of some of the variables, which is possible using the direct command mode of BASIC. Just type in what you want to do without line numbers and it will be done without altering your program's ability to start running again at the point it stopped. A command such as

```
PRINT A
```

will display the contents of variable A. To save typing, you may also want to temporarily add the PRINT instruction to your program. Do this on the line just before the STOP instruction. When the program stops, you can also give a command such as the following:

```
A = 5
```

This command will assign the variable A the value of 5, but it will still not affect your program's ability to continue from where it left off. (Do not change any line of code in your program as this will cause BASIC to terminate the run and make it impossible to continue except by starting over.)

When you are at a breakpoint in BASIC and you want to continue, simply type the command CONT. This will cause your program to start up again where it left off and continue running until it runs into another STOP instruction or the program completes.

The main debugging tool missing in BASIC is a cross-reference listing. When you write a large program in BASIC, one of the biggest problems you have is keeping track of variables. They are not declared and can be used throughout the program. You run the risk of inadvertently using the same variable more than once or mistyping the variable name and having two variables in place of the one you intended.

If you need an XREF, and you don't want to purchase one or go to the trouble of writing your own, consider a quick-and-dirty solution. The following program will look for the appearance of a single variable and print the numbers of all the lines it appears in:

```
1       '* ---------------- LOOKFOR.BAS ----------------- *
2       '* - Prints all lines containing desired string - *
3       '* ---------------------------------------------- *
4       '* ------------- Variable list ------------------ *
5       '* --- FILENA$    - Holds BASIC filename --------- *
6       '* --- LINENO$    - Holds current line number ---- *
7       '* --- L$         - Holds current line of text --- *
8       '* --- V$         - Holds desired string --------- *
9       '* --- ERRF       - Error flag, holds error type - *
10      '* --- T??        - Are temporary variables ------ *
98      '* ---------------------------------------------- *
99      '* -------------- Initialization ---------------- *
100  ON ERROR GOTO 10000
110  KEY OFF
120  SCREEN 0,1 : WIDTH 80
999     '* -------------- Start of program -------------- *
1000 CLS
1010 PRINT : PRINT : PRINT "                LOOKFOR"
1012 PRINT "Displays all line numbers in a BASIC program"
1014 PRINT "file that contain the string in question."
1016 PRINT "May be used to find program variables and "
1018 PRINT "labels." : PRINT
1020 PRINT "BASIC file must be saved as an ASCII file."
1022 PRINT "To do this save program with ``A'' switch."
1024 PRINT "      ( SAVE ``filename.BAS'' , A )"
1026 PRINT
1028 PRINT "Type labels in UPPERCASE as they appear in"
1030 PRINT "program listing." : PRINT
1040 PRINT "Type desired string followed by <CR>"
1042 LINE INPUT V$
```

continued...

...from previous page

```
1050 PRINT "What is the complete program filename"
1052 INPUT FILENA$
1060 OPEN "i",#2,FILENA$
1062 IF ERRF=3 THEN PRINT "Bad filename" :  BEEP
1064 IF ERRF=3 THEN ERRF=0 : FILENA$="" : GOTO 1050
1070 CLS
1080 PRINT "File ";FILENA$;" has string ";V$;" on lines:"
1199   '* ------------- Start of main loop ------------- *
1200 LINE INPUT #2, L$          '* ---- Get next line --- *
1202 IF ERRF=1 THEN PRINT " Done " : GOTO 9900
1210 GOSUB 4000                 '* -- Get line number --- *
1260 T = INSTR( 1, L$, V$)      '* ---- Process line ---- *
1270 IF T<>0 THEN PRINT LINENO$,
1290 GOTO 1200                  '* ----- End of loop ---- *
3999   '* ------------ Get line number ----------------- *
4000 LINENO$ = ""
4010 FOR T = 1 TO LEN(L$)
4020    TN$ = MID$(L$, T, 1)
4030    IF TN$<"0" OR TN$>"9" THEN 4090
4040    LINENO$ = LINENO$ + TN$
4050 NEXT T
4090 RETURN
9899   '* --------------- End program ------------------ *
9900 CLOSE #2
9990 END
9999   '* ------------ Error trapping ------------------ *
10000 IF ERL=1060 AND ERR=53 THEN ERRF=3 : RESUME NEXT
10010 IF ERL=1200 AND ERR=62 THEN ERRF=1 : RESUME NEXT
10080 ON ERROR GOTO 0           '* --- Error abort run -- *
```

You could improve this program by allowing it to look for multiple strings simultaneously.

Debugging with C

Knowing C as you do by now, you realize that it is not overly concerned about helping or making debugging easy for the programmer. If you make a mistake, it is your problem, not C's. You are in the "real" programmer's world now, and C is not going to hold your hand, although the Turbo C Integrated Environment does assist you slightly by showing you which line has the problem that is causing the error message or at least which line it thinks is causing the problem (see "Error Messages in TC" in Chapter 3).

Perhaps the best approach to make debugging easier in C is to increase your knowledge of C. By reading through this book, you are certainly working toward that goal; however, there is something else you could do to speed up this process: know the common errors that are made and keep an eye open for them. The following precautions will prevent bugs that appear with great regularity, especially with someone new to C:

- Make sure you remember to insert the ending semicolons.
- Remember that = is used for assignment and = = is used for comparisons.
- Be careful with uppercase and lowercase. For example, in C the variables var, Var, and VAR are considered three different variables.
- Remember to include an extra byte for the null character when you are declaring the size of a string.
- Be careful with braces {}, parentheses (), square brackets [ ], and angle brackets < >. Make sure you always have matching pairs and that you use the correct one for each given situation. This is especially important for C arrays, which use square brackets around each separate index.

  Example: var = array[9][2];

- Be careful with address pointers, and remember that some C library functions require that you pass an address instead of a variable. A good example is scanf().

In a professional programming shop that is using C, you will usually find an assortment of software tools to help debug code. These tools either will have been developed in-house or purchased from outside and are used to speed up the programming process. In fact, large programming operations will often have a "tools" group to develop and maintain the software that the development team uses to produce and debug code. If the resource is not available, you can always write your own. You have a feel for the types of debugging tools that are used, and there is not much a C program can't be made to do. That includes building debugging tools.

APPENDICES

APPENDIX A: BINARY NUMBER SYSTEM

The logic of today's digital computers depends on the binary number system. To the digital computer, a light is on or off. The computer doesn't try to measure how bright the light might be; it only notes that it is on. A spot on a diskette is magnetized or is not. A switch is on or off. Electrical current is flowing or is not. Everything in a digital computer is one of two states: on or off. Because of this fact, the binary number system is the natural language of the digital computer; the binary number system also has only two states or digits: a one and a zero. A one (1) is defined as meaning the current is on. A zero (0) is defined as meaning the current is off. When engineers designed and built the digital computer, they wired it to recognize ones and zeros as small switches turning current on and off throughout the computer.

Because the binary number system is the natural language of the computer, to really understand the digital computer you must know its language. Understanding the concept of number base is fundamental to understanding any number system. Our everyday decimal number system has a base ten. This means that each position in a number such as 7352 has a value that is some multiple of the number base—in this case, ten. The following example breaks this number apart:

```
7352 =  7000     + 300     + 50   + 2
7352 =  7*1000   + 3*100   + 5*10 + 2
```

In this case, the 7 does not have a value of seven, but has seven times the value of the position it holds. The position values in this case are as follows:

```
1000    100     10      1
7       3       5       2
```

Each digit takes the place value as well as the value of the digit. These place values are arrived at as follows, where ten is the number base:

```
10*10*10      10*10    10     1
7             3        5      2
```

Note that if you wanted to write the number six hundred and four, you would write 604. You wouldn't write 64 because that would change the value. It was necessary to put a zero in the tens position to hold the position. The zero is a vital number, even though it has no value. It is a place holder. Without the zero, the concept of place value would not work. This is true of any number base. The zero is a digit you must have.

There is no magical reason why you must use the base ten. You could choose any base. The most probable reason for using ten is that people have ten fingers and count up to ten on their fingers before starting over.

Other bases are actually easier to work with than base ten. The number ten can be divided evenly only by two and five. On the other hand, twelve can be divided evenly by two, three, four, and six, and a number system based on twelve would eliminate many fractions from our day-to-day life.

A base five would look like the following:

1 would be one
2 would be two
3 would be three
4 would be four
10 would be five
11 would be six
12 would be seven

Remember that the place value in base five is a multiple of five. So the 12 (pronounced one two, not twelve) really means you have one times five plus two more for a total of seven. What value would the number 1302 base five have?

The place values of the number 1302 would be as follows:

5*5*5	5*5	5	1
125	25	5	1
1	3	0	2

1302 base five = 1 * 125 + 3 * 25 + 0 * 5 + 2 base ten
= 125 + 75 + 0 + 2 base ten
= 202 base ten

The computer only has two "fingers": on and off. It makes sense that a number system based on two is used. How does this language of the computer appear? Analyze the base two number 110101 to see what value it has in base ten. First, the place value for a binary number is as follows:

2*2*2*2*2	2*2*2*2	2*2*2	2*2	2	1
32	16	8	4	2	1
1	1	0	1	0	1

Now convert the binary number to its base ten value:

110101 base two = 1*32 + 1*16 + 0*8 + 1*4 + 0*2 + 1 base ten
= 32 + 16 + 0 + 4 + 0 + 1 base ten
= 53 base ten

Note that in base ten, you can write any numeric value you want with just the digits 1, 2, 3, 4, 5, 6, 7, 8, 9, and 0. In base five, you can write any numeric value you want with just the digits 1, 2, 3, 4, and 0, and in base two you use just the digits 1 and 0. Note that in each case you don't have a digit symbol for the base value. In base ten you don't have a digit symbol for ten. In base five you don't have a digit symbol for five, and in base two you don't have a digit symbol for two. In each case, the base is represented by 10. If you wanted to work with a base larger than ten, you would need some new symbols.

Suppose you wanted to use base sixteen. You would have the digit 1 for one, 2 for two, and so on up to 9 for nine. But how would you write the digit ten? You could not use 10 because in base sixteen that would have a value of sixteen, so you need to invent some new symbols. The computer industry has adopted the following conventions for the base sixteen:

1 is one	A is ten
2 is two	B is eleven
3 is three	C is twelve
4 is four	D is thirteen
5 is five	E is fourteen
6 is six	F is fifteen
7 is seven	10 is sixteen
8 is eight	11 is seventeen
9 is nine	12 is eighteen
	... and so on

You will find both base eight and base sixteen used on a regular basis around computers. The reason for this is that base two is easily converted to either of these bases. Take the base two (binary) number 101111011, and convert it to a base eight (octal) number. Simply divide the binary number into groups of three and convert each group separately:

binary	101	111	011
octal	5	7	3

Starting from the right, the 011 binary means there are 0 fours, 1 two, and 1 one for a total of three. 111 binary means there is a four, a two, and a one for a total of seven. You should be able to see where the 5 comes from.

To convert to base sixteen (hex, or hexadecimal), divide the binary number into groups of four from the right and again convert each group separately:

binary	1	0111	1011
hex	1	7	B

Converting to octal or hex allows the binary, machine language numbers to be written in less space.

If you want to convert the base ten number of 1276 to base eight, you must first know the place values for base eight:

8*8*8*8	+	8*8*8	+	8*8	+	8	+	1
4096	+	512	+	64	+	8	+	1

Take the largest base eight place value that will go into the number 1276 and divide. The result will be your most significant base eight digit. Take the remainder and divide again with the next lower base eight place value. Continue this process until you are done, as in the following example:

1276 / 512 = 2 with a remainder of 252

252 / 64 = 3 with a remainder of 60

60 / 8 = 7 with a remainder of 4

4 / 1 = 4 with no remainder

The answer is that 2374 base eight is equal to 1276 base ten.

APPENDIX B: TEXT CODES AND ATTRIBUTES

ASCII Character Codes

Decimal Code	Octal Code	Hex Code	Character (or control character)
000	000	00	NUL
001	001	01	SOH
002	002	02	STX
003	003	03	ETX
004	004	04	EOT
005	005	05	ENQ
006	006	06	ACK
007	007	07	BEL
008	010	08	BS
009	011	09	HT
010	012	0A	LF
011	013	0B	VT
012	014	0C	FF
013	015	0D	CR
014	016	0E	SO
015	017	0F	SI
016	020	10	DLE
017	021	11	DC1
018	022	12	DC2
019	023	13	DC3
020	024	14	DC4
021	025	15	NAK
022	026	16	SYN
023	027	17	ETB
024	030	18	CAN
025	031	19	EM
026	032	1A	SUB
027	033	1B	ESC
028	034	1C	FS
029	035	1D	GS
030	036	1E	RS

Decimal Code	Octal Code	Hex Code	Character (or control character)
031	037	1F	US
032	040	20	(SPACE)
033	041	21	!
034	042	22	"
035	043	23	#
036	044	24	$
037	045	25	%
038	046	26	&
039	047	27	’
040	050	28	(
041	051	29	)
042	052	2A	*
043	053	2B	+
044	054	2C	,
045	055	2D	-
046	056	2E	.
047	057	2F	/
048	060	30	0
049	061	31	1
050	062	32	2
051	063	33	3
052	064	34	4
053	065	35	5
054	066	36	6
055	067	37	7
056	070	38	8
057	071	39	9
058	072	3A	:
059	073	3B	;
060	074	3C	<
061	075	3D	=
062	076	3E	>
063	077	3F	?
064	100	40	@
065	101	41	A
066	102	42	B

Decimal Code	Octal Code	Hex Code	Character (or control character)
067	103	43	C
068	104	44	D
069	105	45	E
070	106	46	F
071	107	47	G
072	110	48	H
073	111	49	I
074	112	4A	J
075	113	4B	K
076	114	4C	L
077	115	4D	M
078	116	4E	N
079	117	4F	O
080	120	50	P
081	121	51	Q
082	122	52	R
083	123	53	S
084	124	54	T
085	125	55	U
086	126	56	V
087	127	57	W
088	130	58	X
089	131	59	Y
090	132	5A	Z
091	133	5B	[
092	134	5C	\
093	135	5D	]
094	136	5E	^
095	137	5F	_ (underline)
096	140	60	`
097	141	61	a
098	142	62	b
099	143	63	c
100	144	64	d
101	145	65	e
102	146	66	f

Decimal Code	Octal Code	Hex Code	Character (or control character)
103	147	67	g
104	150	68	h
105	151	69	i
106	152	6A	j
107	153	6B	k
108	154	6C	l
109	155	6D	m
110	156	6E	n
111	157	6F	o
112	160	70	p
113	161	71	q
114	162	72	r
115	163	73	s
116	164	74	t
117	165	75	u
118	166	76	v
119	167	77	w
120	170	78	x
121	171	79	y
122	172	7A	z
123	173	7B	{
124	174	7C	|
125	175	7D	}
126	176	7E	~
127	177	7F	DEL

Hex Keyboard Scancodes

Key	Scancode	Key	Scancode	Key	Scancode
Esc	01	J	24	Num Lock	45
1	02	K	25		
2	03	L	26		
3	04	;	27	Scroll Lock	46
4	05	'	28		
5	06	‘	29		
6	07	L Shift	2A	Home	47
7	08	\	2B		
8	09	Z	2C	Cursor Up	48
9	0A	X	2D		
0	0B	C	2E		
-	0C	V	2F	PgUp	49
=	0D	B	30		
Backspace	0E	N	31	-	4A
Tab	0F	M	32		
Q	10	,	33	Cursor Left	4B
W	11	.	34		
E	12	/	35		
R	13	R Shift	36	5	4C
T	14	PrtSc	37		
Y	15	Alt	38	Cursor Right	4D
U	16	Spacebar	39		
I	17	Caps Lock	3A		
O	18	F1	3B	+	4E
P	19	F2	3C		
[	1A	F3	3D	End	4F
]	1B	F4	3E		
Enter	1C	F5	3F	Cursor Down	50
Ctrl	1d	F6	40		
A	1e	F7	41		
S	1f	F8	42	PgDn	51
D	20	F9	43		
F	21	F10	44	Ins	52
G	22				
H	23			Del	53

Text Screen Attribute Bit Positions

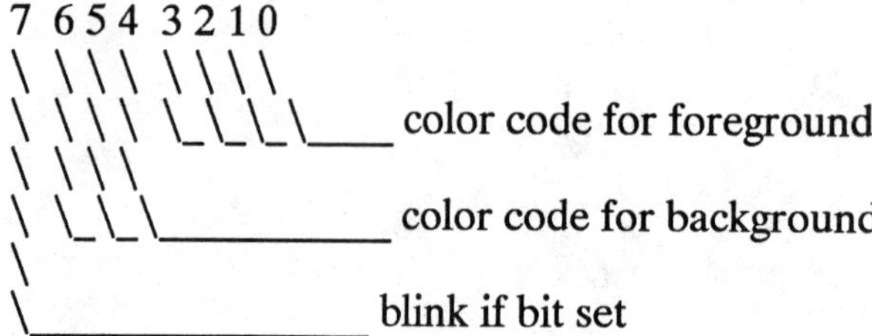

Text Screen Attributes

Color	Background Color Code Blinking Off	Background Color Code Blinking On	Foreground Color Code
black	00	80	0
blue	10	90	1
green	20	A0	2
cyan	30	B0	3
red	40	C0	4
magenta	50	D0	5
brown	60	E0	6
lightgray	70	F0	7
darkgray			8
lightblue			9
lightgreen			A
lightcyan			B
lightred			C
lightmagenta			D
yellow			E
white			F

(Just add the desired foreground code to the appropriate background code, and you have the hex attribute.)

APPENDIX C: REFERENCE SUMMARY

Arithmetic Operators

Operator	Operation
+	addition
-	subtraction
*	multiplication
/	division
-	unary minus
%	modulo
++	increment
--	decrement
()	ordering
=	assignment

Order of Precedence

<table>
<tr><td>parentheses</td><td>( )</td></tr>
<tr><td>unary operators</td><td>-- ++ ! ~ * & - (* for pointer)
(& for address)</td></tr>
<tr><td>multiply and divide</td><td>* / %</td></tr>
<tr><td>add and subtract</td><td>+ -</td></tr>
<tr><td>shift</td><td><< >></td></tr>
<tr><td>relational</td><td>> >= < <=</td></tr>
<tr><td>relational</td><td>== !=</td></tr>
<tr><td>bitwise AND</td><td>&</td></tr>
<tr><td>bitwise OR</td><td>|</td></tr>
<tr><td>bitwise XOR</td><td>^</td></tr>
<tr><td>logical AND</td><td>&&</td></tr>
<tr><td>logical OR</td><td>||</td></tr>
<tr><td>assignment</td><td>=</td></tr>
</table>

Relational and Logical Operators for Conditional Statements

<table>
<tr><th>Operator</th><th>Test</th></tr>
<tr><td>= =</td><td>equal</td></tr>
<tr><td><</td><td>less than</td></tr>
<tr><td>></td><td>greater than</td></tr>
<tr><td>! =</td><td>not equal</td></tr>
<tr><td>> =</td><td>greater than or equal</td></tr>
<tr><td>< =</td><td>less than or equal</td></tr>
<tr><td>&&</td><td>both conditions must be true</td></tr>
<tr><td>| |</td><td>one condition must be true</td></tr>
<tr><td>!</td><td>condition must not be true</td></tr>
</table>

Escape Sequence Character Constraints

Code	Character
\a	alert (BEL)
\f	form feed (FF)
\r	carriage return (CR)
\v	vertical tab (VT)
\'	single quote (')
\?	question mark (?)
\xH	any character (where H is a 1- to 3-digit hex number)
\O	any character (where O is a 1- to 3-digit octal number)
\b	backspace (BS)
\n	newline (LF)
\t	horizontal tab (HT)
\\	backslash (\)
\"	double quote (")

Data Types

Type	**Bytes**
int	2
float	4
double	8
char	1
void	0
Modifiers for type int:	
unsigned int	2
signed int	2
short int	2
unsigned short int	2
signed short int	2
long int	4
unsigned long int	4
signed long int	4
Modifier for type double:	
long double	8
Modifiers for type char:	
unsigned char	1
signed char	1

printf() Conversion Specifications

Conversion Specification	Output Description
%d	signed decimal integer
%i	signed decimal integer
%u	unsigned decimal integer
%o	octal integer
%x	hexadecimal (lowercase alphabetic)
%X	hexadecimal (uppercase alphabetic)
%f	signed floating-point
%e	signed exponential format
%g	shortest of either %e or %f
%c	single character
%s	string of characters
%%	single % sign
%p	pointer
%n	argument will receive integer count of characters printed

scanf() Conversion Specifications

Conversion Specification	Input Description
%d	decimal integer
%i	decimal integer
%h	short integer
%o	octal integer
%x	hexadecimal integer
%f	floating-point
%e	floating-point
%c	single character
%s	string of characters
%p	pointer
%n	integer count of characters input

C Keywords

(Words reserved by C for special use. May not be used as an identifier.)

asm *	auto	break
case	cdecl *	char
const	continue	default
do	double	else
enum	extern	far *
float	for	goto
huge *	if	int
interrupt *	long	near *
pascal *	register	return
short	signed	sizeof
static	struct	switch
typedef	union	unsigned
void	volatile	while
_cs *	_ds *	_es *
_ss *		

* Keywords unique to Turbo C

Stream Modes

Mode	File Status
"r"	open existing text file for reading
"w"	create new text file for writing *
"a"	open or create text file for appending to end
"rt"	open existing text file for reading
"wt"	create new text file for writing *
"at"	open or create text file for appending to end
"r+t"	open existing text file for update **
"w+t"	create new text file for update * **
"a+t"	open or create text file for update at end **
"rb"	open existing binary file for reading
"wb"	create new binary file for writing *
"ab"	open or create binary file for appending to end
"r+b"	open existing binary file for update **
"w+b"	create new binary file for update * **
"a+b"	open or create binary file for update at end **

*	Erases any existing file with same name
**	Both read and write are possible if separated by an fseek() or a rewind()

A

B

C

D

E

F

G

H

Q

R

S

T

RELATED TITLES FROM MIS:PRESS

DOS 4.0 Customizing The Shell
This sensational new book is written for users who want the freedom to "do it their own way." Author Thomas Goodell reveals DOS 4.0's arsenal of power-packed features and demonstrates how to master its new pull-down menu system. This book gives details on how to customize the Shell for specific applications; build, replace, and modify DOS menus; and go beyond the Shell to manipulate the DOS environment.
Thomas Goodell 1-55828-003-0 $22.95

Running DOS 4.0
This essential desktop reference is an invaluable resource for beginning and advanced PC- and MS-DOS users alike. It tells new users everything they need to know to use the system successfullly. Power users will find it a comprehensive command reference and application development guide. Covering all major DOS commands, this book goes in depth on all the new 4.0 commands—including 4.0's new menu-driven shell.
Carl Siechert and Chris Wood 1-55828-005-7 $22.95

Advanced DOS
An indispensable resource and reference guide for serious DOS programmers. Includes sections on data storage, BIOS and DOS interrupts, utility programming, and memory-resident utilities.
Michael I. Hyman 0-943518-83-0 $22.95
44.95 w/disk

Hard Disk Management
This new, revised edition is the practical guidebook for PC, S/2, and compatible users. It reveals how to successfully se popular application software on hard disk systems, cluding how to master DOS, install programs, write menus, manage memory, and integrate software pplications into a single powerful management tool. Covers fundamentals of DOS and OS/2 along with word rocessing, spreadsheets, and database management.
alph Blodgett and Emily Rosenthal 0-943518-82-2
21.95

C Data Base Development
All the tools programmers need for writing C data base programs—with complete, detailed instructions on how to use them. Explains DBMS concepts, C data utilities, the C data compiler, and using C as a data definition language. Includes a billing system program as a sample data base application.
Al Stevens 0-943518-33-4 $23.95
$43.95 w/disk

Turbo C
Everything Turbo C programmers need to get the most out of this fast and powerful programming language. Covers topics and techniques including memory management, ROM BIOS functions, programming screen input/output, and writing memory-resident utility programs in Turbo C.
Al Stevens 0-943518-35-0 $24.95
$44.95 w/disk

QuickC
QuickC is the latest compiler from Microsoft. This book provides a C language development environment for use by both beginning and advanced users. Includes an integrated editor and debugger. The code you develop is upward-compatible with the Microsoft C compiler.
Al Stevens 0-943518-80-6 $24.95
$49.95 w/disk

C/C++ Expert Systems
The most lucid expert systems reference book ever written for professional C programmers, this book exposes the concepts and program components necessary to unleash the power of artificial intelligence with C/C++. Loaded with sample programs, it demonstrates how to create expert systems or shells, make programs "intelligent," introduce uncertainty of knowledge, and embed reasoning capabilities into programs. Includes LISP and Prolog utility programs in C.
David Hu 0-943518-86-5 $24.95
$49.95 w/disk

MANAGEMENT INFORMATION SOURCE, INC.
O. Box 5277 • Portland, OR 97208-5277
03) 222-2399

all free
-800-MANUALS

Available where fine books are sold.

ANAGEMENT INFORMATION SOURCE, INC.